W9-CCT-459

Praise for *Grounded*

"Based on his previous groundbreaking book *Healthy Companies*, Bob Rosen has tackled the issue of how leaders in the workforce can adapt to the changing values and ethos of contemporary, far-seeing, and successful companies. Additionally, he draws up with great delicacy and understanding the very best of Positive Psychology and applies it to the new challenges of 21st century organizations. I have no hesitation in predicting that Rosen's book will be one of the top, most important books on leadership for the 21st century."

—**Warren Bennis,** Distinguished Professor in Business Administration and University Professor at the University of Southern California; author of *Still Surprised: A Memoir of a Life in Leadership*

"*Grounded* argues that we all have the capacity for personal leadership. Bob Rosen provides insights for becoming more alert, engaged, decisive, resilient, and inclusive leaders which organizations need."

—**Kay Koplovitz**, founder of USA Network; entrepreneur; author of *Bold Women, Big Ideas*

"Bob Rosen's timely, well-written new book goes to the heart of what it takes to lead in today's complex world: being grounded in your roots through self-awareness with resilience is the essence of sustaining success. Rosen's message deserves to be widely read and followed to produce better leaders for the 21st century."

—**Bill George**, professor of management practice, Harvard Business School; bestselling author of *True North*

"Today's business climate is the epicenter of some pretty powerful 'winds of change.' Read Rosen's groundbreaking new book *Grounded*, which offers corporate leaders and their teams shelter from the storm and new ideas for success."

—**Marshall Goldsmith**, million-selling author or editor of thirty-four books, including the *New York Times* bestsellers *MOJO* and *What Got You Here Won't Get You There*

"Great leadership is the most difficult and worthy challenge of our times. Bob Rosen, backed by a wealth of experience working with CEOs, knows that leadership is fundamentally personal—and that the ability to drive change begins inside. I recommend that every leader take his advice and adopt the daily practice of focusing on their six dimensions to a greater degree. Not only will this deliver everyday gains at eye level but you will also stay rooted, become more adaptive, and achieve more no matter what uncertainties lay ahead."

—**Jorgen Vig Knudstorp**, CEO, the Lego Group

"*Grounded* reminds us how important it is to balance every piece of our lives—personal, spiritual, family, work, exercise, and more—into one life, which becomes our life's work. Living authentically better enables us to serve and lead with a compelling vision, comprehensive strategy, and relentless implementation. Thank you, Bob, for helping leaders to be their best!"

—**Alan Mulally**, president and CEO, Ford Motor Company

"Leadership is learned through life and experience. And you must be your own teacher. Bob Rosen's *Grounded* lays out a compelling, personal, and proven path for you to take responsibility for your own learning and development. The secrets lie in the six dimensions of leadership health and your commitment to practice them daily. This is a powerful global book, relevant for leaders all around the world."

—**Silas S. S. Yang**, Asia Pacific Chairman and Global Network Leadership Team member, PricewaterhouseCoopers

"Bob Rosen knows the world of leadership. This book puts all that experience and wisdom at your fingertips. *Grounded* provides a map that helps you unlock your knowledge, and open your head and your heart as a leader. If you've ever wanted one book that talks to you personally and professionally, this is it."

—**Beverly Kaye**, founder, Career Systems International; coauthor, *Help Them Grow or Watch Them Go: Career Conversations Employees Want* and *Love 'Em or Lose 'Em: Getting Good People to Stay*

"Bob Rosen's *Grounded* helps top leaders understand that by taking off their mask and being their true and complete self, they can take their personal and company performance to a level never imagined! Rosen teaches us to purposely *not* resist the turbulence, but rather to accept it, and ride it to a new high."

—**Tom Waldron**, senior vice president/people, Walmart

"My advice to newly minted MBAs, entrepreneurs, and CEOs alike is this: volatile times require returning to the fundamentals of business. That includes leadership. Thank you, Bob Rosen, for showing leaders at every level the lasting value of staying rooted—and the critical investment we must all make every day to strive for our healthiest, most human, and most productive levels of leadership."

—**Bob Bruner**, dean, Darden Graduate School of Business Administration

"*Grounded* delivers a new leadership model that's desperately needed today. Bob Rosen doesn't treat leaders as heroes, but as real people who are hungry for new tools and practices that really work in our uncertain times. His stories from the C-suite are fresh. His advice on dealing with constant change is road-tested. And his focus is global. Anyone, at any level, who wants higher performance and greater personal satisfaction will benefit from getting this bold new book."

—**Kevin Oakes**, CEO, i4CP

"Rosen nails it. The metaphor of the unseen and invisible (i.e. underground) roots being the very foundation and source feeding visible success is powerful and accurate. In the new normal, it is critical for leaders to know themselves, respect themselves, question themselves, and believe in themselves. That's what their teams and organizations want and embrace."

—**Paul McCurdy**, chair, Kelley Drye

"World-class corporations need world-class leaders. In *Grounded*, Bob Rosen treats each and every one of us as leaders who have greater untapped strengths and capabilities—no matter where we are in the organizational hierarchy. Thank you, Bob, for providing a roadmap on how employees at all levels within a company can achieve individual fulfillment and success."

—**Wayne Burton,** corporate medical director, American Express

"They say that the trees that live for a thousand years have the strongest roots. The same applies to leadership: to soar high, a leader needs to have their feet on the ground. *Grounded* shows how leaders can increase their staying power and contribute meaningfully to the world by being like the bamboo: strongly rooted and yet super flexible."

—**Navi Radjou**, innovation and leadership strategist; bestselling author of *From Smart to Wise: Acting and Leading With Wisdom*

"The only thing certain these days is *uncertainty.* In *Grounded*, Bob Rosen provides leaders with the best practices, the case studies, and the insights to navigate through what now appears to be the permanently murky waters of our global economy and reminds us all that healthy leadership must be built on a multidimensional and diverse platform of skill sets and a commitment to lifelong education. This is a must-read for global leaders and those who aspire to be leaders."

—**Andrew J. Sherman**, partner, Jones Day; author of twenty-four books on business growth, including the critically acclaimed *Harvesting Intangible Assets*

"Bob Rosen reveals the roots of lives well lived and companies well led. Leaving leadership fads behind, *Grounded* takes us on a compelling journey to first know—and then better—who we are."

—**Ralph W. Shrader**, chairman and chief executive officer, Booz Allen Hamilton

BOB ROSEN

GROUNDED

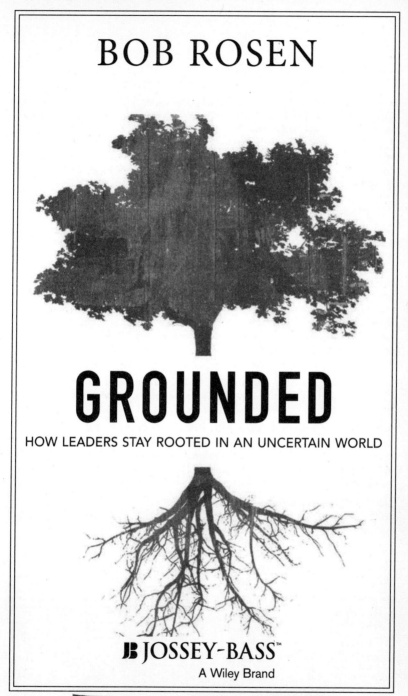

HOW LEADERS STAY ROOTED IN AN UNCERTAIN WORLD

JB JOSSEY-BASS™
A Wiley Brand

Jacket design and artwork by Gearbox

Published by Jossey-Bass
A Wiley Brand
One Montgomery Street, Suite 1200, San Francisco, CA 94104-4594—www.josseybass.com

Jossey-Bass books and products are available through most bookstores. To contact Jossey-Bass directly call our Customer Care Department within the U.S. at 800-956-7739, outside the U.S. at 317-572-3986, or fax 317-572-4002.

Wiley publishes in a variety of print and electronic formats and by print-on-demand. Some material included with standard print versions of this book may not be included in e-books or in print-on-demand. If this book refers to media such as a CD or DVD that is not included in the version you purchased, you may download this material at http://booksupport.wiley.com. For more information about Wiley products, visit www.wiley.com.

Library of Congress Cataloging-in-Publication Data

Rosen, Bob, 1955–
Grounded : how leaders stay rooted in an uncertain world / Bob Rosen.
pages cm
Includes bibliographical references and index.
ISBN 978-1-118-68077-3 (hardback); ISBN 978-1-118-68089-6 (ePDF);
ISBN 978-1-118-68087-2 (ePub)
1. Leadership. I. Title.
HD57.7.R657 2013
658.4'092–dc23

2013025202

Printed in the United States of America

FIRST EDITION

HB Printing 10 9 8 7 6 5 4 3 2

To Jay

Contents

PART III
PUTTING LEADERSHIP INTO ACTION

GROUNDED

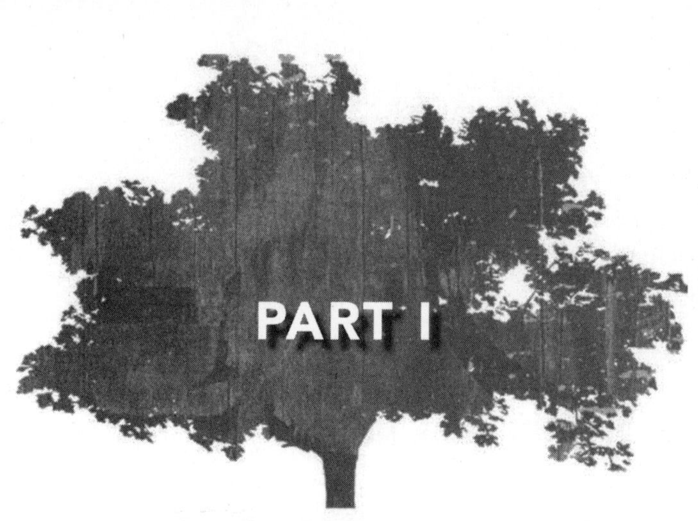

PART I

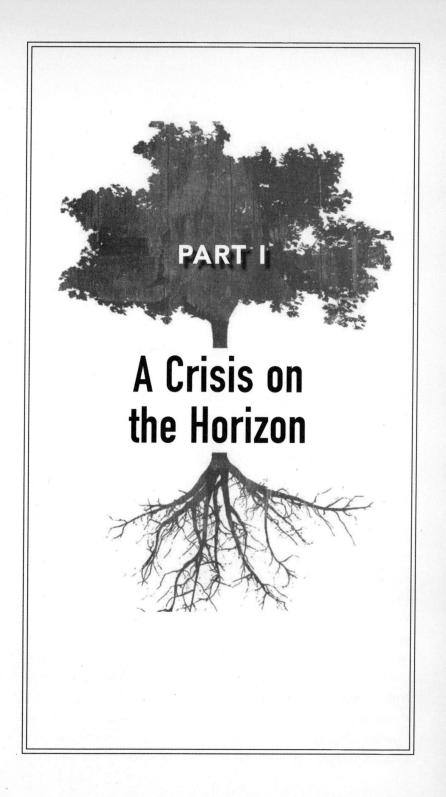

A Crisis on the Horizon

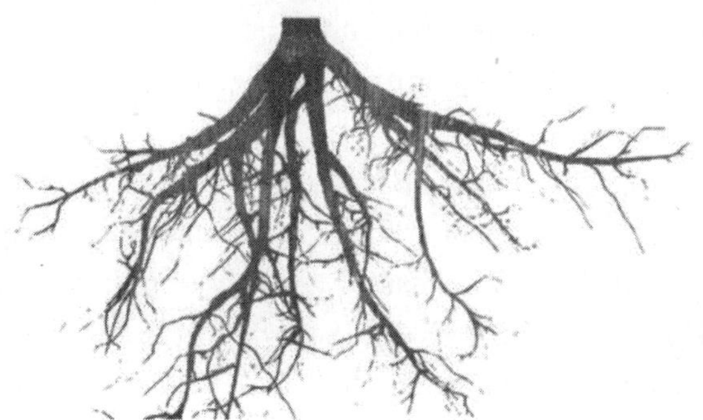

CHAPTER 1

The Winds of Change

Imagine the last time you went to an event or party. You strike up a conversation with someone you don't know. If you are like most people, after the initial back and forth, you ask, "So, what do you do?" This innocuous question naturally elicits an impersonal title, a description of work activities, and the mention of accomplishments.

What if you asked instead, "Who are you—what's important in your life?" This is a question we rarely ask, maybe because it is so personal. And that is precisely our point. In this book, we would like to make the case that what is most personal to people and their leaders is at the heart of their health and happiness. When it's neglected, it can be the source of major problems in business and society. To explain this further, let's first talk about the consequences.

We are in the middle of a crisis. The winds of change are flaming both a personal and public emergency in leadership. Just think about your life and your world: The debt crisis. The obesity epidemic. Stagnant growth. Climate change. Tax reform. Rampant foreclosures. An archbishop arrested. Product recalls. Indicted

CEOs. Adultery in the military. Scientific forgery. Childhood malnutrition. Crisis management. Doping allegations. Ponzi schemes. Business bankruptcies. Medicare fraud. Gun control failures. Bargaining deadlocks. Environmental disasters. Executive terminations. You get the picture.

These winds are coming at us from all directions. Many of our so-called leaders are having trouble leading under these conditions. They feel tossed and turned by the wind, afraid of taking responsibility, being wrong, missing opportunities, or searching for a way out. They may be getting pummeled by violent turns in the economy or dramatic shifts in the global marketplace. Or they may be feeling a change in atmospheric pressure inside themselves. Turmoil of doubt, uncertainty, or stress could be besetting them personally as well as professionally. You may be that leader.

Turbulent winds are unnerving because they have a huge capacity to destroy. They alter landscapes, their paths are unpredictable, and their gusts can demolish everything in the way. This is the climate that you're facing today as a leader. Whether you lead a multinational conglomerate, an entrepreneurial start-up, or a modest-size nonprofit organization, you are encountering forces of change that are as dramatic and potentially life altering as any violent storm.

All of us trying to lead a team or organization today are being thrust into survival mode, tapping into our natural state of "fight or flight" and habituating to a level of turmoil rarely experienced in our lifetime. As the winds intensify, our need to protect and prove ourselves becomes greater. Many of us slowly lose our inner strength. Beneath the winds is a pervasive atmosphere of fear. People are afraid of losing their jobs, of economic collapse, of not growing fast enough, or any number of vulnerable scenarios. As we explain a bit later, this fear can derail individuals as well as entire organizations.

It's likely you already have encountered the winds of change as they are impeding your progress and maybe even jeopardizing your career or company. We at Healthy Companies have found that leaders at all levels, across all industries and sectors, and around the world are buffeted from every direction by six forces: the speed of change,

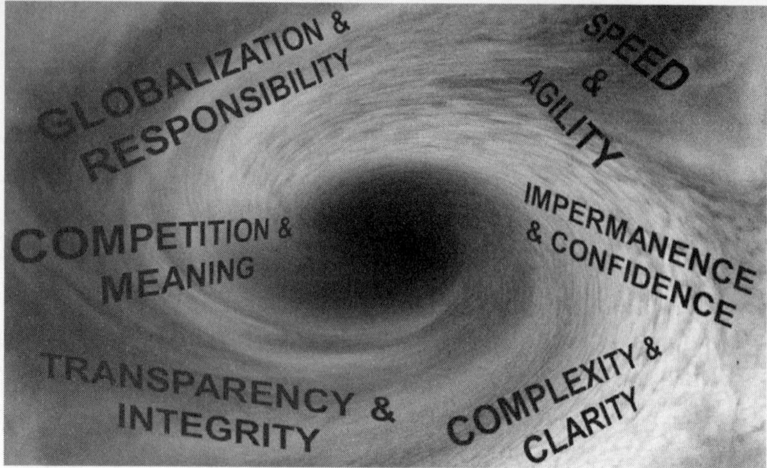

Figure 1.1

impermanence, demands for transparency, complexity, intense competition, and a new world order of global interconnectedness.

BUFFETED FROM EVERY DIRECTION

One of the more powerful forces is **speed**—people can't keep up with the pace of change. The world is changing faster than our ability to evolve, raising the question, How do we keep up while maintaining the ability to balance our lives and bounce back in the face of adversity? The marketplace is changing, workers are changing, product cycles are changing, even the nature of business is changing. Here are some dramatic examples: one in four workers today has been at his or her current company less than a year;[1] ten years ago, Facebook didn't exist; ten years before that, we didn't have the Web. And Google's CEO Eric Schmidt predicts that by 2020, the entire world will be online. If you happen to be in the technology sector, you are being truly whipsawed. Apple offers this head-turning nugget: roughly 60 percent of its revenue is currently generated by products that are less than four years old.[2] Some of us, especially those who are perfectionists, try to keep pace with everything while getting everything just right. This unreasonable standard makes it impossible to stay agile, and eventually leads to burnout.

Another force is the constant state of **impermanence** and instability. You are probably wondering—how can you move forward while staying grounded in the middle of all that's unpredictable? Jobs no longer last a lifetime, and even universities are doing away with tenure. Uncertainty is the new normal. Trend watchers predict that children in school today will have ten to fourteen jobs by age thirty-eight.[3] No segment of business is immune from insecurity. Turnover among managers and CEOs has been rising. In 2011, more than 14 percent of the CEOs at the world's largest companies were out.[4] Companies like Yahoo, with three CEOs in three years, are no longer unusual. For many of us, our natural reaction to uncertainty is to resist change. However, letting yourself be driven by fear, denying the realities around you, or trying to control the unknown only undermines your confidence.

The greatest challenge we all have, and it seems to be coming at us at a faster clip, is information. And we have to be able to hear it, absorb it, truly listen to it, react to it. It's daunting.

—Jim Wainscott, CEO, AK Steel Holdings[5]

Complexity in the business world is also adding pressure to your job. We often hear this question: How do we navigate the intricacies of work while defining, prioritizing, and focusing our leadership? Everyone loves gee-whiz technology, but it has become a double-edged sword for many. On the one hand, it has enhanced communications, manufacturing and design, and workplace efficiency; on the other hand, it is a relentless taskmaster. Business leaders often struggle to keep up-to-date with its uses and stay on top of its applications. One facet of complexity is an explosion of information. Today's business leader must juggle mountains of news and facts. Every eighteen months, according to one global survey, the world's volume of data doubles.[6] Some of us react to this complexity by oversimplifying the world, reducing complex issues into smaller parts while failing to see the big picture. Others overcomplicate the situation and lose their ability to focus and prioritize.

At the same time, you are facing increasing demands for **transparency**, along with more scrutiny and a greater need for integrity and accountability. Regulations are demanding it, consumers are demanding it, and employees are demanding it. JPMorgan Chase CEO Jamie Dimon had to explain and offer copious mea culpas for company trading losses, not only to federal regulators and investigating committees on Capitol Hill but also to the public at large.[7] Not so long ago, a company's internal financial activities were considered confidential and private. Today's attention on a company's activities and the decisions of its leaders has been intensified by social media and the ubiquitous cellphone camera, which guarantees that little a leader does goes unnoticed or unreported. And when something does happen, word gets out fast. Consider this: more text messages are sent and received in one day than the number of people on the planet.[8] All this raises the question, How do you maintain genuine openness while safeguarding your business and yourself?

In this environment, your natural reaction may be to hide and build a moat around yourself. But by isolating yourself you exacerbate the problem by generating suspicion, alienating people, and interfering with your ability to inspire others.

One of the biggest problems in our society is the level of mistrust and cynicism, which is at an all-time high.

—Frances Hesselbein, past CEO of Girl Scouts and Peter Drucker Foundation[9]

A common question raises the next force: How can you ensure a healthy bottom line and pursue profits in the context of inspiring meaning and purpose? Almost every leader must contend with intense **competition**, and it can come from anywhere and at any time. In recent years, the playing field has begun to tip in favor of non-U.S. companies. Chinese enterprises are challenging U.S. businesses at every turn. The fact that China's annual GDP has been averaging 10.5 percent over the past ten years, compared with 1.7 percent in the United States, only highlights its powerhouse status.[10] Perhaps no other industry has felt the lash of global competition more than the auto business. Once-dominant automakers are fighting to hold on to market share. General Motors a few decades ago owned half of the domestic U.S. car market; it now is battling to keep 20 percent. When London's *Financial Times* first began tracking top business schools around the world, twenty of the top twenty-five were in America. Now, only five are in the United States.[11] Some of us deal with this competition by becoming obsessed with winning and losing. Being driven by competitiveness at any cost will preoccupy you with short-term results at the expense of creating long-term value, and you may even lose yourself in the process.

There are two kinds of people, those who do the work and those who take the credit. Try to be in the first group, there is less competition there.

—Indira Gandhi, late former Prime Minister of India[12]

You have probably wondered, "How can we succeed individually while thriving as one planet and global society?" This often-heard question goes to the heart of the final trend: the **globalization** of markets, people, and communities. Work and business are no longer local. If you have a website, you are part of the global economy. Further, work is no longer a means to an end but has been woven into our lives and lifestyles. Both leaders and employees want more from their daylight hours. They want a sense of purpose and community on top of the satisfaction of doing a good job, making money, and building something that lasts.

A sign of this force is the changing workplace. People are demanding the freedom to work wherever they like, whether they are blogging from the back of a camel or crunching data on their laptop on the back porch. Some companies are eager to accommodate their higher-purpose-driven employees. In a survey involving more than 4.5 million employees, almost half of their companies were beginning to offer alternative work arrangements.[13]

Another sign of this force is the rise of corporate social responsibility and what's called "ethical consumerism," such as buying green and building sustainability into your products and footprint. In Great Britain, before the recession, ethical consumerism was rising at a compound rate of 19 percent a year, which was three times faster than the overall economy.[14] No longer can you act as if only you matter in the world. Doing so will not only impede your happiness but also alienate you from the rest of the world.

Any time you have rapid change, it's destabilizing and you look for your roots. And when the financial markets collapsed, all of a sudden, all these things people had come to believe they started to question. And it has this sort of spiral effect.

—Ted Mathas, Chairman and CEO, New York Life[15]

None of these forces are developing in isolation, and many of them are not new. Indeed, some leaders are energized by the positive impact of many of the forces. But today they are creating a confluence of enormous power, and leaders are caught in the middle. Numerous CEOs and executives have told us that they feel stretched and inundated like never before. Even though stress, demanding workdays, and a steady stream of problems are standard fare for executives, the force and pace of these demands have become unrelenting. Leaders are juggling the best they can, but many see that their results are falling short.

FINDING A SOLUTION BY DIGGING DEEP

We at Healthy Companies have been looking for more than twenty-five years at the challenges leaders have been facing—conducting ongoing research, advising, and talking to leaders around the world. We have interviewed more than five hundred CEOs in forty-five countries. Along the way, we have written five leadership books highlighting some of our findings. In *Grounded*, we bring together all these findings to present a comprehensive and highly personal solution to the leadership crisis.

Our approach to learning what makes a successful leader has taken a unique tack. We have been delving into leadership qualities that have been overlooked or discounted. Rather than examining only performance and profit metrics, we have focused more on the leaders themselves. With hard data as evidence, reinforced by extensive one-on-one interviews, we have been able to delineate what makes an extraordinary leader. As you will find here, we have tried to peel back the layers of leadership to understand what drives great leadership at any level of organizational life.

In the course of our research, we made remarkable discoveries. Leaders who are truly healthy in all senses of the word are evolved human beings *and* extremely effective leaders. As we dug deeper into the qualities that make up this healthy leader, we unearthed three unequivocal truths. These findings form the themes and substance of *Grounded.*

Who You Are Drives What You Do

This finding is deceptive because the "Who you are" part is complicated and has layers of meaning. It also turns on its head the traditional idea of leadership being all about action and doing. We found quite the contrary: quality leadership stems not from what a person does but who that person is inside himself. Meaningful actions can take place only after a person has looked deep inside himself and knows what he's all about. "Who you are" refers to individual aspects of you as a person, or what we call your "healthy roots."

These roots consist of your physical health, emotional health, intellectual health, social health, vocational health, and spiritual health.

In the rest of Part One, we provide context and a high-level view of the roots in defining who you are. We also share supporting science here and throughout the book to confirm this shift in thinking. Finally, we discuss how these roots inform our second finding: for a completely healthy self, a leader needs to develop subroots within each root. This makes you grounded.

Who You Are Is Grounded in Your Healthy Roots

"Health" is the key word here, and one that many leaders overlook. Too often, people consider intelligence or experience or other qualities, such as connections and who you know, to be the secret to successful leadership. These qualities are essential, no doubt about it. However, they are just parts of the bigger picture and what constitutes "Who you are."

In Part Two, we discuss our findings in regard to what healthy roots are made of, and we offer suggestions for how you can strengthen them, advice on how to avoid pitfalls, and stories of leaders who have mastered these qualities in their own professional and personal lives. Each chapter focuses on individual, distinctive qualities. In the chapters on physical health, you read about body-mind awareness, energy management, and a peak-performance lifestyle. The chapters on emotional health highlight self-awareness, positive emotions, and resilience. The chapters on intellectual health cover deep curiosity, an adaptive mindset, and paradoxical thinking. In the chapters on social health, you will read about authenticity, mutually rewarding relationships, and nourishing teams and communities. The heart of vocational health consists of having a meaningful calling, personal mastery, and a drive to succeed. Last but not least, in the spiritual health chapters are descriptions of what it means to have a higher purpose, global connectedness, and generosity of spirit. All together, these roots lead to our third finding that the healthier a leader is, the better she will perform.

Healthy Leaders Build Teams and Organizations That Outperform

This third finding speaks to the outcomes and benefits of having healthy roots. With healthy roots, leaders not only are more fulfilled and reach their potential but have an effect on other individuals and organizations. Our data show that leaders with vibrant, healthy roots have a positive impact throughout organizations. They motivate people around them to perform at their best, and they inspire companies and even the communities in which they operate to benefit the greater good. Along the way and not incidentally, their healthy leadership has been shown to produce tangible results in a company's operations and bottom line.

Part Three, Putting Leadership into Action, reveals the ways in which leaders' healthy roots affect how organizations excel. Each chapter highlights a leader whose healthy roots have enabled him or her to outperform in a distinctive way. These leaders tap into a higher purpose, forge a shared direction, unleash human potential, foster productive relationships, seize new opportunities, and drive high performance.

• • •

Before we dig into how individual roots contribute to a leader's performance and what you can do to nourish your own roots, we need to step back. In the next chapter, we look more closely at what the winds of change are doing to your personal leadership and offer a perspective for understanding the ways you respond.

CHAPTER 2

Are You Bending, Breaking, or Staying Rooted?

ONE LEADER'S STORY

Leaders occasionally experience the winds of change as a personal battle. For a host of reasons, personal and professional, they are beset by doubt and demons. Although almost everyone at moments questions themselves or must confront personal issues, some leaders can feel weighed down by their own baggage of being human. Such was the case with Jim Hardy, a professional golfer, legendary instructor, and CEO of a worldwide golf training company.

Hardy remembers early in his career being awakened by a recurring nightmare. In the dream he was at the U.S. Master's with a three footer to win. "I know the putt; it's just a right center putt," he says. "But I would miss it, and I would never make that putt to win the Master's. One day I woke up and realized that that dream was the truth, that I was playing out the realities. If you can't make a three footer and win the Master's, why would you be doing this?"[1]

At this point in his career, Hardy was miserable and felt his life had little purpose. Fear, not joy, had been driving him. He had a fierce desire to excel, but it was not propelled by love of the game. He was more motivated to show others that he was just as good as they.

Hardy did not know how to transform himself, but he knew he had to fix himself before he could fix his personal or working life. Foremost in his struggle was a tremor that erupted during competition, especially when putting. Golfers commonly battle what's been dubbed "the yips," an uncontrollable jerk of the hands. The general assumption has been that the yips are all in the head and that a player needs only to control his nerves. But Hardy's shakes increasingly sabotaged his game, and he plunged into despair. Soon after these nightmares, he quit the tour.

He remembers, "I equated it with such things as 'You're gutless, you can't control your nerves, something's wrong with your mental approach' or something. 'You're not manly, you're not a warrior,' whatever crap we want to throw at ourselves."

Hardy bounced around the golf world, working as a club pro but not playing. "I didn't play golf because of the shame attached to it and how utterly defeated I had been by golf."

He drank too much, having figured out that alcohol quieted the shakes. He started playing again, usually loaded so that his hands would not shake. Increasingly he put more effort into instructing and programs for teaching pros as well as amateurs. To his surprise, he liked teaching. It gave him a higher purpose, something more meaningful and satisfying than prize money. "I realized my calling is teaching. And I could kind of go, 'You mean I don't have to try and make $100 million and satisfy everything and everybody in the world? Woo-hoo, this is kind of fun!' "

Seventeen years after quitting the tour, Jim Hardy learned that the tremors that had derailed his career were not psychological. They were neurological and genetic in origin, a condition called an "essential tremor." Not only do such tremors, which resemble Parkinson's, run in families, but they are intensified by adrenaline. The competition of a high-pressure tournament just added fuel to them.

Learning that his tremors were not caused by his being mentally weak was immensely liberating. He could now trust his new found self-awareness about what was important. He became emotionally stronger and healthier. “I understood that it’s more about personal mastery than how I stood with competitors or other people. I started to have peace with myself.”

He dedicated himself to teaching and developed a unique approach centered on teaching students how to discover their own strengths and weaknesses. His philosophy was simple: “It’s got to start with you the golfer and not necessarily you the teacher.” Students flocked to him, including numerous tour pros.

Today, he and his network of coaches advise nineteen tour pros among the PGA, Champions, and LPGA tours. He’s also CEO of Plane Truth, the world’s largest international training and certification company, which has 260 instructors from eighteen countries.

Hardy knows that developing core values based on intellectual flexibility, positive emotions, and personal fulfillment works. He has seen what an opposite approach, a winning-is-everything philosophy, does to people.

“Tiger used a phrase that shows the depth of his despair that I believe he still buys into, and that is, ‘Winning takes care of everything.’ Winning takes care of things economically, takes care of the hole in your heart for about thirty minutes, and then that’s it. Then that hole is still there, big enough you can drive a truck through.”

• • •

Every leader confronts the personal aspects of leadership in his own way. As Jim Hardy discovered, a leader’s personal and work lives are tightly intertwined. Each puts stress and pressure on the other. When he realized that he had to take control of what was happening inside himself and become truly healthy, he found personal fulfillment and his leadership blossomed.

Whether internal or external, the gale-force winds of change add layers of uncertainty and frustration to life. They have an insidious way of finding the cracks and crevasses in a leader’s character and approach. They can make it particularly difficult for the leader to find balance in life while she is having to pursue growth and higher performance.

INSIDE YOUR WORKING WORLD

As Jim Hardy discovered, the personal is not far from the professional when it comes to leadership. You may not have experienced the same hurricane-force winds that wracked Hardy's life, but you may have gone through situations that swirl around your working life and require personal insight to solve. Here are examples of common situations in which a leader is being battered by competing forces and the needs of many:

- A president seeks to introduce new levels of urgency and risk-taking to drive innovation and growth.
- A senior manager looks to improve teamwork among a group of disengaged managers.
- A CEO wants to gain support from her board while raising the quality of board members.
- An executive realizes the need to upgrade executive talent and his succession plan, but has a weak bench and feels guilty because of his loyalty and friendships.
- A vice president is mistrusting, has trouble delegating, and is micromanaging his team.
- A CEO is perceived as cold and disconnected from her organization yet wants to be more in touch with people.
- A junior executive is frustrated that his team does not take responsibility for decisions.
- A business group leader sees customers leaving and her culture deteriorating, but doesn't quite know what to do.
- An executive working 24/7 believes he has no time for his family and feels burned out and guilty.

How do these winds show up in your life, and what effect do they have on your leadership?

A GIGANTIC GAP

Many leaders are not adapting well to these situations, and feel stressed and defeated. Frequently, they cling to old mindsets and accept outmoded ways of thinking, assuming that what worked in the past will work in the future. As a result, there is an ever-widening gap between the leaders we have and the leaders we need.

Primary among their misconceptions is focusing too much on action and too little on introspection. They haven't examined what it is inside them that is informing, motivating, and inspiring their actions. Theirs is a skewed perspective that looks only at "what leaders do" and not enough at "who they are" as people. They pay scant attention to their health, be it intellectual and emotional health, social skills, or spiritual and humanitarian values.

Another reason that leaders are foundering is a climate of acceptance and tolerance of dysfunctional behavior in themselves and others. Turning a blind eye to dysfunction and underperformance; allowing toxic, negative people to infect the workplace; and refusing to challenge closed minds can undermine even the most well-intentioned leader.

Too often a leader gets seduced by the need to solve problems and take immediate action. Stepping back to examine flawed ways of thinking, personal biases and areas of ignorance, and assumptions about self-image and reputation can be difficult and painful. It's much easier to take quick-and-dirty, superficial approaches to leading, and hope that things will work out.

As a consequence, they are unable to cope with the storm enveloping them. What they have learned so far about leadership is not doing the job. Short-term, predictable strategies have become unsustainable and a source of friction in their organizations. Dysfunctional underperformance, stagnant growth, cynical customers, and disengaged employees are common. This is happening across the world, not just in business.

Politicians and Capitol Hill refuse to do their job, failing, for example, to tackle the country's physical and social infrastructure problems. Sexual abuse scandals reveal that religious institutions and church leaders have lost their moral compass. Regulators and government watchdogs turn a blind eye to fraud and consumer needs. Nonprofit groups struggle for funding and can't find people to serve on their boards. So-called role models in the sports world avoid talking about performance-enhancing drugs, and leaders in the entertainment industry appear indifferent to flagrant moral lapses of powerful celebrities.

The problem for many is a fundamentally flawed belief that their status and actions alone determine the quality of their leadership. They have been chasing profits, wealth, reputations, and accolades without realizing that healthy leadership stems not from all they do but from who they are as human beings.

This leadership gap has persisted despite organizations' having invested billions of dollars in developing leaders over the past twenty years. At best, the results have been mixed. Absolutely we have made progress as individuals and institutions. But development programs have been too segmented and not integrated and holistic. Leaders attend classes, hire coaches, and conduct 360 assessments, but they don't change. Sometimes leaders dismiss these efforts as irrelevant to business, adopt new approaches only temporarily, or do not "walk their talk" and instead display a cynical disregard for issues of health and character.

In short, many leaders are ill-equipped and uncertain as to how to withstand the fierce winds that are wracking their personal lives and their organizations. Of course, some will survive and even thrive, but only those who possess a singular combination of personal qualities become superlative leaders.

HOW DO YOU HANDLE IT?

Leading is difficult, we know. In our experience, leaders react to these forces in one of three ways. A large proportion choose to ignore the obvious. They put their head in the sand and, whether consciously or unconsciously, pretend it is business as usual and continue thinking and acting as if nothing is changing. They may do this because of overconfidence, believing that their way has always worked before, from cautiousness and underconfidence, or from feeling defeated by the enormity of their job. They adopt a rigid attitude toward personal change, avoiding introspection or soul-searching that might threaten long-held values or unexamined goals.

The best return for companies is when things are really going the wrong way and you're willing to go against the tide. If you're risk averse, you get left behind.

—John Chambers, CEO, Cisco[2]

Another reaction is to try to attack the strong winds in a chaotic way. These leaders make halfhearted, uninformed attempts to handle all that's coming at them, and when these fail, they move on to another task or simply give up. Desperate attempts and short-term fixes are part of this reaction. While they are stuck in the old way of doing things, arrogance and hubris or doubts about their competence, courage, and commitment plague them. Ultimately, these leaders get frustrated, stop trying, blame others, or burn out.

There is a third response to these winds, one that involves foresight and adaptability. Our data show that the leaders who recognize the forces battering an organization and its people see reality clearly, anticipate future pressure points, and get ahead of the storm. Time and again, these leaders have told us that they consider the winds of change to be an opportunity, not an obstacle. These individuals are not only flexible and able to adapt quickly but also personally grounded. By grounded, we mean firmly rooted, with well-established qualities and values. These leaders are healthy in all senses of the word.

• • •

You will read more about what it takes to be a healthy and grounded leader. Right now we'd like you to meet Tom Schievelbein, chairman and CEO of The Brink's Company, whose reaction to the winds of change typifies this third response.

Brink's is in the center of the crosscurrents. As a global provider of security-related services, Brink's has been battling the storm every day. It is having to deliver its product and services in increasingly shorter periods of time. Where it once could take a week to move money, it now must deliver within hours. Impermanence and complexity are regular fare as ever-changing technology alters how money is transferred. Transparency has become an especially acute issue given recent global events affecting financial institutions. As Brink's continues to expand overseas with customers in more than one hundred countries, it is also encountering more competition and more criminals trying to gain access to other people's money.

In some ways, Brink's is an old-fashioned company having been founded as a security firm best known for the armored trucks that pick up and deliver money across a city. When Schievelbein took the top spot in 2012, he was tasked with accelerating growth and productivity and reducing operating costs. With a clear vision and deep values, Schievelbein set about to lead the company into the twenty-first century.

He redefined the company's 2015 vision, expanding its core security business into more customer-centric security solutions, providing cash management and retail solutions, and incubating a range of new products and services. His rootedness has given him the ability not only to withstand the winds of change but also to use them as inspiration for improvement. "When there is change in the environment," he says, "many people view it as a problem. I view it as an opportunity. There will be winners and losers—but there's always a pony in that pile of manure."[3] From Bogota to Brussels to Bangkok, Tom Schievelbein's job is to navigate through the storm as he transforms the company.

SCIENCE SUPPORTS THE HEALTHY LEADER

If we had to point to one quality within a leader that can almost guarantee the prospect of success, it is a belief in the power of self-awareness and adaptability. Discovering who you are and taking steps to improve your healthy roots demand an appreciation for self-discovery and the power of change. This may sound like a self-help platitude, and we have encountered more than a few leaders who question their ability to alter what's inside themselves.

However, we have found that among exceptional leaders, self-knowledge and change are a constant in their lives. They not only believe that they can evolve and become more conscious but then they actually do it. Science backs us up on this. It regularly gives us new perspectives about who we are and about the profound influence we have on the environment and that the environment has on us. The fields that are especially fruitful in helping us understand ourselves as healthy leaders are biology, neuroscience, psychology, and physics.

Biology

A field dedicated to systems, biology continues to teach us more about our physical selves. For instance, scientists say that contrary to old beliefs, our bodies—down to the cellular level—are in constant communication with our environment. Our bodies are always looking for better ways to survive, gathering information through intercellular communication via electrical and chemical pathways.[4]

Cell biology also reveals that our genes are only part of what makes us who we are. Researchers like Bruce Lipton have discovered that DNA is controlled by a biochemical awareness initiated by the interaction of cell membranes with the outside environment.[5] This means that cellular activity depends on complex communication via energy fields—including our thoughts and beliefs. In this way, we can influence our biology.

Our cells sort through information to select life-enhancing options while avoiding life-destroying ones; we can't grow when protecting ourselves, and we can't protect ourselves while growing. And, perhaps most important, individual cells interact with other cells to benefit the whole organism while retaining individuality and functionality.

Drawing on these findings, we see it is critical to recognize the influence of external realities on our overall health, and the benefit of factoring them into corporate decisions to create win-win solutions. We must also realize the role of energy in health and disease, the need to balance protection and growth—for ourselves and our organizations. We have the potential to improve our own health through behavior and thought modification, and to expand our collective ability to adapt while working together for a greater good.

Neuroscience

Neuroscience continues to inform us about the brain and how it functions. Long-standing assumptions that the brain consists of complementary systems of "hardware" and "software" have been blurred of late. Our hardware—brain structures, neural pathways, neural chemicals, and neural electrical systems—is not as fixed as previously thought. And our software—our thoughts, beliefs, emotions, and memories—is more than an operating program, and it possesses a certain amount of autonomous intelligence. It can learn and teach itself, and lay down patterns that become fixed, more like hardware.

The concept of neuroplasticity—the brain's ability to rewire itself in the advent of physical or psychological trauma or injury—has been expanded to reveal that we can affect the brain's architecture through practice and repetition.[6] Neuroplasticity can be especially active in the cognitive part of our brains where thinking, planning, and decision making occur, as well as consciousness. Recognition of the potential of neuroplasticity is at the heart of changing our leadership and engaging in company-wide efforts to change.

Our ability to retool our minds can also be brought to bear in the realm of our emotions. Findings about how we process emotions are showing that our more primitive, instinctive survival emotions—the fight-or-flight reactions that keep us safe from danger—aren't always in charge. More evolutionarily advanced emotions that originate in the neocortex, especially the frontal lobe, are also essential to our survival. These are positive emotions, like love, kindness, compassion, joy, and hope. They are vital to healthy leadership.

Psychology

Psychology has recently shifted its attention to the role of positivity in human experience. Instead of focusing on what's wrong with people and trying to fix it, many branches of psychology are focusing on what's right, positive, and functional as the key to our self-improvement and happiness. The field as of late is also looking less like a "soft" science and more like an electron microscope revealing the secrets of personal behavior.

Particularly intriguing is research by the HeartMath Institute showing that the heart has its own intelligence and that peak performance and resilience are enhanced when the heart and brain are in sync.[7] The heart's "intelligence" enables you not only to improve physical performance but also to be more psychologically resilient, especially in handling stress. Those who engage their hearts as well as their minds, and focus around their strengths (rather than weaknesses) have a much better chance of leading a healthy, productive life. This makes it easier to be a healthy leader. The best way for you to inspire passion and performance in others is first by aligning your own head and heart.

Physics

Even physics is changing ideas about ourselves. Scientists are shoving aside the principles of Newtonian physics and classical mechanics and looking to quantum physics for insights. Its concepts about the dynamic unity of energy and matter and how reality can be altered by observation and expectation are readily transferable to businesses and organizations.

A quantum viewpoint is helping people understand how they affect each other's thought processes and problem solving, and confirming the fact that we all live in a world of uncertainty.

Findings like these point to the need for a leadership approach that is dynamic, holistic, and integrated. They strongly suggest the importance of agility and adaptability and of paying more attention to relationships inside and outside the company. They also underscore the need to understand your impact on others, consider the bigger picture when solving problems, and become comfortable with unpredictable change. The best strategy for doing this is to understand who you are, as we explain in the next chapter.

CHAPTER 3

Who You Are Drives What You Do

Picture a large oak tree, like the one on the cover of this book. Notice that it has three parts: lush foliage, a sturdy trunk, and thick roots. These represent essential facets of leadership. The leadership crisis has demonstrated that people have been preoccupied with the wrong part of the tree. The problem is that too much attention is being paid to all the showy stuff aboveground. What's below the surface, those nourishing roots, has been largely ignored. We at Healthy Companies have decades of research, mountains of data, and thousands of hours of interviews with leaders from around the globe, and all that information points to a persuasive conclusion: the only way a leader can withstand the gale-force winds of change is by relying on his or her deep, healthy roots.

The roots of the tree represent what's inside a leader—the values, beliefs, experiences, emotions, and thoughts that define who a person is. When we say a leader must be grounded, we are affirming that a person possesses a strong root system. Well-developed roots are important to a leader for the same reason they are essential to the tree. They support and nourish what you see—the stately trunk and the beautiful branches. In leaders, this aboveground portion is their behavior or actions. It is what they do, yet we have found that what a leader does will inevitably fall short or fail unless it is supported by healthy roots. These roots define who you are and who you aspire to be—your life purpose, your character and deepest values, and your true self.

Now some will say that actions speak louder than words. And in many cases they do. Why should you be so concerned about what's going on inside you? Because actions come from somewhere, and your principles, intentions, thoughts, and emotions determine whether these actions are genuine or insincere.

The leadership deficit is a direct result of people's preoccupation with outcomes, competencies, short-term metrics, and external personas. This preoccupation fundamentally ignores the internal drivers of human behavior. When a leader isn't up to the job, there is little if any discussion of the underlying source of the person's deficiencies.

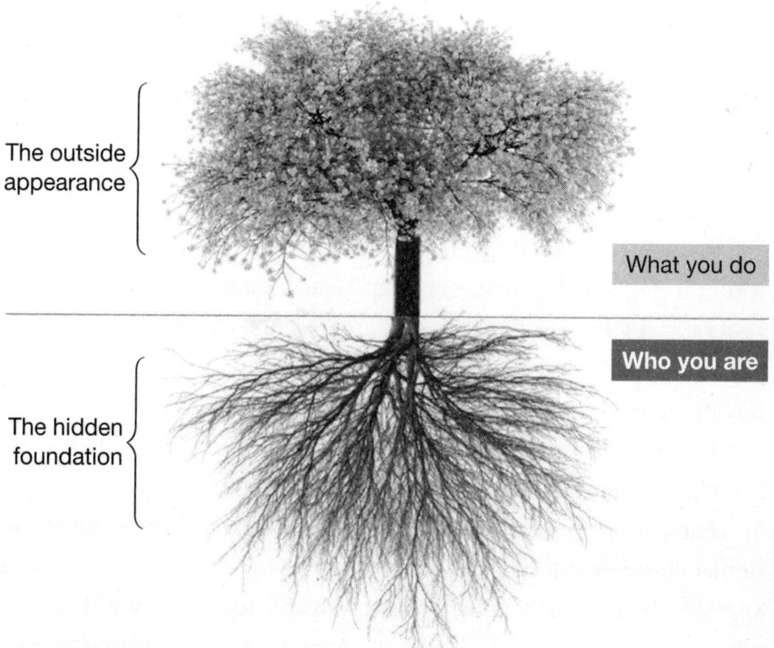

Figure 3.1

We hope to shift your focus and scrutinize the source and origins of problems and inadequate leadership. We are advocating a much deeper examination into the nature of leadership.

INSIDE THE HEALTHY LEADER MODEL

Health is a state of being in which people function on all cylinders to their highest potential.[1] Our organs and bodies naturally aspire to health. We have an inborn desire to grow and adapt to the world around us. We have a fundamental good nature as human beings and want to be part of something bigger than ourselves. Whether we tap into this potential or not depends on who we are and what we focus on.

When people focus on the roots of who they are, they are better able to align their personal emotions and thoughts with their behavior. Leaders who pay attention to and develop the roots of their personal health have a clarity and honesty about who they are and what they can accomplish. They know to measure themselves by what's inside, not by the flashy, superficial exterior. It is also an opportunity to rejuvenate themselves and reframe how they see the world. The result is leadership that is highly personal, deeply grounded, and strong enough to handle the pressures of relentless change without resorting to a style that leaves a person arrogant, drained, or fearful.

We use the tree metaphor to show that what makes a healthy leader a grounded person are deep-seated roots. For leaders, these roots are distinctive because each represents a dimension of their personal health. In fact, we have found the state of people's personal health to be the best way to capture the quality of their leadership. Leaders with healthy roots are strong and thriving, and this is what influences their health, performance, and resilience.

Each root represents an entire field of study, with hundreds of books and experts, but no one has yet brought them together in a way that looks at the whole person and whole leader. As we identified what "who you are" looks like in a leader, we have been able to craft a revolutionary new paradigm for leadership, what we call the Healthy Leader Model, illustrated in Figure 3.2.

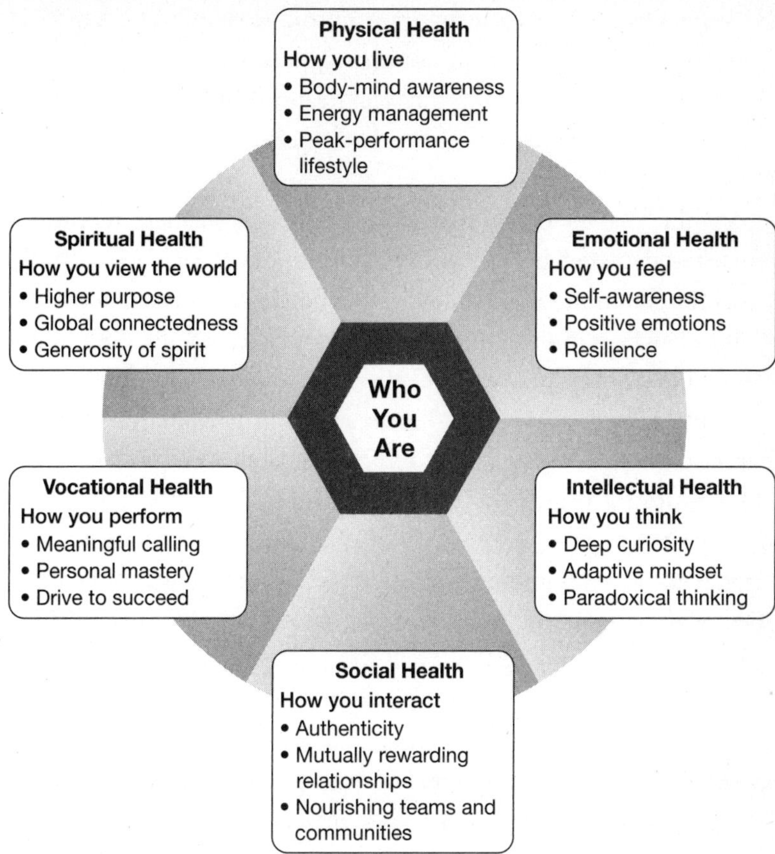

Figure 3.2 The Healthy Leader Model

Here's an overview of the chapters that explain how these roots give you the inner strength and mindset needed to handle all that is coming your way. Our research into the healthy leader also introduced us to individuals who possess especially well developed, healthy roots. We profile these people later and for now want to introduce you to some of them and the facet of their healthy roots they exemplify. You may find some surprising personalities in our pantheon of leaders, the well known as well as the lesser known and people who have overcome tremendous odds.

Physical health (covered in Chapters Four through Six) enables you to be aware of your mind and body, best use your mental and physical energy, and stay focused on a peak-performance lifestyle. It ensures that you are capable of pursuing a healthy life. The energy and stamina that come with physical health enable you to keep up with the amplified *speed of change* that's accelerating in every part of working life.

In the chapter on body-mind awareness, you meet renowned dancer and choreographer Judith Jamison, and the CEO of PBS, Paula Kerger. In the energy management chapter, you read about the global chairman of PwC International Ltd, Dennis Nally. And in the discussion of peak-performance lifestyle, you learn how a pharmaceutical industry CEO, Joe Jimenez at Novartis in Switzerland, handles this challenging aspect of physical health.

Emotional health (covered in Chapters Seven through Nine) deepens your self-awareness. It enables you to understand your strengths and shortcomings, to tap into positive feelings and jettison the negative ones, and to engage just enough anxiety to challenge yourself without causing too much stress. When you are emotionally healthy, you are comfortable asking difficult questions, comfortable living with uncertainty, and able to bounce back from adversity. Emotional health creates confidence, a quality essential to coping with *uncertainty and the impermanence of life.*

The story of Congressman Tim Ryan offers an enlightened account of self-awareness, especially in the rough-and-tumble world of politics. From Nando Parrado, who's not only the CEO of Parrado Multimedia but a survivor of a deadly plane crash high in the Andes, you read about positive emotions. Linda Rabbitt, founder and owner of Rand Construction, also offers a unique perspective on positive emotions. And who better to learn from about resilience than Mike Puzziferri, deputy chief with the Fire Department of New York (FDNY).

Intellectual health (covered in Chapters Ten through Twelve) allows you to expand your mental capacity, to imagine and think deeply. You are able to break out of your mental comfort zone, understand and accept contradictory or paradoxical thoughts, and change what and how you think. It's mental adroitness coupled with far-reaching curiosity. Intellectual health also strengthens mental clarity so that you can innovate faster and meet the demands of a *complex marketplace and workplace.*

In the chapter on deep curiosity, you encounter two different approaches in Mike Petters, CEO of Huntington Ingalls Industries, and Kumar Birla, chairman of Aditya Birla Group. The chapter on the adaptive mindset offers the remarkable story of Headmaster Kashiwazaki of the Ofunato Elementary School, Japan. And a stimulating example of paradoxical thinking is Jørgen Vig Knudstorp, CEO of Lego Group.

Social health (covered in Chapters Thirteen through Fifteen) gives you the confidence to be who you want to be in your relationships. You are able to be principled and true to yourself while at the same time forging intimate ties with others. With a large capacity to feel empathy and compassion, you can build mutually rewarding relationships and be part of nourishing teams and communities. Social health also empowers you to become *more connected and transparent in business.*

The chapter on authenticity features Ken Samet of MedStar Health, and Mitch Kosh, senior vice president of Ralph Lauren Polo, who both live and breathe this quality. In the chapter on building mutually rewarding relationships, you read about Per-Olof Loof, CEO of KEMET. Individuals from two different worlds—Christoph Lengauer, chief scientific officer at Blueprint Medicines, and Eric Schoomaker, former surgeon general of the U.S. Army—show you what goes into nourishing teams and communities.

Vocational health (covered in Chapters Sixteen through Eighteen) is your ability to tap into a personal calling that reflects who you are and what you want to be. This quality gives you the wherewithal to harness energy and skill in order to push yourself toward success. Through personal mastery, you fulfill your highest potential. This healthy root also equips you with the resolve required to *handle the forces of competition* and stay focused on producing lasting results.

The chapter on finding a meaningful calling presents the inspirational profile of Ingrid Srinath, CEO of Civicus. For the chapter on personal mastery, we feature Brian Cornell, head of PepsiCo Americas Foods, and Ted Mathas, CEO of New York Life. The career of Kay Koplovitz, founder of USA Networks and chairwoman of Fifth & Pacific, offers a vivid account of the drive to succeed.

Spiritual health (covered in Chapters Nineteen through Twenty-One) opens up the part of you that recognizes a higher purpose, something more meaningful than your personal needs. This is the quality that gets you outside yourself so that you live with gratitude and generosity and can share with diverse groups of people from different cultures. With spiritual health, you feel connected to the world and strive to make a lasting contribution that betters people's lives and improves the environment. Leaders with strong spiritual health are able to *tackle the powers of globalization* and avoid chasing small-minded, selfish aims.

For personal viewpoints of what it means to have a higher purpose, we profile Jack Stephenson, pastor of the Anona Church in Florida, and Wai-Kwong Seck, executive vice president at State Street Bank in Hong Kong. The chapter on global connectedness tells the inspirational story of Armand Diangienda, director of the Kinshasa Symphony, Democratic Republic of the Congo. Two outstanding representatives for the chapter on generosity of spirit are David Rubenstein, founder of the Carlyle Group, and Klaus Kleinfeld, CEO of Alcoa.

STRONG ROOTS FEED PERFORMANCE

Your performance does not arise de novo but emanates from how you translate what's inside yourself into decisions and actions. Your healthy roots have an immediate and direct impact on how you lead. There is a link between each of your healthy roots and what you do. Roots stimulate a tree to branch out, and in the same way, leaders with healthy roots nourish not only individuals around them but entire organizations.

Those closest to a leader—teams dedicated to discrete projects, board members, or informal groups with a common cause—are the first to feel the impact of the leader's healthy roots. Perhaps the most obvious impact is on how people feel about what they are doing. Leaders with healthy roots inspire and motivate others in a variety of ways. Through words and deeds, they communicate values, beliefs, and a sense of purpose that are bigger than any individual or any company's bottom line. Being around healthy leaders, people see how strong physical, emotional, or vocational roots, for instance, improve their lives and inspire them to do the same.

The power of healthy roots extends even further, influencing the direction and performance of entire organizations, from small nonprofits to giant corporations. A single leader with well-developed, healthy roots can reshape the culture, mission, and day-to-day operations of a company. Such a leader is especially adept at doing things that build successful enterprises.

An important element of our research has been to identify how who you are influences what you do and the impact that healthy leaders have on their organizations. We have found that the healthiest of leaders are adept at six essential leadership actions, which are the topics of Part Three: Putting Leadership into Action.

The chapter on the ways a leader can **tap into a higher purpose** features the story of Bob McDonald, CEO at Procter & Gamble, who's been doing this for years. **Forging a shared direction** is another action, and we profile the classic example of Alan Mulally at Ford Motor Company, who famously turned that company around. The leadership action of **unleashing human potential** is vividly typified by the experiences of David Novak, CEO of Yum! Brands. Sally Jewell, former CEO of REI and secretary of the interior, presents a consummate case for **fostering productive relationships**. The action of **seizing new opportunities** is solidly demonstrated by Ben Noteboon, CEO of Randstad Holding N.V. The sixth action, **driving high performance**, is described through the story of serial entrepreneur John Kealy, CEO of Decision Lens.

These actions produce far-reaching results—namely, an enhanced market reputation, outstanding shareholder value, profitable growth, greater attraction for talent, and a positive social impact. These findings have been confirmed by our research, and much of the data we have collected confirm their validity and help us make the business case for the Healthy Leader Model.

HEALTHY LEADERS ARE HIGHER PERFORMERS: THE BUSINESS CASE

Our mission is to help CEOs and executive teams build healthy, high-performing organizations. Our higher purpose is to help transform the world one leader at a time. In the leadership area, our work involves assessing, developing, and coaching executives and senior managers and their teams.

The foundation of our work is a robust research program studying hundreds of CEOs, looking at their leadership and their business and life challenges. There are two aspects to our research. The first is qualitative: sitting face-to-face with hundreds of CEOs from such companies as Toyota, Canon, Fosters, and Singapore Airlines in Asia; Deutsche Bank, ING Group, and Novartis in Europe; and Boeing, Procter & Gamble, PepsiCo, Cemex, and Ford in the Americas. The Healthy Leader Model emerged from these best-in-class interviews, and in turn has been used as the primary measurement tool for leader evaluations.

The second aspect to our research is quantitative, stemming from our research-based 360 Healthy Leader Assessment. The assessment combines a psychological approach with behavioral parameters that measure a person's leadership character and performance as gauged by who they are, what they do, and how they perform.

Healthy Companies is now developing an extensive database that we are sharing with leaders to help them appraise their effectiveness; shore up areas where they need to improve; and help companies with selection, performance management, and career development issues. Built to be psychometrically sound, the survey is showing amazing results. These data were collected across several industries, multiple levels and job titles, and different levels of leadership health and performance. These are our most provocative findings:

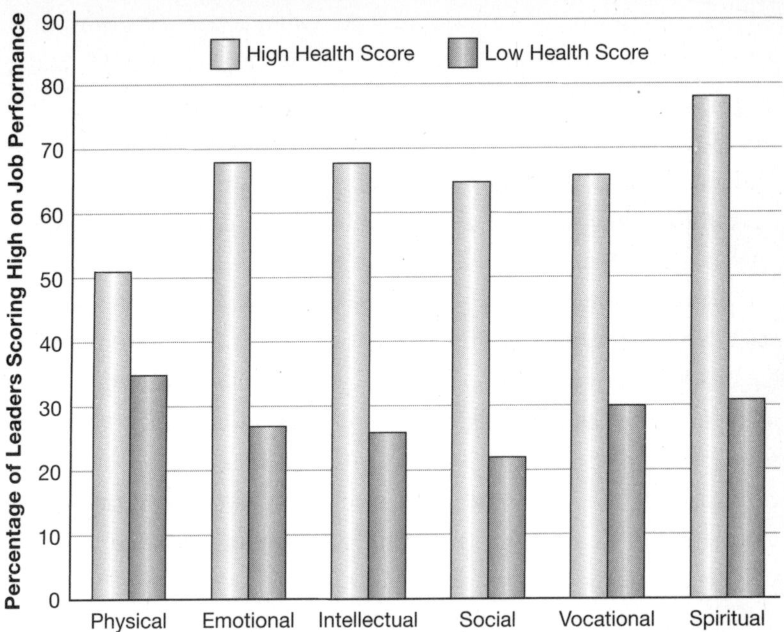

Figure 3.3 Leadership Performance in Relation to Health Score

- Leaders perform significantly better when they score higher on the roots of healthy leadership. The higher the score on leadership health, the better the leadership performance score as rated by bosses, peers, and staff.
- Each person has his or her own unique, personalized leadership profile of strengths and vulnerabilities.
- Each area of health correlates highly with other people's reports of a leader's performance.

Figure 3.3 illustrates these findings, showing how leaders with higher health scores in all six major areas were also the higher performers. Who you are truly drives what you do and how you perform.

This is the business case for healthy leadership. Healthy leaders are more resilient and fulfilled; they build healthier, higher-performing organizations and help build a healthier society. These leaders are able to achieve great market reputation, provide outstanding shareholder value, create profitable growth, serve as major talent magnets, and have a positive societal impact.

Much of this success is the result of shedding old ideas about leadership and how a leader should act. Shibboleths about leadership have been sabotaging even the best-intended leaders for decades. We don't suggest that leaders keep changing what they do, adopt the newest management strategy, or copy what's working for somebody else. Behavior is only half the story. You can retain the best of what is already working while learning to adopt a new mindset. There is no need for wholesale abandonment of what you do well. Instead, try to see the world and your place in it with a new set of eyes. This comes about by tapping into your true self, reaffirming your deepest values and individual strengths, and letting who you are drive what you do.

MAKING YOUR LEADERSHIP PERSONAL

Think of your leadership as a system of health.[2] Your body is an intricate, interconnected system in which everything influences everything else. Your respiratory, circulatory, skeletal, and immune subsystems must work in harmony to be fully functioning. If one of these subsystems is out of line, the entire system can come undone.

Leadership is the same way. Each leadership root is in constant interaction with the others and can positively or negatively affect how the other roots are expressed and managed. All the roots are essential for strong leadership and important to your overall health, well-being, and performance. Poor leadership is a failure or breakdown of the whole or of part of the system.

There are going to be priorities and multiple dimensions of your life, and how you integrate that is how you find happiness.

—Denise Morrison, CEO, Campbell Soup Company[3]

Our approach to leadership is a personalized one. One size doesn't fit all. Each individual has her own portrait and her own strengths and vulnerabilities. What's ideally healthy for one person may not be optimally effective for someone else. But being healthy in all the roots is critical to great leadership.

This is not rocket science. So why have people ignored leadership health? A misunderstanding of human nature is a good place to start. What makes people tick? What drives happiness and success? What does a healthy adult look like? How can we inspire people? What's the connection between health and productivity? These are questions leadership experts have not given nearly enough attention to.

There are other reasons as well. People tend to compartmentalize their personal and work lives and not see themselves as whole human beings. Leaders are reticent about talking about these issues because they might be penalized as being too soft; they are afraid of looking weak or "too human." We also tend to idealize or demonize our leaders and don't allow them to be real people on the public stage. Too often society rewards unhealthy behavior, and as a result many people become too accustomed to unhealthy cultures. It's time to confront these issues head-on and look at leadership in a fresh way. Now let's dig into the roots that will nourish and support your healthy leadership.

The Roots of Healthy Leadership

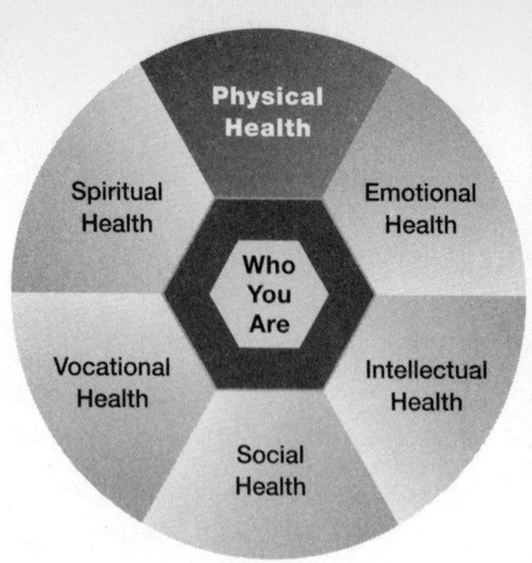

Physical Health

Your physical health is vital to your role as a leader. We're talking not just about the absence of disease but the presence of health. You can't be an effective leader without paying attention to your body; it needs constant care and maintenance, just as your company does. We want you to get deeply in touch with your amazing body, including all its imperfections.

Your body can do remarkable things: It can repair itself, when bones knit together after a break or when the brain rewires after the nervous system is damaged. Organs can coordinate lifesaving activity, as happens with the respiratory and cardiovascular systems. It can tell you when it has been compromised, as happens with infection. And it can lift your mood through the production of endogenous opioids—those wonderful endorphins that ramp up when you push yourself physically.

But the body is not perfect, and people find lots of reasons to ignore its health. It takes time away from "leading" and frequently demands a commitment to breaking unhealthy habits and finding new routines. Unfortunately, at some point in your life, you will face a health crisis or have to deal with a chronic health condition. Cancer, diabetes, arthritis, hypertension, a herniated disk, depression, a traumatic event—it's just a matter of time. Nevertheless, millions are already coping with these while still accentuating the healthy part of their lives.

Robust physical health is also essential in your role as you deal with the fierce pace of change. Today's leaders grapple with longer work hours, excessive job stress, diminished job security, and dwindling work-life balance. Their companies toil daily with the typical upheavals in business. Product cycles are now just months, not years. Marketing projects get torpedoed by the Internet and require instant corrections. A client wants a blueprint delivered ASAP. An executive vice president suddenly quits, and you need a replacement yesterday. A long-term currency hedge taken only hours ago has turned south. Dynamic physical health gives you the agility and stamina to respond to all that's coming at you.

Strong personal health begins with body-mind awareness, which gives you the personal insights and knowledge to develop a healthy lifestyle specially tailored for you. A healthy lifestyle has numerous benefits, not the least of which is a kind of self-protection and self-perpetuation. The results of good health are cumulative. With it, you feel more energetic, and this energetic spirit infuses every facet of your life. When you are able to do more, you simply feel better, and the inevitable result is a peak-performance lifestyle.

WARNING SIGNS OF DECLINING PHYSICAL HEALTH

- Insufficient energy and stamina
- Increased stress and unhappiness
- Inconsistent ability to think clearly
- Lifestyle habits that undermine work
- Loss of work due to illness
- Decreased concentration and attention

CHAPTER 4

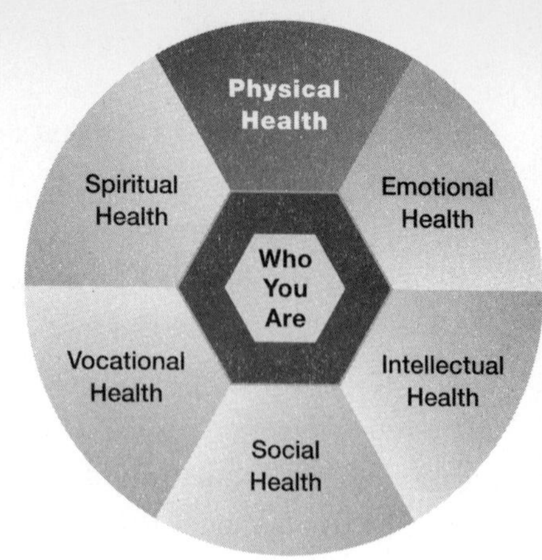

Body-Mind Awareness

A HARMONY WITHIN YOURSELF

Picture a strong, solitary dancer onstage. Tall and sinewy, she is constantly moving. Her hands and fingers seem to speak as she glides, leaps, and fills the stage. Your eyes are riveted to her, seeing both grace and power. You feel the rhythm and sensuality of her movement. Although the dancer's movements appear effortless, you intuitively know that they are the result of countless hours of practice, an iron-willed determination to ignore pain, and an acute awareness of her physicality.

The dancer is Judith Jamison, one of the world's premier modern dancers and choreographers. She began dancing at age six, and her professional home for most of her life has been the Alvin Ailey American Dance Theater. On top of her career as a principal dancer, she also has been the artistic director of the company. Under her leadership, the company performed around the globe, reaching twenty-three million people in seventy-one countries. In 1999, Ms. Jamison (as she is fondly known at the company) was presented a Kennedy Center Honor recognizing her lifetime achievement to the performing arts, and in 2008, Congress named Judith and the company as U.S. cultural ambassador to the world.

Jamison's career is built on her ability to express the interplay of body, mind, heart, and spirit—an interplay born of talent, passion, hard work, and relentless discipline. Every performance she gives and every piece of direction she offers epitomizes this unique convergence.

A dancer uses her mind to extend the body's limitations. Jamison offers an example: "Physically, we don't know where anything ends . . . Inside us is an infinity, so that when I'm telling people to have their arms absolutely at their sides, this arm does not stop at the fingertips. It reaches all the way to the ground . . . and beyond."[1]

The mental, the physical, and the spiritual sides of dance are always present. "Yet it's always mind over matter," she says. "A dancer doesn't go onstage thinking 'I'm going to connect my mind, body, and spirit.' It just happens."

Judith's life has been full of awards and accolades as an international diva, but she's quick to remind us, "I still have to do my own laundry." She remembers fondly her Broadway debut with Gregory Hines in *Sophisticated Ladies*. "As I walked out on stage to the throngs of appreciation and applause, I tripped on my own dress and fell flat on my face. Now that was a lesson in humanity."

Ultimately, Judith Jamison's body-mind awareness enables her to integrate her thoughts and feelings with her physical expression into a vibrant, healthy self. "No matter what you're doing, if you are doing it excellently, then you're in touch with who you are; this is the heart and the soul, why you're here in the first place. Otherwise, what's the point?"

OUR BODIES ARE UNIQUELY SIMILAR

The Human Genome Project was a thirteen-year effort to identify all the estimated twenty-five thousand human genes and to sequence the estimated three billion pairs of genes that make up human DNA. This gargantuan task was completed in 2003 and presented a remarkable finding: 99.9 percent of the DNA sequences were identical across the human population.[2]

This means that leaders everywhere are very similar, but not identical. They differ in who they are, bodies and minds, and how they live their lives. For a moment, let's examine your physical makeup and how it functions as a collection of interconnected systems that drive all that you do as a leader. Your health depends on how you play the four "cards" in your hand. They are your

1. Genetic makeup, which determines your physical vulnerability to stress and diseases
2. Personal development, which mostly encompasses childhood and family experiences
3. Life experiences, which include all the stressors and circumstances you encounter and what they do to you
4. Beliefs and expectations—your attitudes toward your health and how much, or little, control you take[3]

One of the biggest threats to your health, which can arise from a genetic predisposition or life experiences, is chronic inflammation. As with so many internal functions, there is good inflammation and bad inflammation. The good type delivers fluids that repair tissue or remove toxins. The bad type is chronic, which stresses tissue and organs over the long term and leads to their breakdown. Think of chronic inflammation as internal rust that can corrode everything from blood vessels to spinal disks. Understanding chronic inflammation is a good place to start talking about being resilient.

The body's primary systems (nervous, musculoskeletal, circulatory, gastrointestinal, respiratory, immune, endocrine, and sensory) depend on each other. The heart does not beat without direction from the brain. Your bones and muscles depend on the gut for energy and growth. Your senses constantly send signals to the nervous system that are essential to survival. And because these systems are holistic and function together, if one malfunctions or is weak, others suffer, too. We offer this singular proposition: they act as one—as a magical, interdependent system that sustains health and life. As Dr. Deepak Chopra has noted, our physical bodies are not many separate parts but a solitary process.[4] Therefore, doing everything you can to promote this harmony is a cornerstone of resilience.

MORE POWERFUL THAN ANY SOFTWARE: YOUR MIND

The mind is a vital partner in this integrated system. It has a powerful and ongoing conversation with your body. Consider that there are numerous ways the mind and body communicate: chemicals, electrical signals, hormones, and genes. Adding to the traffic is the two-way nature of these messages. Information goes back and forth, at various times amplifying, diminishing, and turning on or turning off particular signals.

What connects the mind and body is energy—a steady flow of electrical signals that activate cells and muscles in the body and neurons in the brain. This energy initiates actions—it sparks movement and consciousness. Also, energy is self-regulating via a feedback loop spearheaded by our genes and inputs from our environment. This dynamic flow of energy influences everything you think about and are aware of, and all that you do.

An amazing feature of this torrent of communication is our mind's incredible influence. The human mind is our greatest distinctive asset—it gives us cognitive capacity, creativity and commitment, courage, a desire to collaborate, and our deep ability to learn and adapt in the world. Science continues to discover the multitude of ways the mind affects the whole person. For a rough idea of what researchers are delving into, consider these pilot studies under way at the Johns Hopkins Center for Mind-Body Research:[5]

- Neuroimaging of catastrophizing and pain across states of consciousness
- The relationship of depression and hopelessness to platelet activation following acute myocardial infarction
- Psychophysiologic effects of yoga on rheumatoid arthritis
- Depression, cardiac arrhythmias, and implantable cardioverter defibrillators
- The psychological leading indicators of various cancers

Numerous other researchers are examining the mind's special qualities. For instance, South African sports scientist Dr. Tim Noakes has looked into the mind's effect on a runner's ability to push beyond normal limits.[6] He has found that the mind can be trained so that a person can physically handle more. This is how Roger Bannister broke the four-minute-mile barrier and declared, "The great barrier is the mental hurdle."

When you are engaged in a Herculean task, something that seems insurmountable, you may be tempted to give up and declare it impossible. Research tells us that often your mind quits before your body does. Physically you are probably more able than you realize, but optimizing your physical health means getting your mind on board. The body-mind partnership will elevate your ability to accomplish more. For a sense of your body-mind awareness, ask yourself:

- When I feel physically fit, how does it affect my moods? Does it make me feel happy or content?
- How aware am I of my physical strengths and weaknesses, such as muscle strength and cardio endurance, and how does my physical health affect my leadership performance?
- If I do not feel well, do I take immediate action to find a remedy, or am I likely to work right through the illness?
- What are my most vulnerable organs or body systems under stress (for example, stomach, nerves, back, head)?

Live Like an Athlete

Our research shows that business executives who participate in competitive sports say that there are lessons immediately applicable to work—namely, it's all about winning and losing; teamwork is essential; you need discipline, perseverance, and the courage to take risks; you learn from mistakes and failure.

THE PULSE OF THE INTELLIGENT HEART

A critical way station between your mind and body is your heart. Surprisingly, your heart generates over one hundred times more electricity than your brain, and it has a magnetic field that is five thousand times stronger.[7] Heart signals affect how you process emotions and rebound from stress, and key mental processes like paying attention, memory, and problem solving.

Your heart rate rises and falls depending on your level of emotional and physical health and fitness. When you are under stress, your heart responds. If you are resilient, your heart readily adapts its rhythm to help your entire body handle the added pressure. At other times, when you are joyful and loving, your heart rate smoothes out and the intensity diminishes.[8]

When your heart works well, other physiological systems become more synchronized with your heart and nervous system and this makes your entire body feel better. You feel not just better but healthy and vital. Scientists in the new discipline of neurocardiology believe that the neural network between the heart and brain is so developed that it functions as an intelligent system, like a "little brain."[9]

The implications of this for you as a leader are profound. Physical fitness won't come with just a strong heart or a resilient immune system or great muscle strength or wonderful stamina. You must attend to it all as a whole. We are fairly certain, for instance, that Judith Jamison, even with all her aches and pains, has so schooled her body that she rarely thinks about how each element contributes to a flawless performance. Nevertheless, they function together as a single, healthy entity. To maximize your body's full health, do not obsess about individual elements, but step back and consider how they work together as a whole.

In the chapters on emotional health, we delve further into this connection between your body and your mind, and focus on how your emotions often determine what kind of leader you are.

A BODY, MIND, AND HEART TRANSFORMED

When Paula Kerger became president and CEO of the Public Broadcasting Service, she was reasonably healthy and eager to tackle all the issues that the country's preeminent nonprofit media organization might encounter. To be sure, it would be a colossal job—PBS is America's largest public media enterprise and serves more than 350 television stations.

Kerger must wear many hats. She's the public face of PBS and does countless interviews with other media outlets; spends considerable time on Capitol Hill, fundraising; ensures fresh programming; and provides leadership for the organization's employees.

At the same time, Kerger has had to contend with fierce external forces. She describes the environment: "Great turbulence and extraordinary change. We are certainly in the midst of both on the media side as well as on the philanthropic side. That is both an opportunity and a challenge."[10]

Kerger's position was physically demanding from the beginning, involving constant travel and nonstop meetings and interviews. Like that of many executives, her fitness regimen fell by the wayside as she devoted longer days and weekend work to her job. As a result, she often got sick and felt "crummy." But she was self-aware enough to realize that she had to do something about her physical health, so she returned to the gym. She challenged herself to compete in a triathlon.

"I looked around, and I saw women my age and older as well as a lot of younger women. And I thought, Wow, I wonder if I could actually do something like this. And so I quietly started training," she recounts.

It took Kerger a year of stealth workouts before she felt that she was ready to compete in a triathlon. The experience has been phenomenal, she says. "I really love the opportunity, and I do consider it an opportunity to be healthy enough that I can participate in races like this and stand alongside women my age and older who are not going to allow the calendar to define who they are."

Her training and triathlon competitions have not only boosted her mental toughness and well-being but also changed her attitude as a business leader. She says that putting herself "in circumstances that were indeed challenging has given me a very different perspective on work. It helps you manage fear as well as stress . . . It's really so much about life, and you're constantly confronting fear."

Kerger offers an insightful perspective on how her physical health and mental outlook intersect and touch every facet of her life: "There's an intellectual part because it's parallel to some of the challenges that you wrestle with in life or certainly in business. You go as prepared as you can. You know that something is going to happen, and you hope that you'll have some good luck. And then you just do the best that you can. And, for me, it's just given me a lot of real energy, and it's impacted a lot of my life."

Her remarkable transformation has also enabled her to bolster PBS. During her time there, she has grown PBS's audiences across genres and has tapped into new media such as iTunes, YouTube, Netflix, Amazon, and Hulu while expanding the organization's arts and children's programming. And PBS has remained enormously vibrant.

Fortunately for Kerger, she's also benefited from participating in demanding competitions with confidence. Regardless of what happens at home or at work, she knows she's in the best shape ever to deal with whatever life throws her way. Her body, mind, and heart are in sync, and she's a better leader and person for it.

CHAPTER 5

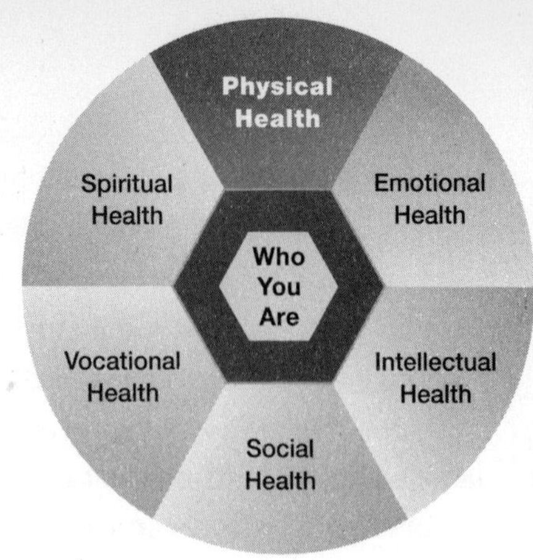

Energy Management

Think about your typical workday, which may look something like this: You arrive early to get a jump on the hundreds of emails and voice messages waiting. Soon people begin to show up at your office with problems and issues that need your immediate input. Next it's back-to-back meetings where you stay focused for a couple of hours, concentrating on what everyone needs and says. Your energy may flag because of jet lag, a bad night's sleep, or having spent most of the previous night on the phone dealing with an overseas crisis. To pump yourself up, you take a mental break, drink a couple cups of coffee, or go for a short walk.

Lunch is quick and at your desk, but you avoid heavy foods that slow you down. During the afternoon, you're on your feet visiting departments and checking on projects while juggling phone calls. At the end of the afternoon, you're back in your office to go over budget figures with the CFO. It's early evening, people are starting to go home, and you sit down with your right-hand person to hash out tomorrow's work and future travel schedules. And if it's a good day, you get to leave for home before 7 PM.

Impressive just to think about—all the energy you marshal to propel you both mentally and physically through the myriad demands of being a leader. The details may be different, but the pace of your day is likely similar to what this scenario describes. Being a leader requires enormous physical energy—energy to handle long days, energy to mentally juggle priorities and tasks, energy to concentrate and think clearly, energy to manage people's personal issues, and energy to be active, whether you're getting around corporate headquarters or traveling the globe.

Mental energy enables you to counteract a steady stream of these stressors. Getting people to buy into your strategy and dealing with work deadlines, disgruntled customers, and complicated team dynamics are just a few. But soon enough you quickly bump up into the tougher challenges—a lack of engagement and accountability, overactive egos, a demanding board member—and throw into the mix your own career ambitions and anxieties. The list is almost endless.

Energy management is a twofold challenge. It's contending with the physical and mental stress of running a team or organization, and it's using these demands as a springboard for renewing and reinvigorating yourself. Whereas body-mind awareness looks largely inward, energy management asks you to think about your inner physical and mental reserves and then use your interactions with your environment in order to create positive energy. So it's both inward and outward. You are harnessing personal energy while simultaneously generating organizational energy.

REPLENISHING YOUR ENERGY AND RECHARGING YOUR COMPANY

The sheer size of Dennis Nally's job would intimidate a weaker soul. As global chairman of PwC International Ltd, the world's largest professional services network, he leads more than 180,000 people in 158 countries.

Nally is presently engaged in a massive effort to create and execute a global 2016 strategy to encapsulate the company's identity into one global network and an iconic brand. The source of Nally's prodigious energy is both his PwC life and his personal life. Over the years, he has learned the fine art of energy balance. He knows what depletes his energy and what replenishes it.

Energy management is like a three-legged stool: it tips over if one leg is shorter or weaker than the others. Nally makes sure each leg of his stool—personal life, family life, and work life—is strong and on solid ground.

He has kept his personal and family life sound and centered by taking care of himself physically and mentally. Some internal meter tells him when he needs to recharge, disconnect from emails and work demands, and get away, literally, by taking time on his powerboat. Married for thirty-five years, with four children and three grandchildren, he knows that family time is vital for recharging and balancing a person. Family vacations are essential to his well-being as a leader and a grounded human being.

Now, you might not make Dennis's salary or own a boat, but that should not stop you from asking yourself how well you balance the three legs on the stool of life.

We've known and worked with Dennis and his senior partners for over ten years, as they continue to build a high-performance culture. Nally's personal stamina has helped him communicate a global vision and strategy for the international network even in turbulent times. The global accounting industry has gone through great upheavals in the past decade, from the collapse of client firms, like Enron, to a rapidly evolving regulatory climate and consolidation among some of the big players. Nally has had to adjust to these tsunamis of change while also making sure that he has the stamina to cope with radical changes in how his company does business, deploys technology, services demanding clients, and globalizes the business. Most challenging, however, is inspiring and engaging his partners and associates.

Over the years, he's learned how critical it is to keep his work and life balanced. He wasn't always good at it. Early in his career, his approach consisted of driving hard and ignoring the impact this had on himself and others. As happens with many leaders, the job threatened to consume him.

He recounts, "If you don't know who you are and you don't have a good sense of what you're trying to do . . . it's pretty hard to deal with the changes that are out there. You've got to understand what's going to work for you as an individual. And if you don't, you're at everyone's mercy because in any one of these key leadership jobs, you know it is 24/7 if you want it to be . . . You need to understand what your priorities are as an individual."[1]

Key for him is "setting the tone for the organization and surrounding yourself with individuals who share the same mindset." Energy management, not only in himself but in those around him, has been fundamental to achieving excellence. It's taken him years to understand how to find that balance. He describes the process: "Everybody is different and can handle various amounts of stress. You need to recognize that and make sure you deal with people according to their personal tolerance levels. A good leader constantly recalibrates himself and takes the pulse of the organization to know whether he's ahead of the game, behind the game, or just about right."

Excellence matters a lot to Dennis, and he is constantly striving to instill it throughout the organization. "You need to exert positive energy so that change is viewed as an opportunity. You can always do better, you can always learn from your mistakes, but it's the positive energy that makes all the difference."

CAN YOU GO THE DISTANCE?

What do NFL football players, Wimbledon tennis champions, World Series baseball pitchers, and great rugby and cricket players all have in common? You might say they perform and compete at a world-class level. And you would be right.

Professional athletes employ a variety of strategies to develop their strength, stamina, and skills. They routinely expose themselves to stress. During training, they repeatedly push themselves to the point of near collapse when their bodies want to quit.

At the same time, successful professional athletes have a full repertoire of rituals they go through between training sessions to help them renew themselves. They will dedicate themselves to an activity unrelated to their sport, like the professional tennis player who plays golf, the NFL lineman who practices yoga, the baseball player who studies acting, or the Olympic skier who pilots planes. They may spend their off time playing chess or becoming a great Italian cook; the activity itself is less important than taking time to redirect themselves into something that uses other muscles and other mental abilities. Their rituals let them mentally decompress so that the stress of regular high-caliber performance does not become chronic. The balance in Dennis Nally's personal and professional life is similar to that of a professional athlete. Even though Nally never has an off-season, he manages energy expenditures in a way that optimizes his ability to react quickly and sustain this effort while allowing himself recovery and renewal time.

People need time for renewal, especially hard-charging leaders. Rejuvenation alters your brain patterns so that your mind, heart, and body can refresh and reinvigorate themselves. Without this renewal, you are unable to bolster your immune system, readjust your routines, maintain your productive energy, or adapt to life's changing conditions.

Research confirms what common sense tells us: people would be happier and healthier if they took more time off and spent it with family and friends, reduced commuting time, and took longer vacations.[2] Without relaxation and renewal, we eventually experience chronic stress, burnout, and breakdown.

MANAGING YOUR ENERGY

Eastern philosophy has long regarded the human body as a holistic organism. All the expressions of your energy, whether it's your ability to move, handle stress, or take action decisively, depend on your entire physiology working in concert. An array of internal activities—eating, breathing, digestion, metabolism, sensory experiences, thinking, feeling, remembering, and even dreaming—all function together as a single process. This perspective is contrary to that of Western medicine, which tends to think of people as a collection of separately functioning biological systems.

The holistic perspective helps explain the amazing things the body can do and how personal energy, both physical or mental, can determine the course of your leadership. It is energy that enables you to adapt well to changing conditions, stretch yourself to think faster and clearer, and work harder and faster than the competition. But as you stretch yourself, you must find a way to maintain physical and mental balance. The scientific term for this balance is *homeostasis*, which means equilibrium. The body has a natural desire for homeostasis, but the change around us is constantly challenging this natural state. Much of how you perform as a leader is influenced by your energy homeostasis. That's why being grounded is so important.

As physicians and researchers have found, the right balance produces vibrant energy and long-term health. For instance, balancing your mental energy can affect how your body ages. Genetic researchers have discovered how your emotions can alter the expression of your genes to the point of accelerating or decelerating the body's aging process. Research has actually found that four months of meditation can increase the genetic production of telomeres, which naturally decrease as we age.[3] Meditation, as most people know, touches every facet of your mental energy, including attitudes, motivation, and burnout.

The impact of balancing our physical energy is more familiar to us. There are numerous diseases and conditions that may be influenced by your energy management. One interesting study shows that chronic sleep deprivation (less than six hours a night for a week) affects hundreds of "circadian genes" involved in immunity and inflammation, altering a person's attention, thinking, and risk for coronary heart disease.[4] Knowing how to combat fatigue, handle stress, and build up stamina can also help prevent heart disease, asthma, obesity, diabetes, headaches, depression, gastrointestinal problems, Alzheimer's, aging, and even early death.[5]

How people balance their lives is also influenced by national culture. On the one hand, Americans are often considered out of balance, particularly given our inclination to overwork, take shorter vacations, and ignore personal health. We certainly appear to pay the price for this imbalance with high rates of divorce, heart disease, obesity, and alcoholism. On the other hand, other cultures, especially those in tropical climates, are known for being much less productive and more inclined to take lots of leisure time. They too pay a price with an assortment of health problems that come with a lower standard of living.

Achieving the right energy balance comes with avoiding extremes and finding a middle ground that works for you. This is your personal homeostasis, a state where your energy production makes you optimally healthy and productive. This positive energy naturally influences the decisions you make and the interactions you have during the course of the day.

As you can see from the following suggestions, Eastern and Western philosophies complement each other when it comes to personal health. Examine your life for the forces that can upset your personal homeostasis. Possible culprits might include too many prescription drugs and supplements, an erratic sleep routine, too little exercise, an out-of-control appetite for sweets or carbs, or too many "relaxation" drinks after work. Consider these energy boosters:

- When you feel stressed and out of balance, turn inward and examine the sources of your stress. Slow, deep breathing activates parts of your nervous system that can calm you.
- Use visualization to discover what a balanced energy system feels like. Imagine your mind and body feeling just enough stress to be engaged and productive.
- Find new ways to get fit. Alternate daily exercise routines; try taking a brisk walk in the park during the day; practice intervals on the elliptical machine; try swimming, tennis, or racquetball and simple weight training.
- Manage your habits and circadian rhythms. When and for how long you eat, sleep, work, and relax all have an impact on

your energy. Take Sunday off and enjoy a quiet day reading a book.

- Discover ways to recharge your energy, such as by pursuing long-postponed interests or engaging in a spiritual activity.

A JOURNEY OF FINDING BALANCE

Northwestern Mutual may look like a typical large corporation, given its 156-year history, recent revenues of nearly $25 billion, and four million policy owners. But it is not. As chairman and CEO John Schlifske explains, it is a mutual company owned by its policyholders and has a longer time horizon for reaching its goals than does a public company. Similarly, John has found that a long-term personal strategy for his own health and fitness is giving him the best results. And the core quality behind making the company and himself more productive is balance.

In his personal life, Schlifske has discovered more energy as he has added balance. This journey began soon after he took over. "The biggest surprise for me being CEO is the level of energy that is required 24/7. I just had no idea about this."[6]

To reenergize himself, he turns to activities that nurture and strengthen him—spending time with his family and reading. He best describes what his wife and six children do for him: "I'm a huge believer in work-life balance . . . Going home every night is a huge refuge for me . . . Our youngest kids, two six-year-olds, don't know that I am a CEO. If they do, they don't know what it means. It's just a totally different life at home, and it's a good thing. I love it. It's a total distraction."

He's ruthless about making sure he does not shortchange his family. "Certain things come first with respect to the family—vacations, coaching my ten-year-old's baseball team . . . I don't let anything interfere with that."

Reading also sparks his energy through intellectual stimulation. "I love to read. I like to read either autobiographies of great leaders or articles about what companies are doing to make themselves better. That, to me, is recharging."

Schlifske's balanced, high-energy life has made a difference. The company has been voted by Glassdoor's annual employee survey as one of the best places to work in the industry. It looks as though everyone is benefiting from John's energy management.

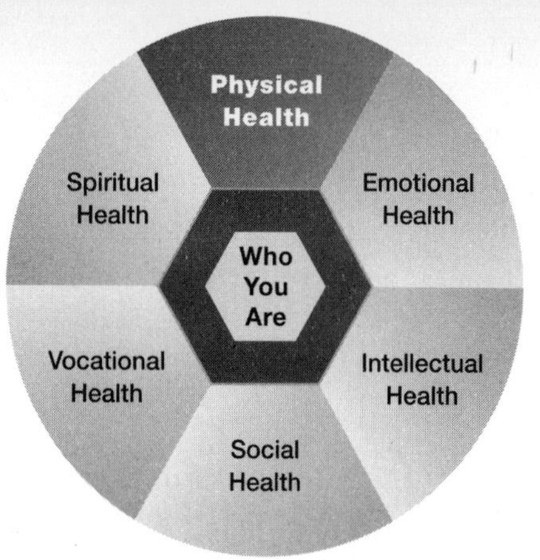

CHAPTER 6

Peak-Performance Lifestyle

A PLAYBOOK FOR LEADING

Bill Johnson, CEO of H.J. Heinz Company, learned about health from his father, a professional football coach for the Cincinnati Bengals. He applies this philosophy to himself and to his efforts to build a high-performance company at Heinz.

"If you plan each play in your drive meticulously and execute it flawlessly, you can make one first down, then another, then another, until you've taken the ball across the finish line," he reasons.[1]

An example of this was his approach to streamlining the company, a sprawling consumer products business that has manufacturing operations on six continents and markets to more than two hundred countries. "I changed our focus from driving profits at any cost to growing over a period of time to sustain performance"—not unlike an athlete who wants a long career on the playing field.

Although Heinz is best known for its ketchup, other offerings, such as Ore-Ida, Lea & Perrins, and Weight Watchers, have become global staples. Johnson's goal was to enhance the company's famous brands, so he sold factories, got rid of noncore products, and accelerated the company's purchase of sauce and snack businesses. Then he turned to mainstays, like Heinz Ketchup, and set a goal to introduce new features to them every twelve to eighteen months. This incremental, one-play-at-a-time strategy could explain why the company's earnings per share grew 11 percent from 2006 to 2009, despite the economic downturn.

Johnson believes in the value of stress. Not chronic stress, but just enough pressure to push him to excel. And he advocates it for himself personally as well as for company employees. "I'm uncomfortable with the status quo," he declares. So push yourself just enough that you can meet a challenge before reaching total fatigue. In this way, you build up your physical strength and endurance while also making yourself mentally tougher.

"If you're not prepared to question and challenge yourself, then you have no value," Bill says. "You have to keep renewing yourself in order to renew the company. You have to embrace discomfort, which creates sleepless nights and anxiety. Without the ability to channel this anxiety appropriately, it's impossible to succeed."

Johnson challenges himself physically by putting himself against much younger executives. "I just turned sixty. You don't know anybody younger at sixty than me—I mean, I can run with most of the guys who work for me who are in their forties. I can also outwork most of these guys. It makes me very unpleasant at times."

So how does a sixty-something CEO maintain his personal health? With balance in his life. By paying attention to his life outside Heinz as well as inside. And knowing the value of this balance, he also insists that those around him are equally attentive to their work-life scale. He tells this story to illustrate: "I have lunch with summer interns every year . . . Our HR people dread this because I'm always asked about work-life balance . . . They know my answer is going to be 'There's no such thing unless you create it.' What that means is that you don't fill the void with work. When there's an opportunity, take time to do what you need to do."

By pushing himself as well as those around him, Johnson has instilled an appreciation of staying in shape. He makes sure he's physically able to maintain the brutal pace of managing a global consumer products company, and he conveys the value of maintaining a peak-performance lifestyle to everyone around him. Maybe that is why his fifteen-year tenure as CEO at Heinz makes him the longest-serving chief executive in the food industry.

DO YOU HAVE WHAT IT TAKES?

Think about your own personal and work life—are your attitudes and habits geared to peak-performance living? Ask yourself:

- What changes do I need to make to advance my physical health?
- Do I make sure I have time to exercise regardless of where I am or what is going on?
- Does my schedule include regular breaks for rest and relaxation?
- Do I set a good example for my team and my organization?
- What gets in my way balancing my life or managing my time?

The average American who hits fifty or sixty in reasonable health is likely to live well into his or her eighties. Some 70 percent of premature death and aging is lifestyle related. In the popular book *Younger Next Year*, Chris Crowley and Henry S. Lodge, MD, make the most provocative suggestion of all: exercise six days a week for the rest of your life.[2]

AN OUNCE OF PREVENTION = A TON OF BENEFITS

Maintaining a peak-performance lifestyle like Bill Johnson's demands more than a daily run or having salads for lunch. It's also about prevention—keeping illness at bay and your immune system strong. Investing in prevention is much less costly than undergoing treatment once you are sick or on disability. Western and Eastern approaches to health are valuable for understanding the many facets of prevention. On the one hand, prevention means focusing on individual diseases and conditions, like heart disease or hypertension. On the other hand, prevention also entails balancing your internal health with a lifestyle that emphasizes activities and habits that can prevent illness while boosting your well-being. Here's what the latest science of prevention reveals about the ingredients of a peak-performance lifestyle:

- Seventy-five percent of medical costs are preventable, and the single biggest threat to our own well-being and peak performance is ourselves.[3]
- Diets with five to thirteen servings a day of fruits and vegetables lower your risk of stroke, cardiovascular conditions, cancer, and diabetes.[4]
- Thirty minutes of moderate physical activity, such as a brisk walk, each day can reduce the risk of a heart attack by up to 50 percent and help burn fat throughout the day.[5] However, only 27 percent of people get thirty minutes of exercise five times a week.[6]
- Your immune system becomes impaired with too little sleep. People who sleep less than seven hours a night are three times more likely to get a cold.[7]
- Excessive drinking, defined by the Centers for Disease Control (CDC) as consuming more than two drinks a day for men and one for women, can lead to chronic liver disease and alcohol-related injuries. The CDC reports that seventy-nine thousand deaths annually are attributable to excessive drinking.[8]
- The rise in the incidence of dementia, particularly Alzheimer's, has been linked to lifestyle risk factors including smoking, physical inactivity, midlife hypertension, diabetes, and midlife obesity. The risk factors account for 54 percent of diagnosed cases of Alzheimer's in the United States.[9]
- Dr. James Rippe of Tufts School of Medicine found that 40 percent of Fortune 500 executives are obese and 73 percent have a sedentary lifestyle.[10]

WHAT'S YOUR PERSONALIZED FITNESS PLAN?

Clearly, it's possible to run an organization and ignore your personal health. It's just not optimal. We also understand that the stress and demands of being a leader can get the better of a well-intentioned individual. Sometimes the business climate makes it doubly difficult. Some people think that sacrificing their health is the price they pay for being the leader—whether they're leading a big corporation or a small starving nonprofit, or managing in the middle and being pulled in all directions.

The problem with this reasoning is that it overlooks a key finding of business and health economics: unhealthy executives produce unhealthy companies, and unhealthy companies produce unhealthy employees. And unhealthy workers are costly workers, whether they are in the corner office or on a factory line in Asia.

The human value chain goes something like this: employee health and well-being leads to engaged, highly productive, high-performing people. People truly are a company's most valuable assets, and there are numerous ways to appreciate their value and invest in human capital. They begin with preventive programs, such as screenings, immunizations, health risk appraisals, behavioral coaching, and health education. Overall fitness programs run the gamut from company subsidies for healthy meals and gym memberships to flexible work policies and financial incentives attached to particular activities.

The payoff to a company from investing in the health of workers is huge. The benefits can be seen in worker attitudes and commitment, productivity, and a financial return on the investment.

One study by the Centers for Disease Control focused on company strategies for preventing individual conditions, like cardiovascular disease. Over a two-to-five-year period, companies with comprehensive workplace wellness programs and health plans saw each dollar of their investments yield three to six dollars.[11] Other groups have confirmed that companies reap a substantial return on investing in the health of their workers. Health Fairs Direct analyzed more than fifty studies related to worksite wellness and found that the ROI on wellness programs ranged from $1.17 to $6.04.[12] These yields come from a variety of improvements, such as reduced absenteeism, improved morale and loyalty, higher revenue per employee, lower health and disability costs, and lower turnover and recruitment costs.

Here are some ideas for getting started in creating a culture of health and productivity:

- Flexible leave and flexible work schedules
- Sick-leave pools
- Child care and elder care
- Employee assistance plan
- Telecommuting
- Job sharing
- Healthy food choices in company facilities and vending machines
- Educational programs—possible topics include nutrition and smart eating, smoking cessation, chronic diseases, and individual risk factors
- Fitness programs—gym discounts, lunchtime classes, incentives, free memberships

FROM THE POOL TO THE CEO'S OFFICE

Being a high-achieving athlete in an individual sport like swimming may not sound like the kind of experience to equip a person to lead a pharmaceutical giant that operates in 140 countries and has more than 120,000 employees. But for Joe Jimenez, CEO of Novartis, headquartered in Basel, Switzerland, the fit has been perfect for a host of reasons. By applying lessons learned as captain of Stanford's swim team, he has honed his personal leadership style and infused the company with a culture that knows the value of physical hardiness.

Jimenez's personal leadership philosophy is focused on three concepts: self, team, and the organization. First, he begins with an inward assessment. He believes that before he can lead an organization, he must be able to lead himself. A feature of his "lead yourself first" attitude is being disciplined about keeping himself physically fit and helping others achieve their individual peak health.

He explains why fitness is so crucial: "This is a global company; I'm traveling probably 50 percent of the time. I'm constantly jet-lagged because I'm in different time zones. I'll be in Asia and North America and in Latin America in the same week. And so physical activity and maintaining physical stamina is a very important piece that's become part of the way that I manage myself."[13]

Another facet of his leadership is paying attention to his own skills and abilities, and recognizing where he's strong and where he's weak. It's the attitude of a competitive breaststroker who knows he's not so good with all the four strokes of an individual medley and so helps build a team in which individuals complement each other.

"Leading yourself and making choices means understanding where you are very strong, where you're weak, and how you back-stop yourself," he explains. "You need to focus on the team and surround yourself with the right people . . . with people who are taking more of a positive outlook versus a negative outlook."

Jimenez's personal fitness and discipline, plus a management team with remarkable stamina, came into play during a struggle over the looming expiration of a drug patent with a $30 billion sales basis. The effort first required thinking ahead and planning. Although the expiration was a couple years away, in the Big Pharma world, that's like tomorrow. Jimenez assembled a team and fixed a goal—no sales decline come expiration day.

"Everybody said, no way, that's impossible, we're going to see a dip," he recounts. He insisted: "The pharmaceutical division will move through this period without a dip in sales. And I think it's that same mentality of nothing's impossible, of getting people around you who share the same goal. The team needs to increase their comfort zone and really see themselves moving through this period, performing at a higher level. Then you can make it happen."

Since becoming CEO in 2010, Jimenez has made sure that everyone in the company knows the value of strong physical health and takes the steps to ensure it. He created a company-wide program, Be Healthy, that offers workers a variety of ways to improve their own well-being. It includes fees for health clubs, company cafeterias offering healthy items, and individual screening for conditions such as high cholesterol and high blood pressure.

He explains why having a physically fit workforce is so important: "We're a company that cares about patients. It's the reason we come to work every day. We want to care equally for our associates who work for the company. If you look at our organization, and many organizations, the people who are able to adapt to changing environments the fastest are the people who demonstrate high levels of learning agility."

For Jimenez and Novartis, peak performance is best expressed by three priorities: to innovate, drive productivity, and accelerate growth. He helps achieve this by making sure that he and the organization have the physical agility and stamina to accomplish his business goals.

• • •

The components of physical health—body-mind awareness, energy management, and a peak-performance lifestyle—don't come immediately. They start with commitment and develop with discipline and persistence. Some of us are natural athletes and stay healthy, fit, and balanced over our lifetimes. Others of us go back and forth between being in shape and dropping our routine. Still others are simply bored by it all and unmotivated to stay in shape. If you are one of them, know that your greatest enemy is becoming discouraged. Regardless of where you start, keep it personal, choose your activities carefully, and do what is challenging and fun. The goal is to stay vigilant and make a genuine and sustainable commitment to your physical health. The benefits will cascade into many aspects of your life.

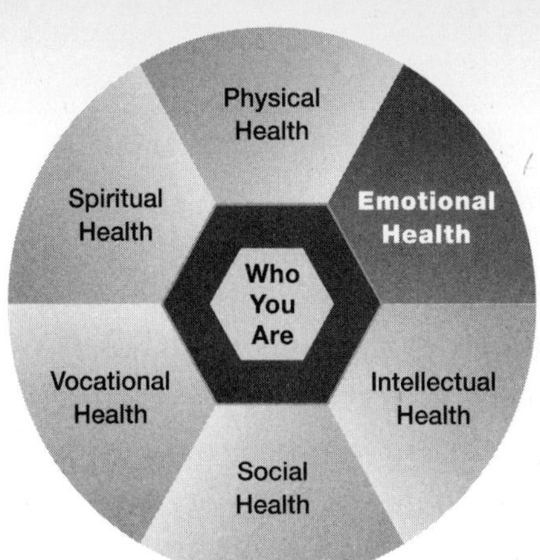

Emotional Health

Have you ever been in a business meeting with an executive who makes everything about him? You want to talk about staffing problems, and his contribution is a series of one-liners, such as "That wasn't me who hired her" and "Send him to my department—I'll show him hard work."

Self-centeredness, bluster, arrogance, ego—these are just some of the signs of someone who is emotionally immature. As people, they are annoying to be around. As leaders, they are a disaster—which is why emotional health is so vital to the roots of healthy leadership.

People experience a full range of emotions; some are stuck on the negative end of the spectrum, hijacked by fear, anger, and anxiety; others swing to excessive positive emotions. Healthy leaders find a comfortable middle ground, experiencing both negative and positive emotions yet able to manage and control them. They recognize that their emotions can infect a workplace or invigorate it. Their natural preference is to choose positive emotions whenever possible.

For many, the biggest benefit of emotional health is as both a mentality and a skill set; it enables you to adapt to a world that changes with a snap of the fingers. Emotionally healthy leaders have a nimbleness, evident in their reactions, thinking, and behavior. Being light on your feet emotionally is essential in business today as you live in a world of uncertainty. Leaders with strong emotional roots are not derailed by unpredictability, realize that they don't know everything, and fully expect that shit happens. So when it does, they manage their emotions, monitor how others are faring, and do their best to make good decisions. And they do this time and again, knowing that emotional health is a process as much as a state of being.

Before you read any further, pause for a few moments to think about your emotional health and where you might fit on a spectrum from robust to dysfunctional. These questions may get your mind in gear:

- How often do you talk openly about your emotions? Do you have someone you can confide in, both in your personal and work life, and who offers supportive feedback?
- Are you the kind of person who blisters at unpredictable situations and unexpected changes in your routines? Or are you someone who relishes the opportunity to embrace change and manage through adversity?
- When you have a strong emotional reaction to something, do you identify a method to help you stop before acting out your emotions, or are you easily hijacked?

There are many theories as to what constitutes emotional health. As is true of most personal qualities, there are no hard-and-fast formulas. Nevertheless, when we focus on emotional health with executives, three aspects keep showing up: self-awareness, positive emotions, and resilience.

WARNING SIGNS OF DECLINING EMOTIONAL HEALTH

- Increased susceptibility to stress
- Inability to fully express and manage emotions
- Getting caught up in negative thinking
- Disconnection from network of support
- High incidence of conflict and defensiveness
- Feeling victimized or powerless

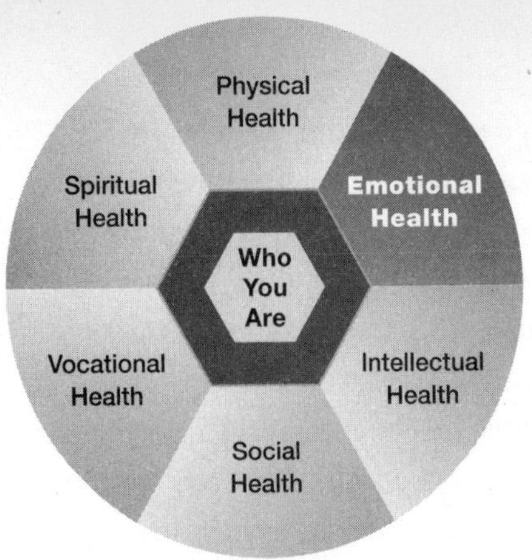

CHAPTER 7

Self-Awareness

A LEADER WITH A MIND OF HIS OWN

When you think of a congressman, self-awareness or mindfulness is probably not the first characteristic to come to mind. Nevertheless, for House Representative Tim Ryan, focusing on his personal mindset and attitudes is making him not only a personally insightful leader but a more effective member of Congress.

Being mindful for Tim Ryan means that he constantly monitors his thoughts, striving to keep them in the present and not allowing himself to get sidetracked by what's happened in the past or worries about the future. Whether debating on the House floor or negotiating with other members of the committees he serves on, Ryan focuses on listening and understanding what motivates others, and where their vulnerabilities and strengths lie. Self-awareness and mindfulness, Ryan says, keep him from "going down roads that lead nowhere."[1]

He wasn't always this way, and vividly remembers a specific conversation with a good friend. They were relaxing at a tavern when the friend, after noting all of Ryan's successes—getting a law degree, being the youngest Democrat elected to the House at age twenty-nine, getting a plum assignment on the Appropriations Committee—asked him what he was going to do when he "really made it."

Ryan's immediate reaction was to laugh, but then he started thinking. He realized that her question reflected most people's mentality—they lived in the future and always looked ahead, and did not pay attention to the here and now. On further thought, he understood the fallacy of always thinking ahead. "You are really disconnected from where you are, and you're living in the future . . . That kind of rips you out of enjoying what's right in front of you."

A major step in Ryan's evolution came during a five-day retreat that included thirty-six hours of complete silence and reflection. This had a profound impact on his thinking: "You start seeing everything outside of the present moment as not real . . . The best thing you could do is to live completely in the present, because you will see opportunities everywhere."

There is a practical streak in Ryan's present-centeredness. He believes that it is preventive: it stops him from saying something that spins out of control and later requires time and energy to reel back in. He also believes that being mindful of the present builds trust among friends and colleagues. They learn that he is not going to say things that are divisive or that cause damage. In discussions with opposite party members, he works to "invite them into a more mindful conversation without throwing gasoline." He can be trusted to be more interested in finding common ground than in venting the latest partisan rant on Capitol Hill.

It's in this spirit that Ryan hopes he can make a bigger impact in Washington. He is convinced that if lawmakers devoted more time to self-reflection and developing self-awareness, their priorities would shift. If they were more mindful leaders, much of the aggression and anger would dissipate, and they could focus more on cooperation and finding lasting solutions to difficult and contentious societal problems. This is his dream: a mindful leadership in Washington inspiring mindful constituents who all come together to create a healthier society.

Ryan reinforces his self-awareness and mindfulness every day, with meditation, yoga, and staying grounded by making time for personal relationships. "Ground yourself in basic goodness that is gentle and tender, kind and genuine," he suggests.

TELLING THE TRUTH TO YOURSELF AND OTHERS

As Tim Ryan's story reveals, developing self-awareness can be an uphill battle against all the pressures of a world that values action over introspection. It's difficult for many people, as Congressman Ryan would surely confirm. Much gets in the way.

According to one of the largest executive recruiting firms, 80 percent of executives have blind spots about themselves, and 40 percent have strengths they are unaware of or not using.[2] Problem areas that could stall or hijack executives' careers include being too narrow, failing to inspire or build talent, and not relating well to others.

Nomi Bergman, president of Advance/Newhouse's Bright House Networks, a midsize cable company with two-and-a-half million customers founded by her father, tells a story about starting work at the company. She had little business experience, so she molded her style after her father. His approach to managing people was classic old school, placing a high premium on bluntness, toughness, and doing things his way. He often told Nomi, "You don't have to be liked; you just have to be respected."

Initially, Nomi tried his way. To say it didn't work is an understatement. Nomi says that being physically small made many of her efforts at leading fall flat. And being blunt or insisting on her way without input from the people she was leading made her miserable.

To her credit, Nomi realized that her father's style was not hers. "I would feel awful at the end of the day," she says.[3] She vowed to develop self-awareness and figure out what worked best given her unique qualities. She offers an example: "In a meeting, I make a point much differently than my father. When it's a lower-level meeting, with people who report to me, I make a point of asking them questions . . . I try to lead them through my questions so they own the direction."

Nomi got trapped by trying to mimic her father's leadership style. She turned herself around by first being honest with herself and recognizing that she wasn't her father and that she needed to acquire skills of her own, beginning with self-awareness. Being honest with yourself also means recognizing when you are in denial about your abilities (strengths and weaknesses), your feelings, and your behavior.

Another hazardous area is the way we think about ourselves and the world. We often fool ourselves and aren't honest about our thinking errors. We all like to believe that we're good critical thinkers and don't let our emotions get in the way of sound judgment. But few of us are consistent in thinking clearly. Instead, we overgeneralize, jump to conclusions, engage in obsessive thinking, ignore the positive, magnify or minimize situations, personalize everything, or rely on self-commands using "should" and "should not" in conversations with ourselves.

ACCEPT WHO YOU ARE

Nothing is more important than knowing yourself and being comfortable with who you are. But be careful. Some people claim to be very self-aware, and they might be, but they happen to be jerks. Accepting who you are can begin with your "story," the internal dialogue most people have about where they came from and who they are. At the heart of this internal communication is self-reflection. This entails asking yourself questions about your values, assessing your successes and failures, thinking about your perceptions and interactions with others, and imagining where you want to take your life in the future.

Consider this: according to research involving forty-one thousand managers, most people are unaware of how their behavior affects others.[4] This is especially the case for those people who operate at "extremes" (people who make quick decisions or, conversely, resist change and diligently follow rules).

We all have imperfections. Central to self-awareness is admitting them not only to ourselves but to the people whom they impact. But this is not always easy. We are hardwired—psychologically and physiologically—to believe the story we have about ourselves. Psychologists call this story-creating process "sense making"—our insights into who we are, how we learn to be that way, ideas about the causes and circumstances of life events, and the internal narrative we have about ourselves.

It's important to remember that stories are created to understand our lives, and they can be rewritten to improve our lives. To deepen our self-awareness, we must understand our story and how we make sense of our life. Our stories influence our self-esteem, personal power, ethics and integrity, and relationships with others. By learning about our strengths and weaknesses and knowing what we like and don't like, we are able to become our true selves.

Nomi Bergman decided to change her story about herself. She used her newfound self-awareness to convert a personal quality once considered a liability into an effective and disarming asset. As she was honing her leadership style, she made an effort to be supportive and collaborative. "If I came on too strong and felt like I missed somebody else's point now, I'll go back to these people and say, 'You know, I came on too strong and I liked your idea. I want to go back to that.'"

Some may misinterpret Nomi as a pushover. Rather than protest or develop a tough exterior, she turned this skewed perception into an asset. Today, one of the main weapons in her arsenal is leveraging kindness. "If I look in the mirror and feel like I've been good in energizing others, I feel like I have been successful . . . It's a very powerful tool. Being a kind person . . . is more about bringing up your ideas in ways that protect the ego of the other person and aren't threatening to them. You try to do it in a way where both could own the new direction."

FAILED LEADERSHIP ARISES FROM IGNORANCE

There is one truism that applies to all of us: we have a lot to learn about ourselves. This may sound obvious, but leaders by nature are confident people and tend to believe strongly in their opinions. We recommend a more Socratic approach to personal knowledge.

Ask questions in the moment, search for answers deep inside yourself, dissect your story, and use critical thinking to assess your emotional health. Use your self-awareness to illuminate what you need to learn, and then seek out the best way to do that.

Harry Kraemer, investor, award-winning business school professor and ex-CEO of Baxter International, says it best: "My style of leadership starts with self-reflection. In my opinion 99% of us are just racing around and in constant motion, and not really taking time to think." Cadbury CEO Todd Stitzer tells of the consequences: "If you think you can make it up the hill and then realize that people are not following you, you're going to be a pretty lonely guy when you're near the top. So you have to know how people are feeling, and you have to monitor what comes out of your mouth. You're always self-correcting."[5]

Going public and admitting what you don't know has the added advantage of signaling to everyone around you that you are open to learning. It also tells people that you do not expect them to know everything.

Of course, self-education is a lifelong process. All of us have blind spots and discover new ones all the time. To address these gaps, engage your mind in a process of discovery. Shed the emotional baggage that is hampering your awareness. We often find ourselves distracted, seduced, or sabotaged by internal conversations that undermine our best selves. We develop attachments to ideas, people, ideals, and things that weigh us down. Our conscious and unconscious conversations keep us stuck in old patterns and dysfunctional habits.

Trying to do it all, expecting it can be done exactly right is a recipe for disappointment. Perfection is the enemy.

—Sheryl Sandburg, COO, Facebook[6]

Attachments come in many shapes and sizes. Some are simple thoughts and feelings. Others are more elaborate philosophies about life, desires for the future, and ideas about success. As they develop, they grow like a dense, tangled psychological web that controls our mind. One day we wake up to find that we have created a compelling story that has hijacked our mind.

Here are a few examples:

- **Attachment to stability.** We believe we can create stability and safety in our lives. But there is no such thing. Scared of uncertainty, we deny this reality and run away or get hijacked by change.
- **Attachment to the past.** Many of us are living in the past, trying to make sense of what's already happened, idolizing or demonizing our memories, and becoming immobilized by old emotional scars.
- **Attachment to the future.** Many of us are preoccupied by the future—striving for more or better, obsessed over what is missing in our life. By fearing that something is missing in our life, we risk enjoying the present moment.
- **Attachment to control.** From early childhood, we are taught to shape our environment. We minimize our weaknesses, maximize our strengths, and develop confidence and courage to be in charge. Then we become controlling.
- **Attachment to success.** Everyone dreams of success. But when our fear of failure or our desire for success turns into a compulsive need for achievement, then we've got a real problem.
- **Attachment to perfection.** Many of us are ruled by the need to be perfect. Perfectionism in ourselves is bad enough. But we tend

to impose perfection on the people around us, and all hell breaks loose.

LET SELF-REFLECTION REIGN, AND SUCCESS WILL FOLLOW

Don't get us wrong. Like you, we value action and achievement. However, we're convinced that true achievement comes from the inside. Put on hold your natural inclination to take action, and instead devote your energy to internal inquiry. As we said at the beginning of this book, extraordinary leadership stems not from your day-to-day behavior but from what's inside you. An introspective survey is an essential step in discovering who you are. Ask yourself:

- What are the core values that transcend both my personal and work life?
- When I go home at night, what thoughts about the day give me the most satisfaction?
- What gets me excited and eager during the day?
- Are there certain people or situations that I consistently avoid?
- What is my typical reaction when I receive feedback about myself from others?
- Do I quickly identify counterproductive thoughts or self-talk?

LEARNING TO BE SELF-AWARE

At this point, we'd like to shift focus from internal self-reflection and move along the continuum to how you can put your newfound self-knowledge to work. Yes, at this point we are talking about actions—things you can do, now armed with a rich, deep self-awareness, so that your emotional health and the unshakeable feeling of being grounded are firmly rooted.

- Look at your schedule and make time in each day—even as little as fifteen minutes—for quiet self-reflection. This may mean meditating or thinking about a problem, becoming aware of your body or senses, or observing your thoughts and feelings from fifty thousand feet. This is called mindfulness. Make this time inviolable and a permanent fixture in your day.

- Keep a journal of entries about life's situations and your emotional reactions. Become accustomed to identifying and naming your feelings. This will make it easier to talk about them. Some days you may log a few sentences and on others write many pages, but add something every day. In this way, you can track how and where your emotions interact with the other facets of your personality and daily activities.
- Test your self-awareness frequently by talking to others about what you and they are thinking and feeling. Especially feelings—don't be afraid to raise the subject of emotions. Promise yourself during these times that you will listen more than you talk or explain.
- Whenever you make a decision or take action, ask yourself questions based on a personal assessment of people or situations, and write them down. Was my decision consistent with my beliefs, values, and philosophy about life? What experiences most influenced my actions and what made me feel vulnerable? What aspect of leadership was most vulnerable for me?

CHAPTER 8

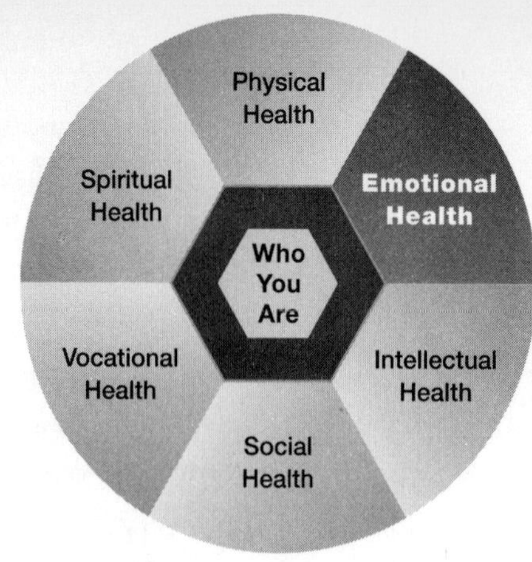

Positive Emotions

TRIUMPHING OVER FEAR

At age twenty-three, Nando Parrado, his rugby teammates, and their family members were flying over the Andes to a match, when their plane crashed at over eleven thousand feet. Parrado lost consciousness for three days. Some of his teammates lay dead, as did his mother. Parrado regained consciousness in time to hold his sister in his arms as she died of exposure. Survival was an immediate issue. The people who remained had no food and only melted snow for drinking. Three of the survivors, led by Parrado, climbed out of the mountains for help and hiked eleven days before spotting a peasant, who led them back to civilization. All told, the group had been missing in the mountains for seventy-two days.

The crash and rescue created a huge sensation around the world, spawning news reports; a bestselling book, *Alive: The Story of the Andes Survivors*; and a collection of feature films and documentary movies. Much of the story is known, including Parrado's role, which he wrote about in *Miracle in the Andes*.

Parrado had to act; he had to conquer his fears. A crisis often alters a person, but not always for the better. Sometimes people crumble. Even common personal crises like divorce or financial difficulties can forever alter you. Nando's experience instilled an enduring confidence, a belief that he could overcome even the worst of times.

Today, his personality is rooted in a belief in himself and his positive emotions. To be sure, Nando possesses other leadership dimensions, especially physical health, social health, and spiritual health. His strongest suit, though, is his emotional health, firmly rooted in positive emotions.

We often talk to CEOs and other leaders about positive emotions, explaining how such seemingly soft concepts can influence decisions. Sometimes we tell them Nando's story and of how his positive emotions transformed him. Nando explains it best: "I was lucky enough to find out at a very early age what the important things in life are."[1]

Not everyone can crash in the Andes, then miraculously climb to safety. You do not need a tragedy to harness feelings of hope, compassion, and joy in the workplace. You do need to appreciate how defeatism and fear can undermine your emotions. Nando refused to let his fear dominate him. Other fears—of failure, the unknown, losing control, making a wrong decision, or being vulnerable—can also wrack a leader.

Nando survived, and experienced a renewal, a deep understanding of the value of love and the role it plays in every facet of his life—even work. After losing his sister, mother, and best friends, he had to start over to find the affection and support he needed in order to find meaning. It took years, and Nando has never forgotten how vital family and friendship are to him. To this day, they come first, no matter what's going on at the office.

Nando could have become cold and distant, vowing never to let love into his life again. But he didn't, not because love makes him a better leader, which it does, but because it makes him a better person.

Today, Nando Parrado is the CEO of Parrado Multimedia, a television production company and host for National Geographic TV specials, and president of Uruguay's largest hardware retailer. It has taken him decades to build up these enterprises, yet the philosophy that has guided him arose in the mountains of the Andes. His philosophy has four tenets: don't be afraid, live in the moment, follow your heart, and never stop changing.

He has devoted thirty years to building up his television and cable companies. He often bases business and hiring decisions on his intuition and his "heart." "I am a believer in giving the best, receiving the best, and sharing things with people," he says.

A few months ago, he spoke at a conference of influential South American business families and talked about how his experience changed his attitude toward business and defined him as a leader. One of the attendees was so impressed that he asked Parrado to talk at each of his companies.

What makes this encounter noteworthy is that the individual was business magnate Carlos Slim, presently the world's richest man (net worth $69 billion) and controlling owner of numerous telecom, technology, retail, and finance companies. The two shared a vision. "He thinks companies are the people that make those companies, not the buildings or the assets," Nando recalls.

Nando teaches us volumes about the importance of positive emotions. His core beliefs form his positive attitude toward life and business. His lack of fear and his ability to live in the moment while applying love and compassion have propelled his ventures to new levels of success.

PART OF OUR HARDWIRING

Positive emotions, like survival emotions, are hardwired into everyone. Psychologists know this, and neuroscientists are beginning to produce a growing body of scientific literature delving into how these emotions are generated and have an impact on our lives.

A person's positive emotions differ depending on experiences, upbringing, genetic makeup, and circumstances.[2] They also may be shaped by a crisis (as Nando's were), good parenting, a spiritual life, or an innate quality. Dozens of subjective feelings could be called positive emotions. Among the successful leaders we have worked with, the most ubiquitous positive emotions are hope, compassion, forgiveness, joy, generosity, empathy, and love. Of course, few people possess all of them, and stellar leaders understand that developing positive emotions requires effort.

Before we go any further, here are several questions to help you gauge the state of your positive emotions and understand how your emotions influence your daily life:

- How aware are you of your emotional life? Honestly?
- When was the last time you laughed so hard you cried?
- How do your emotions shed light or cast shadows on people around you?
- How did your family handle emotions? Did you laugh, scream, cry, or just avoid each other at dinner?
- What kind of people make you smile, and who in your life makes you angry or frustrated as hell?
- How easy or difficult do you find it to forgive others? To feel compassion? To find joy in what you do? To be hopeful? To express love?
- Are you a worrier who is always anticipating problems? Or do you believe that things will turn out for the better and that you can make a difference?

Although there is much about positive emotions that science does not know, we do know that these emotions are hardwired into the brain. At the same time, they are subject to a certain amount of neuroplasticity, which enables the brain and nervous system to change as a result of injury or learning.[3] One emotion that all of us should try to cultivate and hardwire into our brain is love. It is arguably one of the most powerful human emotions, as well as a powerful leadership emotion. We use the word "arguably" because love is not mentioned very often in business. It's the emotion no one talks about, but we have seen how love can transform an individual and a company.

MANY EXPRESSIONS OF LOVE

Love in the workplace may be expressed as love of your job, love for your colleagues, or love of a project. Nando Parrado, for instance, more than once talked about his work life and "living with love."

Love motivates and inspires us. It helps us rise above our personal needs and build organizations with a higher purpose. When you lead with love, you create positive and nourishing relationships and enterprises that endure.

Love is a true survival emotion. This makes immanent sense if you think of love as the glue for essential positive attachments. It's natural: we are hardwired for love because it promotes mating, nurturing and support of the young, and social bonding. It's a powerful emotion that prompts us to live in groups so that we can help each other survive.

Numerous hormones and neurotransmitters stir your emotions. Oxytocin is one of them, sometimes called the "love hormone" because it stimulates hugging, touching, and sex; fosters parental love; and increases feelings of trust. Dopamine is famous for being our naturally produced opiate, which makes us feel better.

We know it is possible to survive your business life without feeling love. But if you make a choice to overcome your fears and let your innate feelings of attachment, affection, or deep concern for others—call it love if you dare—guide your behavior, then your leadership will be stronger and your organization healthier.

IMAGINING THE FUTURE: HOPE AND OPTIMISM

Healthy leaders who express hope and optimism imagine and invest in a better future. They believe in people and give them the benefit of the doubt, and they avoid getting blindsided by crises, using them instead as challenges. Without hope, it is easy to become overwhelmed by your problems. With hope, you are motivated to push past obstacles and strive for something better. Optimism is hope coupled with realism. Often rooted in experience, optimism is the wisdom to know what is possible and having faith in your ability to reach your goals.

Hope and optimism are subtly wired into our brains. A facet of our neurological makeup that may be wired for hope is in our "prospective memory," which is our ability to think about and plan for the future. When you take action to create a more prosperous tomorrow, or pledge that next time you have a problem you'll solve it instead of ignore it, your prospective memory is engaged with your positive emotions. Your outlook for the future, no matter how potentially arduous that future may be, has become more positive.

Optimism affects your sense of well-being too. Psychology researchers report that this feeling has been associated with lower levels of depression, anxiety, and distress, particularly in the face of difficult circumstances. We also know that optimists perform better than pessimists. Psychologist Michael Scheier, whose 1985 research into optimism broke the field wide open, says that such people are problem solvers who try to improve situations.[4]

Looking at leadership under the lens of hope and optimism, you can see that these qualities are essential if you are striving to lead people and inspire others to share your vision. But be careful. This belief that the future will be better than the past gives most of us the tendency to overestimate positive events in our life and underestimate the possibility that bad events will happen. This is known as our "optimism bias."

Tali Sharot is a research fellow in brain sciences at University College London and has produced some striking results. Her research shows that most of us naturally spend less time focusing on negative outcomes than we do positive ones.[5] In one study, she and her colleagues scanned the brains of people who processed both positive and negative information about the future. "When people learn, their neurons encode desirable information that can enhance optimism, but the neurons fail at incorporating unexpectedly undesirable information." All age groups showed the same patterns.

So optimism is a good thing. It enhances your hope, happiness, and odds for survival. But never forget your human tendency to wear rose-colored glasses.

NOT JUST DANCING IN THE STREETS: JOY AND HAPPINESS

Joy is a universal emotion. Scientists from various disciplines, including psychologist and facial expression expert Paul Ekman, neuroscientist Antonio Damasio, and psychiatrist George Valliant, agree that the capacity to feel and express joy is inherent in all of us.

Joy is many things. At its most basic, joy is a triumph over suffering. Making people feel better or improving their lot in life often generates joy. It is the ultimate antidote to misery. Although many leaders are not in a position to relieve suffering, they can stir joy in other ways. The simplest things can stimulate joy at work: praise, compliments, engaging in playfulness. You may flash a smile and big hello in the morning, offer a quiet "Nice job" to a colleague, thank a group of employees who put in an extra-long day, or celebrate special days.

Happiness differs from joy in that it has less to do with easing suffering and more to do with a state of being. For some leaders, happiness is difficult. It's not a dominant part of their genetic predisposition. In fact, happiness is one of the most heritable parts of our personality; over 60 percent of our happiness is genetically determined.[6] In the long run, it doesn't much matter what happens to you. You will generally return to your own personal happiness set point. For example, within a year, lottery winners and paraplegics both (on average) returned to their happiness baseline after the dramatic events in their lives.

Nonetheless, we have seen that DNA is not destiny, and inherent tendencies can be overcome. To encourage those leaders who don't seem wired for happiness, we tell them that happiness is not one emotion generated by a single brain structure. Numerous systems are involved. This makes happiness likely to arise from a variety of experiences and thoughts, giving a leader any number of opportunities for feeling and expressing happiness. And if you have a vulnerable happiness set point, just acknowledge it and don't beat yourself up for it. You just have to work a little harder than others to feel the same level of happiness.

Research also shows that particular attitudes in business can stimulate happiness. Neurobiologist Robin Lester says that workers who are risk-takers or highly motivated are happier in general.[7] Happiness not only brightens your outlook but also has a strong impact on people around you. It is especially infectious for engendering enthusiasm, laughter, and attention.

GIVING OF YOURSELF: EMPATHY, COMPASSION, AND FORGIVENESS

Leadership and business are all about relationships. These relationships only grow stronger when a leader feels empathy, compassion, and forgiveness. Each of these positive emotions has been shown to have strong value for an individual and an organization.

Empathy is being able to share someone's pain and suffering. The neurological center for empathy is the insula, which is also the heart of the brain's reward system. Empathy may be reinforced by a kind of brain cell called a "mirror neuron," which is activated when we see someone in pain. We can truly feel others' pain. Being able to sense when those around you are in distress is important for an empathetic leader; you can sense that employees are stressed, struggling with a task, burned out from working too hard, or hurt by something someone said. We will talk more about mirror neurons in the chapters on social health.

Frequently, empathy is paired with compassion, which is also hardwired into us. Whereas empathy is pure emotion, compassion requires action. Compassion is emotion plus behavior. It moves you to relieve the suffering of friends, colleagues, and family. The brain ensures that you will act this way by releasing endorphins when you act compassionately. As revealed in a brain scan study, the reward system also releases the pleasure neurotransmitter, dopamine, when you make a charitable contribution.[8] This reinforces acts of compassion.

Forgiveness does more than make you humane. It motivates you to avoid fighting or destructive behavior. A simple example of its benefits is what happens when negotiations triumph over war or when an "I'm sorry" halts a feud. Healthy leaders forgive by giving people some slack when they make mistakes; they work hard to get over disagreements quickly, and they try to avoid their own passive-aggressive behavior. It doesn't mean that you let people off the hook when they are wrong, only that you forgive. Without forgiveness, negative emotions can pile up and get in the way of success.

Forgiveness is contagious. In a business environment, if you are known to be forgiving, it inspires others to forget their grudges and revenge scenarios and devote their energies to worthwhile activities. One leader known for her compassion is Linda Rabbitt.

A POSITIVE LEADER IN ACTION

There are no formulas for what positive emotions should look like at work. Linda Rabbitt, founder and owner of Rand Construction in Washington DC has faced numerous challenges in running a company in an industry dominated by men who routinely question her competence. Nevertheless, she has harnessed her positive emotions and made her company into the second-largest female-owned construction company in the country.

She describes her learning curve: "When you're a woman in a very male-dominated industry, the band of emotion you're allowed to display is much narrower than a man's. If you're too tough, you're a bitch. If you're too soft, you're a marshmallow. By process of elimination and making many mistakes, I've learned when I was taking it too far."[9]

A turning point for her and Rand Construction came about ten years after its founding, when Rabbitt faced a two-front crisis: the company was stagnating, and she was diagnosed with breast cancer. At the time, she had a tight-fisted grip on the company, insisting on taking responsibility for everything and doing everything. "I had made the funnel way, way too narrow," she says. The small funnel was inhibiting her employees and holding back the company.

It was a dark time, and whether it was the illness or her own self-awareness that forced her to change, she recognized the importance and meaning of people around her. Relationships became paramount. This not only opened her heart but energized her company. "When I got sick and took a leave of absence and allowed other people to start leading Rand, we just exploded in growth. Out of my illness, my best relationships got deeper and stronger. It was a great thing that happened to me."

Linda Rabbitt devoted years to cultivating positive emotions. Earlier in her career, she led a nonprofit group that "had a really incompetent staff." She toiled for two years, gradually made changes, removed the dead weight, boosted the underperformers. It was a painful task, and Rabbitt struggled to stay positive and hold on to her belief that she could make a difference.

She describes what helped most: "When you're in your darkest hours, you take long walks and you proverbially kick the cat. I'd go find a beach or do something physical or emotional that lifts me up again. It's amazing what a mood changer music is. I'd put my old favorite music on and get on the cross-trainer. I can change my attitude in an hour."

An essential attitude for her is not to be afraid of showing employees that she is just like them—human, fallible, and caring. "One reason people are loyal to me is because I'm honest yet kind with them. Because I'm honest about my own mistakes, it allows them to be honest about their mistakes. If I made a mistake in the way I staffed a project, it's really my fault; we're all in the soup together," she says.

Rabbitt finds great joy in helping others. In her company, this translates into an ethic that couples joy with knowing that she and her employees have delivered the best service possible: "It's so important that people not only be happy with our product but with our process. It's so people-intense. When you're building somebody's office space in Washington, with an entire community of Type A personalities, their office is their home. You're building their soul. And I want them to feel that this process doesn't have to be so horrible. It can be fun and enjoyable. That's why we try to hire people who are natural pleasers, who really get a high from making someone else happy."

POSITIVE EMOTIONS PAY REWARDS

Positive emotions affect both your physical and social health, adding a holistic dimension to your leadership style. The physical rewards are well documented. One of the biggest payoffs is in how positive emotions slow the body's stress response system and help speed recovery.

Positive emotions also help protect you against heart disease. A ten-year study in Nova Scotia found that people who are happy, enthusiastic, and content are less likely to develop heart disease. Furthermore, people who are in a good mood every day and use humor to cope have a stronger immune system.[10]

Positive emotions impact your social health, too. For instance, they give you charisma, which is one of the secret ingredients in leadership. Charisma generated by positive emotions infuses you with the ability to be more persuasive, inspiring, and motivational while also forging intense loyalty. Psychologists who study leadership have found that charismatic leaders are deeply emotional, and this attracts followers. What especially attracts followers are a leader's vision and how he or she communicates that vision. Such charismatic leaders are noted for generating employee cooperation and trust and better performance.

DO YOU HIDE YOUR EMOTIONS?

You may resist showing emotions and communicating feelings like love, joy, happiness, and compassion, especially around the office. Habit and discomfort get in your way. Showing affection, empathy, or compassion can leave you vulnerable and ripe for rejection. But the point of showing emotions is not to gain acceptance. It's to be honest about yourself and what matters, and to let coworkers know that humanity is as important as productivity. The point is to form bonds and relationships based on true personal qualities, not a cold façade.

The business culture is especially uncomfortable with emotions. You want to get raised eyebrows at work? Start crying. We are uneasy with touching each other, even in a light, supportive way, like putting a hand on the shoulder. Only recently have we begun to accept hugging. All these unspoken taboos dampen positive emotions. Showing emotions can make you vulnerable. Being emotional may threaten your self-image, your authority, your control, or your well-being. Or you may think emotions make you look silly, too eager, too excited, or too hopeful. You might also fear wanting something and not getting it.

Likewise, some leaders think that seeking forgiveness signals weakness by admitting a change of mind and a mistake or fault. You may fear that saying "I'm sorry" suggests that your convictions are weak. Nothing could be further from the truth. It requires strength, not weakness, to recognize that we are all imperfect and that everyone makes mistakes, and to have the maturity and fortitude to take responsibility for our actions.

WHAT EMOTIONS DERAIL YOU?

Essential to managing your positive and negative emotions is knowing when you are vulnerable. This way, you can take steps to replace dysfunctional patterns with healthy responses. Although it's natural to experience anger, fear, or sadness, it is unhealthy to slip into these on a regular basis. Negative emotions disrupt creativity, interfere with decision making, and diminish happiness. Further, if you allow yourself to get hijacked by these emotions, they end up coming back in your face.

Here are the three big negative emotions—anger, fear, and sadness—and suggestions for avoiding being hijacked by them.

Anger

- After a blowup, immediately stop and think. Next time, try to think before the blowup.
- Go public—admit to others that you are working on managing your temper.
- Look around for what makes you angry and explore how you might reframe the issue.

Fear

- Don't keep your fears hidden—they will only grow larger. A simple acknowledgment of nervousness helps greatly to calm it.
- Remind yourself that you've mastered similar frightening situations in the past.
- Try exposure therapy—constantly confront what's frightening you. Run toward it, not away from it. With time, familiarity will breed confidence.

Sadness

- Make a list of your positive qualities or ask a friend to do so.
- Keep a chart of your successes and failures so that you don't forget all the good things in your life.
- Commit yourself to spending time every day on something you thoroughly enjoy.

Some of us grew up in families that downplayed our feelings or encouraged us to hide them. Some of us grew up in families that blew feelings out of proportion. Even if you learned to identify and express your emotions in healthy ways, doing so at work can be tough given frenetic deadlines, competing agendas, and toxic colleagues. Practice and patience are the only ways to overcome these barriers. Here are some ways to help you convert negative feelings into positive energy.

Experiment with Your Emotions

Practice makes perfect or at least opens the door to something new. Try expressing a positive feeling that you may be unaccustomed to, like great enthusiasm, gratitude, or admiration of someone. The more you do this, the more natural such feelings become.

Conquer Your Negative Side

Every emotion sits on a continuum facing its opposite emotion on the other end. As you learn to identify when you are tilting toward the negative, imagine yourself an actor and try expressing an emotion that sits at the other end.

Anger — Forgiveness
Envy — Appreciation
Fear — Confidence
Hate — Love
Sadness — Joy

Impose Mind over Emotions

We know this sounds counterintuitive, but once you are aware of your emotions, assert your discipline and self-control. Be firm and resolute, using all your smarts and reasoning to manage your emotions. Your thoughts can prevent stupid mistakes.

We're not saying be a phony, but at least for a while pretend a bit. Negative feelings feed on themselves, so banish them. Assume you are already "there," then take the leap in the positive direction.

Celebrate What's Right in Your Life

Photographer Dewitt Jones of *National Geographic* magazine has a positive vision of people.[11] After taking thousands of breathtaking pictures of landscapes and people, he realized that many of us live by the adage, "I won't see it until I believe it." He challenges us to be open to possibilities, to "believe it before we see it," and to celebrate what's right with the world.

"As long as you have confidence in your heart, you will never be defeated."

—Li Ning, CEO of Li Ning Sports Group, a leading sports brand in China

---

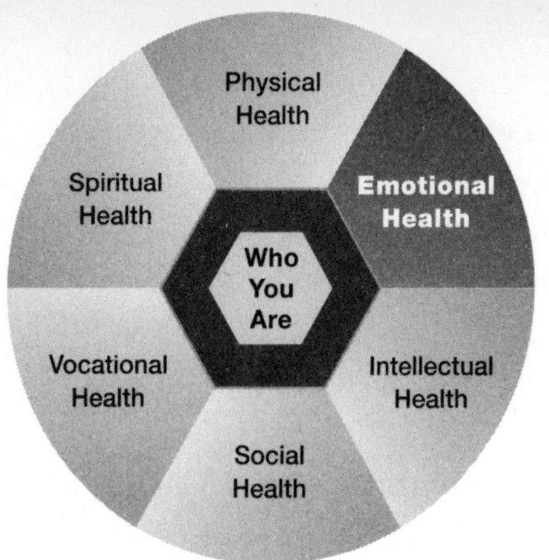

CHAPTER 9

Resilience

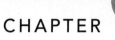

Imagine yourself the co-owner of a small family business that's been flourishing for more than thirty years, with sales steadily rising despite developing markets and setbacks from competitors. The early days were challenging, and adding to your struggles was a reluctant marketplace: it needed education and persuasion to change lifestyle habits before it would commit to your product.

Now you feel that the hard times are behind you. Your company has received widespread recognition and acclaim for its products, you have a growing network of vendor relationships, and you have managed to soothe regulators. Just as your business is about to take off, you learn that a privately held energy company with more than fifty thousand employees and revenues around $100 billion is trying to seize your company's land for an oil pipeline. If it succeeds, you would be ruined.

What would you do?

STAYING CALM DURING THE ONSLAUGHT

Before we tell you how the owner reacted to this threat to her and her company, we want to talk about resilience. Without it, a leader is like an old, dead tree in the middle of a hurricane. Branches snap, the trunk topples, roots pull out. Much has been written about resilience, particularly people's ability to withstand personal tragedies and natural disasters, and it certainly is a vital personal quality. Yet it's perhaps even more crucial for business leadership. As our business owner learned firsthand, without resilience, you are not just traumatized—you are demolished.

Handling the ups and downs of work, along with a constantly changing business environment, requires the presence of mind to calmly assess the true nature of the problem. It could be a personal crisis. There may be a miscommunication. A relationship may need mending. Goals or financial targets may need adjusting. The possibilities are endless. Nevertheless, staying calm ensures that you won't react without careful thought and before collecting relevant information from everyone involved. During this time of calm, you may want to revisit assumptions about you or your reactions to your company's direction and plans for getting there.

By drawing on experience, knowledge, and skills, you can regain your balance and prepare to deal with what needs fixing.

You may need time to recover emotionally, but no doubt your brain will also need time to regain its equilibrium. A challenge or threat triggers a survival reflex in the brain, releasing a flood of neurochemicals that throw you into the classic fight-or-flight mode. We all know the effects of chemicals like cortisol and adrenaline. They rev us up, preparing the brain and body for battle or fleeing. If they are amped up for a long time, which happens with chronic stressors, they can do damage. So it's vital that you take a deep breath and calm down when something has shocked you or your company.

GETTING COMFORTABLE WITH UNCERTAINTY

Resilience is more essential than ever because the business climate is increasingly unpredictable. We live in a time of turmoil, stimulated by churning technologies and a fiercely competitive global marketplace. At any moment, you or your business could be blindsided by anything from a cyber attack to a devastating drought. In practical terms, getting comfortable with uncertainty demands that you prepare yourself emotionally for this type of constantly churning world. The quality that best handles uncertainty and unpredictability is emotional flexibility. This is a readiness to shift gears, bounce back, and move in a different direction when calamity is headed at you.

Buddhist thinking has much to teach us about emotional flexibility. It maintains that everything in life, including our goals, is a moving target and that uncertainty is the reality.

THE POWER OF CONFIDENCE: THE FOUR NOBLE TRUTHS

Buddhism, like all world religions, offers thoughts on how to handle life's hardships. What is different from other religions is its distinctive philosophy about life. The central tenets of Buddhism are the Four Noble Truths, which emanate from the proposition, "Pain is inevitable; suffering is not."[1]

The Four Noble Truths explain why we suffer and how we can overcome it. The fundamental assumption behind them is that everything is always changing—we never step into the same stream twice—and change causes suffering when we resist it or ignore it.

This happens when we cling too tightly to the attachments we discussed earlier, be they wealth, power, status, ambition, or even our own expectations. Uncertainty can become our undoing if we are not open to what's around the corner, whether new ideas and experiences or the latest arrows or disappointments. Someone who is open to uncertainty has learned to be comfortable with being vulnerable. Although the idea may seem counterintuitive, in a business context, vulnerability is a strength, not a weakness. Allowing yourself to be vulnerable says you are willing to take risks, be an imperfect person, and accept reality, whatever that may be.

Another dimension to the power of resilience is the necessity for living and leading with just enough anxiety. Anxiety can be a positive and powerful force in our lives. It challenges us, stretches us, and helps us learn every day. Life would be flat and bland without the right amount of anxiety. The resilient leader senses this, knowing that living with just enough anxiety will fuel higher productivity and greater achievements. When you manage anxiety, rather than suppress it or run away from it, you're much better able to handle all the various kinds of events and experiences that throw you off balance.[2]

Be willing to embrace the unknown. Distinguish between what you can and cannot control. Cultivate self-confidence even when it hurts. Become comfortable with being uncomfortable. And be tough enough to be gentle with yourself, especially when you feel vulnerable.

APPLYING LESSONS FROM THE PAST

Coping with the inevitable ups and downs of business requires a calm, collected, and concentrated mind. Your extreme focus coupled with an inner peace accepts the impermanent nature of things and enables you to draw strength from your past successes.

Now for the rest of the story of the small business owner we mentioned earlier. The co-owner, Atina Diffley, along with her husband, Martin, had devoted more than thirty years to building up an organic produce business—an urban-edge, name-brand farm producing organic fruits and vegetables distributed through natural food cooperatives, a roadside stand, and restaurants. That experience gave Atina the presence of mind to do battle with Koch Industries, considered the second-largest privately held company in the United States.

Diffley's inner strength and courage came from her determination not to be a victim and the knowledge that over her many years in the business, she had acquired a steel-mesh network of supporters and influential allies.

"Koch had the money, but we had the people on our side," she says. "And that is really what it takes. Often to take on this kind of imbalance of power is to find power from a different place, which we had in a huge number of people who just said, 'This is really important, we care about this, this has to be protected.'"[3]

She continues, "When you have healthy roots and healthy soil, you can always recover from life's challenges and difficult situations, because you can go back and draw your nourishment there." The battle raged in and out of court, involving the Minnesota Department of Agriculture and public hearings. In the end, the Koch subsidiary decided not to build a pipeline through the Diffley farmland. And Atina was instrumental in helping the state write, pass, and implement new agricultural guidelines to protect farmers and their soil affected by future such projects.

In hindsight, Atina finds that her strength came from various sources. "I'm observant and flexible. As a farmer, you learn all the rules and then you learn when to break them." Talking about her battle with Koch, she observes, "People see someone doing something brave, and they think that [the person is] fearless. It's not that they're fearless, it's just that they don't let the fear stop them."

RESILIENCE ON THE FRONT LINE

Your brain becomes accustomed to handling challenges to your emotional life. It's like the immune system—it gets stronger as it's exposed to more challenges and contaminants and while learning to adapt. The brain and body can learn not to overreact when you hit an obstacle or are emotionally distressed. Repeated exposure to hard times or crises, assuming you get through them, teaches your brain that your emotions do not need to go into fight-or-flight survival mode. Rather than panic, you can persevere. You will get through the present crisis the same way you did before.

Emotional resilience comes from repeated exposure and trials. Research with adolescents and young adults (ages fifteen to twenty-five) shows that young people need some form of crisis in their life to prepare them for adulthood. Without this experience in learning how to deal with adversity, they are vulnerable to the stresses and uncertainties of middle age.[4]

Someone who acquired resilience from years of exposure and confronting perilous situations is Mike Puzziferri, deputy chief of the Fire Department of New York (FDNY).

To understand Mike's resilience, you need to know a few things about him. He's a second-generation New York fireman, so he had a live-in role model early in life. Before his recent retirement, he had been on the job for thirty-one years. He began on the bottom rung of the leadership ladder in an engine company and climbed to the top of the country's largest municipal fire department.

His life as a fireman has been rich with lessons in how to lead and to handle the unpredictable. It is a testament to his self-awareness that Mike remembers precisely the events that had the greatest impact on his education. The first happened during his rookie year with the department. The fire company was responding to a nasty blaze in a multistory building.

Mike and the company's leader, a man named O'Hagan, were pinned down on a floor with flames over their head and smoke enveloping them.

The two men were trapped for only seconds when O'Hagan said, "Mike, I've got something to do, and I'm going to leave you here so you can make sure I don't get lost . . . You be my marker and make sure I'm safe and know how to get back. Make noise—call out for me every few seconds."

Mike explains why this was so memorable.

"He wasn't going to get lost. He had twenty years on the job . . . He just wanted to keep me there probably because he wanted to go into a place that wouldn't be safe for both of us . . . He was raising me to a level where he made me feel confident. He didn't say, 'You don't know what you're doing; I don't want you to get hurt.' He taught me a lesson about how to lead—you can get things done, and you don't have to burn somebody to get it done."[5]

That day Mike also learned how to stay focused on a goal, like safely surviving a fire, and how to adjust to conditions in order to reach that goal.

"You look at the world changing around you . . . You have to complete your mission and make adjustments inside so that you can complete that mission."

Another mainstay of Mike's resilience is his ability to handle the unpredictable. Of course firemen every day encounter situations that could take a dangerous, unpredictable turn. One particular fire sticks in Mike's mind, an "ass-kicking, dangerous fire."

It was in a high-rise apartment building, and a forty-miles-per-hour wind was flashing through it. The first company arrived, forced open the door, and began searching for trapped residents. Mike, at the time a battalion chief commander, told crews to make sure they had a charged hose line for protection. The firemen entered, glass began to fall because it was so hot, and the wind had created a blowtorch effect in the apartment where they were looking for people. Four firemen got badly burned and retreated. Knowing there was a tiny window of opportunity, Mike moved forward. Telling himself, "This is going to be bad," he left the lobby command post for a position closer to the fire on the twenty-fourth floor.

Another fireman, the captain, was already in the apartment sending out a Mayday. Mike realized that the captain believed that the fire was going to kill him and so acted immediately.

"All my years of training put me in a place where I was confident that I could pretty much handle what might come my way. I started to take the proactive move, saying to myself, 'This is going to be really bad, and I've got to plan for the worst possible scenario,' and I put all my pieces in place."

He continues, "I get on the radio, there's 150 radios out there, every one of them on a different fireman, and they're not only hearing the content of my voice, they're hearing the nuances. I took a step back and was about as cool as we're talking here. I was clear about what I was thinking, clear about what I was saying, and clear about my plan for knocking the fire down. What they were hearing uplifted them emotionally. Everybody was cool."

Nobody died that day, and Mike was able to extract the trapped captain. What saved him, and probably others, was years of experience confronting one of the most uncertain environments imaginable. Mike offers an explanation for how he did it:"You can't panic on stuff like this. You got to take a step back. Instead of reacting to it, you have to respond to it. And that takes emotional flexibility and resilience."

BEND, DON'T BREAK: THINGS TO CONSIDER

For decades, stress was viewed as bad and damaging. Then we began to see the power of resilience. Whether you are coping with adversity, bouncing back from setbacks, or leading through uncertainty, these experiences make you stronger. When you rise to a challenge, you reveal your hidden abilities, strengthen your capacity to suffer through setbacks, and build character. Adversity and resilience also make you more sensitive and empathetic and open to other people's challenges. Your difficulties also have a way of changing your priorities and perspectives about the present, giving you a kind of wake-up call that tells you to stop and smell the roses.

Studies also confirm that resilience can be learned. Researchers exploring psychobiology and neuroplasticity say that a key goal in learning resilience is taming the stress response system.[6] Instead of being derailed by the brain's fight-or-flight reaction to stress and the body's physiological reaction, you can harness them to work for you.

Throughout this chapter, we've mentioned the role of anxiety and how just the right amount is essential for inspiring and motivating people. If you can learn to manage the inevitable anxiety that besets you as a leader, you are much better equipped to react and adjust to the forces that are coming at you. In this spirit, we offer five steps you can take. Bear in mind that these are cumulative—each step builds on the previous one. As you practice them, you may find a big boost in your emotional stamina.

Step 1: Anticipate. Survey your world to pinpoint where the biggest changes are coming from. Are they economic? Personal? In work relationships? In your company industry? Sketch out best- and worst-case scenarios for possible dramatic change. Devise responses for each, plus backup plans. Chances are you've been there before in one way or another. So stay confident and courageous, and keep your perspective.

Step 2: Monitor yourself. It's easy to get wrapped up in external events, especially when there's a crisis. But this is precisely the time when you must be aware of your emotions (panicked? too passive? overconfident? confused?) because they can hijack you. Your emotions affect not only you but everyone around you. Remember Mike Puzziferri—he knew he had to control his emotions and stay cool in order to help everyone survive.

Step 3: Enlist a strong support network. You can't withstand change and build resilience by yourself. Not only are you going to need help in terms of getting things done, but your support network will be essential in giving you realistic feedback on how you're doing and where adjustments need to be made.

Step 4: Sink deep roots. What we mean by this is to nourish and develop your emotional values. Decide what is fundamental to your belief system and sink these beliefs so deep that nothing can upend them. There is frequently no single core emotional value but a complementary collection, such as loyalty, honesty, courage, confidence, and fairness. Embrace and enhance whatever is important to you. Ask yourself: Am I aligned with my values and who I aspire to be? This will ground you in trying times.

Step 5: Practice. How do you practice handling anxiety and withstanding unpredictable forces when all is calm? Seek out situations that are risky and make you vulnerable. We're not talking bungee jumping, but unfamiliar situations and new ventures. For instance, there is little more nerve-racking than being a beginner at something, whether you're trying to master a body of knowledge where you know nothing (How's your accounting knowledge or Spanish?) or a basic skill (Can you do what your employees do?). Perhaps mimic the people in the TV series *Undercover Boss*, who leave the confines of their offices to learn firsthand the skills their employees use every day.

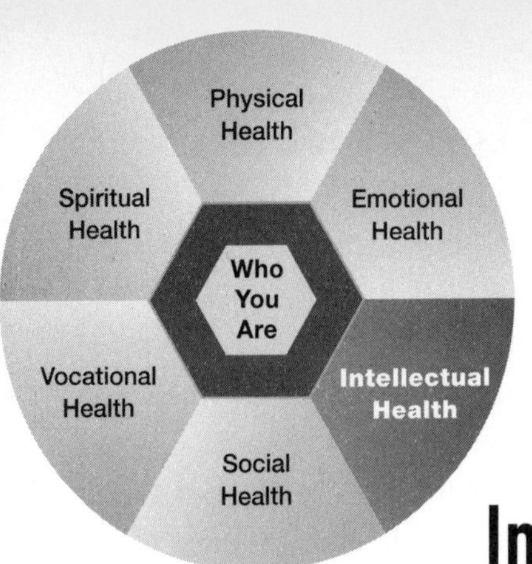

Intellectual Health

Your company is going to be late delivering to its most valued customer. The customer demands your product in six months, and you need at least a year or more. Your computer models, past deliveries, and suppliers' commitments all show the same year-plus timeline.

Do you try to persuade the customer to accept the longer timeline? Do you put the squeeze on your employees? Do you go ahead and hope it will work out by relying on past performance as a predictor of future results? Or do you step back from the entire situation and take a deeper look? Do you jettison the usual way of doing things and tease apart the entire complex manufacturing process step-by-step, talking to individuals about each piece and looking for new ways to cut production time and produce the product on time and within budget?

Leaders experience these complex business dilemmas all around the world every day. Yes, simple problems still require simple solutions, but there are fewer simple problems these days. The world is getting more complex, and there is a growing gap between the demands of work and the people and organizations to solve them.

We need a greater capacity to deal with mental complexity, and intellectual health is the key to enhancing that capacity. By expanding your mental range, you can broaden your thinking, solve complex problems, and focus on what is truly important. Instead of oversimplifying, you make sense of the world by embracing the complexity of it.

Many leaders are linear thinkers, seeing problems as a straight line with direct cause-and-effect explanations. But today's world is not linear; it's weblike and interconnected. Whether you're confronting a manufacturing problem, a process dilemma, or a human issue, the variables are typically arranged in a multifaceted mosaic. Knowing that A leads to B leads to C in a simple linear fashion is not enough anymore. Your thinking needs to be flexible and systemic, able to make jumps that defy logic, and understand the complexity of a multidimensional and multidirectional world.

Healthy leaders understand this. They possess three features of intellectual health—deep curiosity, an adaptive mindset, and paradoxical thinking—that equip them well to handle the complexities that beset an organization.

WARNING SIGNS OF DECLINING INTELLECTUAL HEALTH

- Inability to adapt to changing conditions
- Difficulty thinking critically and solving problems
- Inability to make short- or long-term decisions
- Inability to recover from setbacks
- Decreasing ability to apply skills and knowledge
- Difficulty understanding diverse beliefs

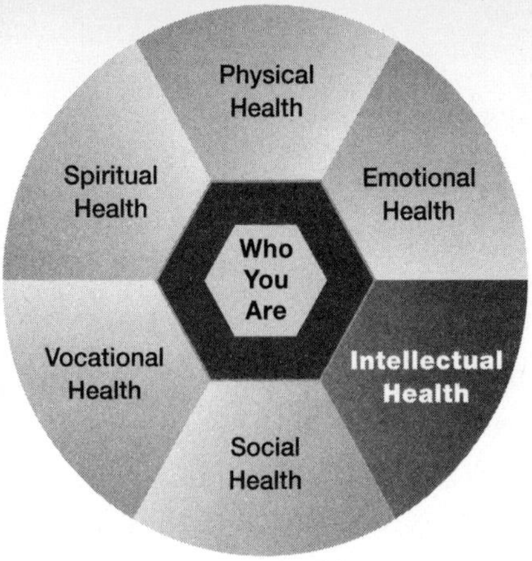

Physical Health
Emotional Health
Intellectual Health
Social Health
Vocational Health
Spiritual Health
Who You Are

CHAPTER 10

Deep Curiosity

HOW A CEO SAILOR NAVIGATES

Deep curiosity is the foundation of Mike Petters's leadership. Petters grew up on an orange farm in Florida and became a sailor. Armed with a degree in physics from the U.S. Naval Academy, he was a submariner on the USS *George Bancroft* before joining Newport News Shipbuilding. That was twenty-five years ago, and since then he has risen through the ranks as the company became part of Northrop Grumman, which emerges today as Huntington Ingalls Industries (HII), the world's largest shipbuilder.

Even though Petters leads a company of thirty-eight thousand people designing, constructing, and overhauling a variety of ships, including nuclear-powered submarines and aircraft carriers, he devotes an enormous amount of time to his own professional learning and growth. We have been advising Petters and his company for ten years, and much of our time has been devoted to helping him explore how to expand his executive mind, to be the best CEO leader he can be, and to build a culture of leaders inside the shipyards.

Mike started his career as a production controller, moved on to work in the business development department, and eventually became the director of the aircraft carrier program. After heading up contracts, he became the chief human resources officer; in this role, Mike discovered his passion for leadership as a "craft of its own."[1] This led him straight into the CEO's office. His story is one that illustrates the power of curiosity and how it can accelerate your career.

Mike extends his curiosity in numerous ways, learning by reading, watching others, asking penetrating questions, analyzing issues from all directions, and "never making a decision before its time."

Here's an example. It takes eight years to build an aircraft carrier. But Mike wondered whether the company could build one faster. So he invested in a computer program to see whether the machine could suggest ways to improve performance. "To my surprise, the computer said it would take ten years, not the typical eight, and I began to really appreciate the power of human ingenuity," Mike recalls.

"It was the curiosity, learning, and intellectual health of the shipbuilders working together that made all the difference." Whereas the computer program functioned in a linear fashion, with each task following on the heels of another, people in the shipyard did not necessarily work that way. They did multiple tasks simultaneously, collaborated as a team to reduce time and waste, and could rush jobs over night.

Whether driven by a personal need to keep informed or a professional need to strengthen the company, Petters thrives on steep learning curves. "There are a lot of people counting on me. And I feel the responsibility not to let them down. If there's something out there that will help me do my job better, I want to know it." Away from the office, whether driving or at the gym or relaxing at home, he's learning. He may be listening to the *Economist* on an iPod, reading a biography, or talking to an old pal from his engine room days.

You need to have a beginner's mind to create bold innovation.

—Marc Benioff, CEO, Salesforce.com[2]

His thoughtful curiosity paid off when HII spun off from Northrop Grumman, and he led the new entity's IPO. Although he had watched the process before from a distance, he had never executed an IPO himself. So he gathered information and adapted. He had lunches with other CEOs, made visits to bankers and analysts on Wall Street, and participated in a Harvard Leadership Program.

He explains, "Like a good shipbuilder, I divided the project into parts. You know, eight lanes is the way I thought about it. Eight lanes to go through to get the spin. There was the SEC lane, the debt lane, the equity lane, the governance lane, the management lane, employees, customers. The last one was training the CEO, and there is only one person responsible for that lane."

Petters's deep curiosity is disciplined, and he deliberately applies it daily. When making a decision, regardless of whether it's big or small, he assembles what he needs to know. "I want to make sure first of all that I've gathered all the information that we can to make the right decision." When Mike gets too stagnant or too comfortable, or if he loses his curiosity or focus, it's time to stir things up or move on.

Mike is curious about what other leaders do too and reinforces what he knows about leadership by reading military history. A book about the North African battles of World War II and accounts of General Patton and General Eisenhower showed him how an individual's personality can impact a large, disparate group. He applies such lessons from military history to his own company.

He also tailors his curiosity to his personal life—his golf game is an example. He freely admits that he's new at the game, so he matches the instruction to the way his mind works. "I'm not good when I've got folks telling me how I should do it. But if I'm reading about it and practicing on the course, then I can internalize it."

Mike would be the first to say that it takes an entire company of curious people to build a great business. "It's our purpose behind the work," says Petters, "that motivates people to stay with the shipyard for decades, often through generations." So Mike found a creative way to tap into people's curiosity and purpose with the company's successful I Am a Shipbuilder campaign.

The campaign was simple: an emotion-packed video that aired around the company and nation, featuring numerous, diverse HII employees talking about what their job means to them and their pride in building ships. Mike beams with pride about the project. "We deliver products, we send them down the river, we make history for fifty years."

• • •

As humans, we are deeply curious by nature. It's the "deep" part that makes curiosity essential as a mark of healthy leadership. This kind of curiosity is intentional, conscious, and focused. It homes in on the knowns and unknowns, sifting through what is necessary and what is extraneous, and settling on the best ways to fill in the blanks. To be curious is to be on a journey of deliberate personal education, one that a leader pursues rigorously and regularly.[3]

Deep curiosity gives you as a leader an optimal avenue for growth, personally and intellectually. Curiosity not only drives you to acquire a body of knowledge but, more important, shapes who you are and how you see the world. Deep curiosity gives you fresh goals and horizons. It enables you to imagine a project from beginning to end. It expands your ability to grapple with mental complexity. And it gives you a route to a better future by enhancing your internal resources.

WHAT TORPEDOES CURIOSITY AND WHAT KIDS CAN TEACH US

Children are intensely curious for much of their childhood, but then it fades. When they are young, curiosity fuels their spontaneity, makes them natural risk-takers, and fires their enthusiasm. Unfortunately, this mentality frequently does not last. Around adolescence, most children's curiosity wanes. Child development experts say that a child's fading curiosity can be attributed to three causes.

Fear kills curiosity by constraining a child's willingness to explore the unknown. If someone's environment is chaotic, unpredictable, or even vaguely unsafe, he clings to the familiar and stays in his comfort zone. In a business situation, fear reigns over curiosity when trying something new might jeopardize a person's job or standing. In such cases, the risk-reward of experimenting is skewed toward risk, so people are afraid of trying it.

Disapproval discourages curiosity. Children are frequently scolded for normal explorations of their world ("Don't touch that!"), and adults are discouraged by others telling them what they can't do ("That's beyond your level"). Disapproval of trying something new may take the form of low expectations ("No way that's going to work") or discomfort with the unconventional ("We've always done it the other way").

Lack of support inhibits curiosity. Detached, unsupportive parents are the third factor that undermines curiosity in children, and bosses can have the same effect on employees. Having someone encourage being curious and trying something new gives a person confidence and a feeling of safety if the exploration doesn't achieve its initial goal. People are more willing to venture outside their comfort zones when they know that no bridges are being burned and that they will always be welcomed back into the fold.

BUILDING A CURIOUS BRAIN

As a child learns, her brain develops structures and neurological pathways that reinforce that learning. This is why, for instance, if you learned a foreign vocabulary as a child, you can tap into that data bank for the rest of your life.

The wonderful thing about the brain's natural neuroplasticity is that you can continue to learn throughout your life. Your brain develops new and expanded neural networks, and with repetition and time, these networks grow stronger. Completely new experiences or facts, however, do not have an established neural network to support them. So when you first encounter them, the details may be hard to retain, and the only way to foster them is through repeated exposure or repetition.

The brain is designed to recognize patterns. When your curiosity encounters something new, the brain attempts to fit it into its existing patterns. It looks for connections and associations. Deep curiosity prompts new learning that actually creates new connections and associations in your mind. It's like building a web of thoughts, information, and mental processes.

If you are continually curious, this strengthens your brain's wiring and communication systems. The opposite is true, too. If you do not stretch your brain, certain regions begin to atrophy. This is the principle behind the "use it or lose" it mantra.

Scientific studies have shown that curiosity enhances various brain functions. Functional brain scans of volunteers viewing trivia facts that piqued their curiosity showed increased activity in structures involved in rewarding emotions and memory. This revealed links between curiosity and increased motivation and pleasure. Put another way, curious people tend to be more eager to learn and tend to remember more.[4]

WHAT'S YOUR LEARNING STYLE?

We are all capable of applying our personal brand of curiosity to learn about something novel or about the unknown. Howard Gardner, psychologist and professor at Harvard University, celebrates this diversity with his model of multiple intelligences.[5] He believes that we each have our own special combination of intelligences. Some of us are naturally gifted in the spatial and logical-mathematical arenas. Others excel in interpersonal and intrapersonal domains. The key is to discover your most natural forms of intelligence.

But intelligence alone is not enough. An in-depth study of "growth leaders" from such companies as Hewlett Packard, Procter

& Gamble, Corning, IBM, and Best Buy, conducted by Healthy Companies International and the Darden School of Business at the University of Virginia, revealed that leaders who are constantly learning and growing have a unique mindset that gives them a distinct advantage.[6] Compared to leaders who avoid complexity, risk, and uncertainty, the business leaders who drive their companies into double-digit growth see learning as their primary task, and they value deep curiosity. They adapt for growth. Their continual learning entails being comfortable with uncertainty and seeking new situations; taking small, immediate risks; and learning from others in their pursuit of solutions. This distinctive learning style is based on embracing the inevitability of change.

Here are questions to help you determine your personal learning style:

- Do you prefer to hear information or capture it visually by reading or watching?
- In what kinds of situations are you most receptive to new ideas or experiences: a crisis, when you are in charge, in the presence of an expert, where you are physically and mentally comfortable, in a completely foreign environment?
- Do personal factors influence your learning? For example, Are you more alert and receptive at certain times of day? Do you have a short or long attention span? How does sleep affect your learning?
- Do you have hobbies that boost your curiosity?
- Are you a public learner who thrives on other people's ideas across the table, or are you a private learner who needs privacy and silence for deep reflection and contemplation?

THE CURIOSITY-CREATIVITY CONNECTION

It's long been accepted that the brain's right hemisphere is in charge of curiosity, experimenting, finding solutions, and thinking related to creativity, like playfulness; the left half was thought to direct logic, math, fact-based thinking, and analysis. But recent research reveals that brain functions are not completely ruled by a single hemisphere. According to Ned Hermann, a pioneer in whole-brain science, creativity springs from processes that tap into both sides.[7] Though the hemispheres have some discrete functions, they are connected by a layer of neurons called the corpus callosum, which makes sure the two halves talk to each other. When you have a creative solution, being curious is often the mental process that links the two hemispheres.

It's your curiosity that makes you imagine a new business venture and seek out useful financial information to support it, and it is curiosity that inspires you to wonder how to make the venture work next year. It's your curiosity that taps into different ways of thinking (analytical and intuitive) and enables you to access old patterns and memories from past experiences. These produce new ways of working for the future and come together to form a creative inspiration. This is why R&D and sales and marketing teams must work together to create real, practical innovation. The engine behind this is deep curiosity.

Some people, like Mike Petters, are natural intellectual explorers. Others need to develop habits to become deeply curious leaders. Here are questions to nudge your curiosity:

- Think of the last problem you faced: How far did you go to seek out its root causes and interconnections? Get diverse perspectives? Look for patterns? Thoroughly explore different options?
- How often do you educate yourself or personally research a topic you do not know much about?
- When was the last time you admitted you didn't know something, and what did you do about it?
- When you do not understand something, do you ask questions until you do?
- What was your last big new idea? How did you explore or promote it?

I have no special talents. I am only passionately curious.

—Albert Einstein

As you assess what makes you curious, be alert for elements in your life or environment that may impede you. Much can get in the way.

A common way of sabotaging yourself is through mental miscalculations or a negativity bias. Do you overestimate the danger of risks, tend to expect the worst, and assume that the unknown is bad and to be avoided instead of explored? This is your brain shutting down your curiosity by letting your negative emotions, namely fear and anxiety, influence your intellectual health.

You can also be deterred by defeatism. You may feel that information is expanding so quickly, the world so complex, that it is impossible to understand or master. It's true that a single week's worth of news in the *New York Times* contains more information than the eighteenth-century individual learned in a lifetime. You need to break problems down piece by piece so that you don't become overwhelmed by the complexity of it.

The most common reason we shut down our curiosity is that we are simply running too fast. We don't take the time out of our busy lives to be curious—to stop and take a breath, read an article or book, take a day off to reflect, get a coach, or simply ask a question rather than rush in with the answer.

THE POWER OF PERSONAL GROWTH

One of India's most successful business leaders is Kumar Birla, age forty-five and chairman of the Aditya Birla Group (AGB), a large global conglomerate operating in thirty-six countries and producing everything from aluminum and copper, carbon black, insulators, and cement to fertilizer and fiber. His induction into the world of business began as a young man watching his father, who turned the family-founded company into an international business.

"Before his untimely death in 1995, my father involved me in all aspects of the business," shares Kumar. "He gave me independent responsibility early on—from running stable businesses, those in the implementation phase, some that were still on the drawing board, and some in crisis . . . My father believed that you will learn to swim if you are in the deep end of the pool."[8]

When Kumar took over the $2 billion company before his time, he had a simple philosophy: "The quality of your future depends on the quality of your imagination." Today the company is generating $40 billion, and his plan is to achieve $65 billion by 2015. Known for his love of strategy and meritocracy, Kumar and his group made twenty-six acquisitions in seventeen years. Many people ask, "How did he grow his company so fast in such a flat global economy?" His business answer is succinct: smart strategy, consistency, reorganizing, cutting expenses, developing people, and leveraging technology.

But his secret weapon is his own learning. He discusses his evolution: "Every day is a new day for me. Every inflexion point has turned out to be a very powerful period of learning. It's like an exploding star that emits a lot of light within a short burst of time." So he pushes himself and everyone around him to always be learning: "Know what you enjoy doing and go after it. Aggressively seek out learning, know what you don't know, which skills you don't have, and what you need to understand better."

Learning in the middle of a storm is especially critical. Kumar reflects, "These are the times when learning is driven deeply into you, by the force of circumstances. Sometimes it comes in the shape of headwinds, sometimes as tailwinds. Each is a moment of truth. When you are passing through the eye of the storm, you are wonderfully focused, because this could be a make-or-break moment."[9]

TAP INTO YOUR NATURAL CURIOSITY: THINGS TO CONSIDER

- **Explore the world differently.** Observe the world in more detail, question the status quo, connect unrelated questions and problems, combine ideas from different disciplines.

- **Experiment and try out new ideas.** Test them with friends, suppliers, customers, and colleagues; develop a hypothesis-testing mind; ask "What if" questions as you imagine new possibilities.
- **Become an information omnivore.** Expose yourself to novel sources of information: books, magazines, newspapers, audiobooks, Internet, TV, radio, libraries, expert lectures and seminars, adult education, community colleges.
- **Share and solicit your creativity and knowledge.** Contact the three most creative people you know and ask them to share their secrets. Talking to others, including your customers—what they like and don't like, and how they use your products and services—is critical.
- **Develop passions.** Few things in life are more rewarding than having a fascination with something and then allowing yourself to wallow in it. Oftentimes people mention something they would like to pursue but keep postponing, like learning a language or reading certain books. Stop postponing and dive in—your business and your life will be better for it.

CHAPTER 11

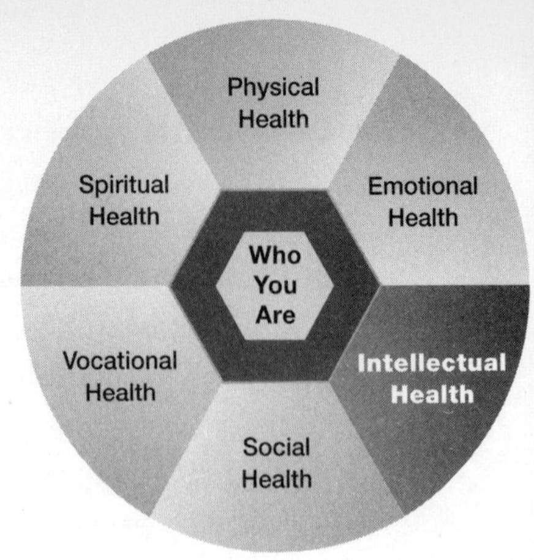

Adaptive Mindset

An adaptive mind is a self-transforming mind. It is agile and flexible, open to the unexpected, and able to handle the uncertainty of change. It possesses a clear point of view, but it's open to other ideas and thus has great capacity to expand in the face of increasing mental complexity.

Why is this mind so important for healthy leaders today? Because the higher you go inside organizations, the more capacity you need for dealing with mental complexity. Over and over again we see this in real-life examples of business successes and failures. The ability to develop an adaptive mentality that course-corrects in real time has a direct effect on your leadership performance.

THINKING IN REAL TIME

One leader who has mastered this ability may surprise you.

Without much notice, the tide began to rise very quickly, finally reaching a height of ninety-seven feet. The entire small coastal town of Ofunato, Japan, was devastated, drowned by the worst of nature's work, the Great Eastern Japan Earthquake and Tsunami of 2011.

The water and debris had swept away all the houses, and hundreds of citizens were missing.

Among the courageous few observing from a small hill were Kashiwazaki, the headmaster of the Ofunato Elementary School, and his teachers and students. "Watching the complete or partial collapse of their houses at a distance, I led the teachers and the 265 kids to higher ground, and we literally saved their lives." Kashiwazaki remembers, "It was so important to act swiftly and adapt to the situation. If we had acted according to the manual, we would have stayed in the school, the designated evacuation zone. Seeing the tsunami approaching, we escaped by climbing over the fence along the school's backyard."[1] The teachers carried the first graders over the fence one by one. All 265 students and twenty-one teachers were saved. That cold snowy night, all the teachers and students cuddled together in blankets at a nearby school, not knowing the fate of their families and homes. Fortunately, in the days to come, all the children made it back safely to their parents.

"In 1960, exactly fifty-two years ago, the Chile Earthquake and Tsunami hit Ofunato. I was in first grade at the time, and I still remember the tsunami climbing up the river," Kashiwazaki recalls. "At the fiftieth anniversary of that tsunami, we paid respect to the victims by having each grade in our current school read essays written by children (like myself) who were in their respective grades at the time of the tsunami. I then asked my students to write about their current experience fifty years later. It's very important not to forget this tragedy and pass the stories from the earthquake to the later generations."

To their surprise, three hundred letters came unexpectedly from the Robert Hunter School in Flemington, USA. The letters said that "people in the world are thinking about you. We are your friends. I told my students that we need to keep all this kindness in our hearts forever."

Headmaster Kashiwazaki reflects on what he and the teachers learned: Act swiftly, think in real time, be flexible and adaptive. Give people room to take initiative. Learn from the past and prepare for the future, and pass wisdom down from one generation to the next.

THINKING ON MANY LEVELS

One of the reasons leaders have difficulty managing through complexity is that their view of their surroundings is often too narrow and too shallow. Subsequently, they fail to take into account all of the available data around them. After decades of research on the topic, Daniel Kahneman, Nobel Prize winner in economics, explains it this way: "What you see is all there is." When your mind makes decisions, it deals primarily with "known knowns," phenomena it has already observed. Rarely does it consider the "known unknowns," what we know to be relevant but about which we have no information. And we stay oblivious to the "unknown unknowns," information unavailable to us and of unknown relevance.[2]

This superficial understanding of our environment leads us to what Kahneman believes is an "optimistic bias" that gives us the impression that we are in control and on top of things. We discussed this in Chapter Eight. This bias can be helpful to us in some ways. Optimists are happier and more resilient, and they live longer. The downside is that many of us naturally run away from complexity, ignore critical information, and overestimate the benefits and underestimate the costs of projects.

In his most recent book, *Thinking Fast and Slow*, Kahneman explains this thesis even further by describing two modes of thought going on inside each of us. System 1 is fast, instinctive, and emotional. System 2 is slower, more deliberative, and more logical. Both systems can cloud our thinking, yet both are necessary for leading in a complex world.

This is why healthy leaders spend so much time cultivating an adaptive mindset: digging deep for data, questioning their mental assumptions, acting with instinct and intellect, learning how to multitask, and asking challenging questions of themselves and others.

The more unknowns they can surface and the more levels they can think on, the more prepared they are.

LESSONS FROM CELL BIOLOGY

The cell is a tiny organism, yet it has much to teach us about leadership, complexity, and adaptability. It is a microcosm of our interconnected world that we can examine to see how different conditions affect it. One distinctive quality of any cell (there are two hundred different kinds) is that its survival depends both on its internal properties and its connections with other cells. Although it can exist as a single entity, it is better equipped for survival when it interacts with other cells.

What happens inside a cell is dictated by how its genes express themselves and how its membrane interacts with its surroundings, namely, various fluids, chemicals, and electrical signals. This membrane is permeable, but not everything passes through it. The healthy cell allows only essential nutrients to enter it, and shuts out toxins and other harmful substances. According to the cellular biology researcher Bruce Lipton, a cell's genes can also be turned on and off by chemical and electrical signals stimulated by a person's thoughts, feelings, and emotions.[3]

At this point, you may be wondering what this has to do with a leader's adaptive mindset. Our goal is to impress upon you a number of truisms that apply to all living things, whether an individual cell bathing in a Petri dish or a CEO of a multinational corporation.

- We are surrounded by complexity. It is unavoidable and a normal part of living.
- Although we can survive on our own, we grow and learn to adapt by joining other organisms and interacting with our external environment.
- Complexity that comes at us from our environment needs to be understood and carefully managed. We don't want every facet to penetrate our membranes, so to speak.

- At times, we generate internal complexity through our feelings and thoughts. These need to be managed as meticulously as outside influences.
- Living systems—both leaders and their organizations—move between stability and instability, order and disorder. When chaos becomes too great, things fall apart. When order is too rigid, things cannot grow or develop.

WRESTLING WITH COMPLEXITY FROM ALL DIRECTIONS

In 2010, IBM surveyed 1,541 CEOs, general managers, and public sector leaders around the world, asking how they were responding to the current competitive and economic environment.[4] In past surveys, the leaders pointed to change as their primary challenge. But in this more current survey, they said another influence had taken the number-one spot in their list of concerns: complexity.

The other major finding was that creativity was the most important leadership quality. To succeed, leaders must take more calculated risks, find new ideas, and keep innovating in how they lead and communicate.

There is a natural tension in our lives between stability and instability. Stable forces, for instance, are people's need for routine and habits, a company's need for cash flow, and a loyal workforce. Instability is evident in our need for variety and excitement, a company's drive for innovation, and an organization's need to adapt to the times. Both forces have a place in our lives and companies. The challenge comes with trying to balance them, as we need both to thrive. We must recognize that stability is a kind of anchor that helps us through an immediate crisis and that instability is necessary for growth and change going forward.

Stanford psychologist Carol Dweck offers a system for determining whether you tend toward one way of thinking or another. She divides people's thinking into two opposite mentalities: a fixed mindset and a growth mindset.[5] The view you adopt for yourself profoundly affects the way you lead your life.

If you have a fixed mindset, you are driven by the need for stability and are more inclined to avoid new experiences, limit your learning and acquisition of skills, be fearful about uncertainty, and work toward maintaining the status quo. You view life as a test of your competence that is better handled with your existing skill set.

On the other end, if you have a growth mindset, you see life as a journey that requires continual growth along the way. With this attitude, you seek out new experiences, regularly broaden your knowledge and abilities, and remain open to change and new ideas.

Scientists are learning that people have more capacity for lifelong learning and brain development than they ever thought. Yet, most people fall somewhere on a continuum between these two mindsets. Look at these statements and ask yourself where, on a 1–10 scale, you might fall.

1 2 3 4 5 6 7 8 9 10

Life is a test.	Life is a journey.
I try to avoid making mistakes.	I expect to make mistakes.
Uncertainty makes me fearful.	I am comfortable with uncertainty.
I try to avoid new experiences.	I seek out new experiences.
I prefer to add to my existing knowledge.	I like learning new things.

Here's the kicker: once you know where you are on these mental yardsticks, recognize that you can change your way of thinking. Just as an individual cell's genetic expression may be influenced by its external environment or your internal thoughts and emotions, so too can you alter your mentality by applying motivation and willpower. What you believe about your ability to grow and adjust to changing circumstances can have a big impact on how you interpret and react to events.

WHY DON'T PEOPLE EVOLVE?

After decades of research, Harvard University researchers Robert Kegan and Lisa Laskow Lahey make a compelling case that we are falling behind in developing workers and leaders who can keep up with growing complexity—and it's affecting our ability to innovate and compete.

They describe three distinct plateaus for development. On the lowest level are people with "socialized minds." These are natural team players who seek direction and fall in line around a strategy or framework. In a complex world, we need them to take more initiative, exhibit more self-management, and understand the economics of the business.

"Self-authoring minds" make up the next level of leaders. They are typically independent and agenda driven, with their own belief systems, ideologies, and personal codes. In more complex environments, these leaders must stay true to their values yet model the organization's values, while generating new ideas and respecting a global and psychologically diverse workforce.

At the highest level are leaders with "self-transforming minds" who learn how to adapt and modify their assumptions about the world. In a world of constant change with disruptive technologies, these executives must live in ambiguity, reexamine their business models, and create a culture of learning at all levels of business.[6]

As you can see, complexity is forcing everyone to move up to the next level of development. We realize, however, that this kind of development is not easy. No one likes to take a leap without knowing what kind of landing is in store. Learning to be comfortable with the unknown is best approached as a gradual process. Yet even the most willing adventurer can unwittingly sabotage himself. In our work with executives from around the globe, we have encountered ways of thinking that impede a person's ability to develop an adaptive mindset. These impediments to personal evolution fall into two broad categories: personal psychology and business practices. Here are some characteristics.

Personal Psychology

- Ignoring the tough issues or early signs of a problem
- Discarding information that doesn't fit into your assumptions or perspective

- Never seeking out other perspectives
- Avoiding ambiguity and conflict when something challenges your values
- Assuming that everyone learns the same way you do

Business Practices

- Developing a detailed plan of action and sticking to it no matter what
- Concentrating on the immediate task at hand and ignoring the bigger picture
- Measuring progress solely by whether your plan has been executed
- Sharing your vision and values infrequently (for example, once a year)
- Focusing only on skills needed for the present situation

OPENING PANDORA'S BOX

Pandora, to briefly refresh your Greek mythology, was the earth's first woman. To punish her, Zeus gave Pandora a clay box with instructions never to open it. Of course, she opened it and so released all the evils of the world. But her curiosity did not create a complete disaster because in the box was also the spirit of hope, and it too was let loose.

The parallel we are making here with Pandora is that leaders too face choices and temptations, and experience the mystery of embracing uncertainty. In our work, we have found that leaders can be separated according to how they think about these issues of control and uncertainty.

There are leaders who rely heavily on their personal power. Confident and courageous by nature, they believe in their ability to master their environment. They have what scientists call a high degree of self-efficacy—an important predictor of how successful people will be. These leaders are usually high achievers and top performers. They accomplish a lot and are widely admired. But they can also overlook key factors beyond their control or end up manipulating people for their own ends. They tend to ignore life's mysteries.

Then there are leaders who enjoy uncertainty and the mystery of life. Recognizing how much of life is out of their control, they rarely try to predict the future. They are agile and flexible thinkers and adapt well to changing circumstances. Like a willow tree bending in the wind, they are able to accommodate to the forces around them. And they are often just as successful as their personal power–minded colleagues. Their Achilles heel, however, is that they can become cynical or feel tossed about by fate. And they tend to ignore their own power. Just as with personal power, some of us love uncertainty, and some of us simply hate it.

As we grow older and wiser, most of us realize that both of these worldviews are valid. Life is filled with uncertainty, *and* we each have the power within us to choose how to navigate its ups and downs. Generally, however, the more comfortable you are with one, the less comfortable you are with the other.

So you probably know where this is going. You're a healthy leader with a strong adaptive mindset if you hold both worldviews (personal power and uncertainty) simultaneously. You pride yourself in shaping your environment, yet you know that life is unpredictable. Just when you think you're on top of the world, something or someone arrives to screw it up. And just when things are going south, a new opportunity shows up on your doorstep. So in a world of increasing complexity, who do you want to be?

LEADING WITH AN ADAPTIVE MINDSET

Leading through complexity demands adapting your own mind to a changing world, and helping others do this, too. If you are the only one in your organization's management who is attuned to complexity and has sufficient confidence to handle it, you won't do well. You need to model adaptive thinking on your team and mentor others who are struggling or not seeing what's happening. Here are some ideas for getting started.

- **Manage your fear of the unknown.** Complexity, by its very definition, is difficult. When it shows up, be aware of passing the buck, blaming others, pretending that you don't have the answers, or being excessively polite by ignoring the problem. Be vocal about your willingness to accept the challenge and acknowledge errors, both yours and others'. Encourage risk-taking by using instances of it for lessons and learning. Recognize the impact of change on people around you and throughout the organization.
- **Be confident that you will land on your feet.** Start by asking tough questions and teach yourself and others about being comfortable with being uncomfortable. Create the right amount of conflict and disequilibrium that keeps people on their toes. Turn backsliding and lack of participation into opportunities for learning. Pay close attention to how you influence others. Regulate with just enough anxiety, inside yourself and in your behavior with others. Be aware that you convey your attitudes through actions and body language every day. Navigate around needless or obstructive actions and those who are resisting changes; support those who are showing excessive stress and frustration.

If you double the number of experiments you do per year, you're going to double your inventiveness.

—Jeff Bezos, CEO Amazon.com[7]

- **Be open to new ways of thinking.** Nurture real-time learning. Adapt current practices and develop new practices. Try to be more flexible and encourage adaptive thinking. Ask yourself: What are the questions we are trying to solve? Why do we have to do it this way? What are our competitors doing? What should we keep, and what should we lose? Be open to trial-and-error thinking and conduct experiments all around. For example, have your operations and tactical meeting on Monday and your strategic and introspective meeting on Friday to allow room for both parts of your brain to flourish.

- **Be aware of old patterns and create new ones.** Get up fifty thousand feet and scan the internal and external environment. Think holistically, where the sum is greater than all its parts. Collect more data when you have to. Ask your team: What information do we need? Who else needs to be involved? What are the innovations and best practices out there? What can't we ignore? What professional networks do we need to tap into? Educate people, making sure they know why change is needed, how it will happen, what their role is, and what they will gain. And don't forget to talk to your customers. They will lead you into the future.
- **Create communities of adaptive people.** Develop pockets of people who are thinking and questioning deeply about the business. Teach people about the importance of intellectual health and their adaptive mindsets. Give them room to incubate and improvise with new ideas. Avoid haphazard execution that has little or no sense of support or buy-in and that avoids the bigger picture and the community at large. Let people challenge your assumptions, give feedback, and focus on building trust through open, honest dialogue. Be conscious of people trying to sabotage your efforts, at the top, middle, or bottom of the organization.

AT THE POINTY END OF THE SPEAR

The higher you go in organizations, the more you need to use an adaptive mindset to handle complexity. Horacio Rozanski, chief operating officer of the professional services firm Booz Allen Hamilton, learned this when he and other top executives initiated an effort to integrate its government and commercial businesses. After much analysis and many good attempts, the concept never fully developed. The company eventually separated the traditional government consulting business (now Booz Allen Hamilton) from the commercial business (operating today as Booz & Company). Today Booz Allen is a publicly traded company.

Headquartered in McLean, Virginia, this ninety-nine-year-old firm has been Rozanski's professional home his entire working life, since receiving his MBA from the University of Chicago in 1992. During his time at Booz Allen, the firm has grown to twenty-five thousand employees, and he has been a commercial partner and served as chief personnel officer and chief strategy and talent officer.

The task of integrating the two parts of the firm encountered strong headwinds. Rozanski had made it his mission to get it done, but there was resistance. The firm's CEO, Ralph Shrader, was his mentor and showed him the benefits of real adaptive thinking.

"A number of times he came to my rescue when the forces that didn't want the integration to happen threatened to overtake me. He was smart enough to be watching for the alternative. While he kept trying, he could at the same time start working Plan B. I learned a lot from that," Rozanski says.[8]

Horacio learned well that if you always think inside the box, you'll box yourself and your organization in. You'll fail to adapt to changing circumstances and lose your competitive edge. Being able to change your mental models, listening deeply to others, exploring options, moving the boundaries of your thinking, and standing back to observe patterns are the only way to evolve over time.

Today, Horacio is leading Booz Allen's long-term strategy, Vision 2020, an initiative to prepare Booz Allen for the future with a broader adaptive mindset. The firm has a special culture. It combines self-initiative, independence, and entrepreneurship on the one hand, with integration, teamwork, and a sense of partnership on the other. Horacio's job is to tap into both sources of human energy. He reflects, "As a leader, if you don't know who you are, how you operate best, and you don't know your own shortcomings, then I don't know how you lead successfully. If you're not grounded, you can't deal with the future."

So Rozanski is always learning and hearing new ideas and ways of thinking. He explains, "The only thing that I ever worry about is what I don't know. Because no matter how bad it is, we'll figure out how to respond—either mitigate, brace for impact, solve it, or deal with it."

He constantly engages people by holding town hall meetings at all levels. "I like thinking in groups. I try to let those groups be as broad and diverse as possible, and set up the environment where people can actually say what they want to say, as opposed to what they think I want them to say." He goes on to describe how this helps keep his thinking nimble: "My ideas get better, to the extent that they're any good, when I articulate them and I hear myself say it. Then somebody will say something, and I will reflect on it. And then have another idea that was better than the other one, or incorporate somebody's idea into my idea."

Rozanski's personal style of leadership guarantees that he's exposed to different ways of thinking every day. His technique? "Ninety percent is asking the right question, 5 percent is listening to others for the answer, and 5 percent is my own thinking. On a day-to-day basis, it can be exhausting, because it's constantly questioning everything, and there's no respite to that. [But if] you step back and look at it, it's a wonderful thing."

HOW TO THINK OUT OF THE BOX: THINGS TO CONSIDER

There are countless ways to keep your mind open and flexible. Here are important behaviors that help jar your thinking away from routine patterns and stimulate novel patterns and ideas:

- Create a trusting environment that makes it safe for people to bring their full selves to the table.
- Ask open-ended questions and listen *closely* to people's answers.

- Encourage differences of opinion and foster constructive conflict among people to deepen the conversations.
- Let people know that their thoughts are influencing or maybe even changing your way of thinking.
- Summarize what's been decided and what's still open ended, and thank people for their openness and good ideas.

CHAPTER 12

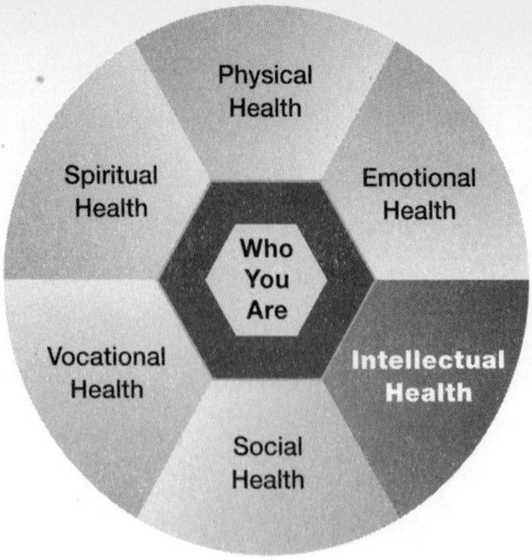

Paradoxical Thinking

LEADING IN A CREATIVE WORLD OF CONTRADICTIONS

Jørgen Vig Knudstorp is CEO of Lego Group in Denmark, a company famous for brightly colored interlocking block toys that spark the curiosity of millions of kids. Like the children who play with its products, Knudstorp is open and curious, qualities that are essential for handling a multidimensional world. Knudstorp is surrounded by complexity, leading a global leadership team of twenty-two in an international marketplace bulging with challenges, from the Internet to video games.

When Knudstorp took over the reins of Lego (whose name is derived from the Danish words for "play well") ten years ago, he had to unwind years of sluggish growth and quickly cast a new strategy to ensure the survival of the eighty-year-old company. He restructured the company, outsourced manufacturing to the Czech Republic and Mexico, and cut twelve hundred jobs.

"Ensuring the company's survival is a CEO's number-one job," says Jørgen. "That means beating the competition and staying relevant through continual exploration and adaptation."[1] Linear thinking, which attempts to apply logic and rules to situations, is inadequate for the increasing complexity of business and life. That's why Jørgen evaluates ideas from many angles and considers seemingly contradictory concepts to make the best decisions. His approach is less regimented and less conventional, and he's especially comfortable with paradox. "There's no single answer to anything anymore."

Jørgen's initial efforts were successful in the short run. But Jørgen warns that "success can turn into a singular culture; you become arrogant, and think you know the one answer to everything." That's really dangerous. You can become a bureaucratic monster where there's little receptiveness to change, no anticipation, and thinking that is too inward. So the more curious you are, the more adaptive you are. And the more competitive you become, the better your chance of success.

Paradoxical thinking is essential to his leadership. It has been a game saver for his company in resolving trade-offs he faces in trying to meet Lego's need for growth while also being realistic about its capabilities.

"What drives me is intellectual curiosity. It's not resolving a trade-off by saying you can get either A *or* B, but rather resolving it by how we can get A *and* B," he explains. "Let's be concrete: Walmart wants better delivery service but also lower cost. Supply chain says I can give you low cost, but then I want high predictability. Sales says I want low cost, but more important to me is that I can be flexible . . . So we can be innovative in our operation setup, maybe how we treat an order when it comes in. So planning techniques may be how we develop platforms."

Knudstorp applies his paradoxical mind to internal management also. One of his favorite mantras, "Take charge and let go," epitomizes this approach. After the company's "manage for profit" period, when all efforts had been focused on the core business, he released the reins of power, flattened the organization by expanding the leadership team from six to twenty-two, and asked executives to help him broaden its domain and find new avenues for growth. Today executives, armed with "incredible autonomy," are encouraged to come up with new ideas. "That's why I must take charge of the strategy and then let go like an orchestra conductor."

His philosophy of leading meetings epitomizes paradoxical thinking as well. "We believe in any meeting there's a rational part and an emotional part." Above the line is the rational part—decisions made and their impacts. Below the line are emotions and relationships—this is how people react to what is being decided and to each other. "As a leader you must manage above the line and below the line. Being explicit about what's going on below the line helps avoid problems.

"By making the emotional side more explicit, we have managed to open up a bit more. And we often say 'That's great,' or 'You think differently than I do,' or 'Say some more,' or 'You're making me very curious now because I had a totally different view on this.'

"I very much believe in embracing the complexity in organizational life and being open to multiple hypotheses—you know, the fact that the same problem can be viewed from many different models of reality . . . We feel as leaders we should be able to give one answer [but] I don't believe that's the truth. And so curiosity for me means to think about how can I create an adaptive organization."

MAKING A MENTAL LEAP: LATERAL THINKING

Lateral thinking, at which Knudstorp is a master, is the opposite of linear thinking. To quote Edward de Bono, the physician and philosopher who coined the term, "Lateral thinking is about changing concepts and models."[2] It generally defies logic, making mental leaps away from analytical, sequential thoughts and arriving at novel and unusual solutions. When you engage in this kind of problem solving, the process of ignoring the obvious and heading into new directions is as important as the final discovery.

Most of the time, people use linear thinking. It is a predictable way of thinking, being a series of steps each depending on a yes or no, correct or incorrect answer before moving on. Yet in a complex world, such thinking has obvious drawbacks—it doesn't create a broad range of options or inspire creative possibilities. Linear thinking works if your business is solely mass production, but not if your organization is grappling with a barrage of complexities and needs to be nimble and innovative, like the Lego Group and most organizations around the world.

EMBRACE OPPOSITES

Paradoxical thinking is apparent throughout the natural world, which is organized into systems that merge contradictory or polar opposite forces. Both are real and have merit. And yet they contradict each other—like good and evil or right or wrong.

One example of complementary opposites is our autonomic nervous system. It is divided into the sympathetic and parasympathetic systems. The sympathetic system prepares the body for movement and reaction, such as self-defense—it accelerates the heart, opens up the lungs, dilates the eyes, shuts down digestion, and constricts blood vessels in the skin. When you panic, it becomes engaged. In contrast, your parasympathetic system is calming—it decreases your heart rate, contracts airways so that breathing slows, constricts pupils for better focus, and stimulates digestion. This ying-and-yang arrangement allows us to react in totally opposite ways, depending on a situation.[3]

Leaders, too, need to be able to tap into cognitive opposites. A leader today lives in a world filled with tension generated by opposite forces. There's a constant tug-of-war between today and tomorrow. You're pressed to meet demands for meeting monthly targets while articulating and pursuing long-term growth strategies. You have to cut costs and boost revenues. You have to improve people's efficiency and motivate them. You have to be an authentic, honest leader and decide whether or not to share sensitive information.

If you examine your thoughts and actions, you will probably find a number of paradoxical forces. It is useful to remember that you need both. They give you balance and shield you from extremism.

Though you may tip more toward one side in certain circumstances, being aware of the other end helps you get back to center.

The following common leadership paradoxes serve as a window into thought processes essential for strengthening your intellectual health.

Constructive Impatience

The constructive side of your thinking aims to create a psychologically safe environment for those around you. It is where people feel good about themselves, feel empowered to take risks, and are open to change and new ways of doing things. You foster this environment through a supportive, strong community in which everyone's well-being is important and self-interest is discouraged. You are understanding and patient, and show people that they are valued.

Another side of you is impatient—you want visible, immediate results. So you push and make demands not only on yourself but those around you. As a leader, you thrive on challenges, defy anyone to say something's impossible, and are accustomed to winning. You want everyone, yourself included, to stretch their abilities and eagerly pursue the organization's vision.

Realistic Optimism

Every leader needs a large dose of realism. Rose-tinted glasses and self-delusion can sink an organization quickly. Your realistic half is honest about business realities and fierce competitors, strengths and weaknesses, successes and failures. You do your level best to assess everybody's actions in the clear light of day. In the same vein, you strive to tell the truth and not sugarcoat obstacles. And when you promise to do something or make a commitment, you work hard to carry through.

Yet alongside your coolheaded realism is a wide streak of optimism. This is what gets you out of bed in the morning and helps you fire up the troops. It's a vision full of hope and can-do spirit that looks ahead and declares that nothing is insoluble and that whatever you put your mind to is possible. Your optimism has the added benefit of being inspirational. It's infectious, and it helps you bring out the best in people around you. When they see you forge ahead, they too become believers and dreamers.

Confident Humility

Leaders by definition must be confident. If they don't believe in themselves and their leadership ability, no one will follow. Bear in mind, confidence at times resembles arrogance, but it's different. Confidence is about your ability and not used as a yardstick to measure how much better you are than others. We all know what confidence feels like, having experienced it at various times—we hit a great round of golf or solve a problem easily or meet a monthly target or accurately assess what a competitor is going to do. In most people, confidence waxes and wanes, but in outstanding leaders, it is their bedrock.

At the same time, being humble indicates that you know you aren't perfect. Even though you are skilled or smart or successful, you understand that you don't know everything. Humility can strengthen your confidence by making you open to ideas and suggestions from others. It has the effect of multiplying your abilities because it makes greater knowledge accessible to you. If you are a confident, humble leader, you can walk into a politically charged boardroom and handle yourself with grace and authority, and then sit down with an entry-level staffer and have an open and honest conversation over lunch about his family and the weekend.

Committed Detachment

As a leader, of course you are committed to your career, organization, and employees. It is obvious from the long days and weekends you work, your fully engaged attitude, and your attention to detail and insistence on excellence. Commitment gives you energy and propels you through tough times. It is the foundation of your success. So where does detachment comes in?

Most people attach failure to something not working out or how people perceive you. My attitude to failure is not attached to outcome, but in not trying.

—Sara Blakely, founder and CEO, Spanx[4]

Detachment is the dispassionate part of your thinking. It knows that you can be blindsided at any time and that there is often a broader context for understanding events. Your detachment makes sure that emotions do not hijack you. With it, you do not get so enamored with an idea or course of action that you are unable to realize that a course correction is needed. It's also vital for your personal well-being. Even though you are fiercely committed, detachment lets you step back from a desired outcome or from work and your responsibilities so that you can get needed downtime and devote yourself to recharging your batteries.

Passionate Rigor

Passion is akin to commitment, but more encompassing. It is an inner quality that infuses an entire personality. It's being so dedicated to a goal that you are prepared to go to any length to achieve it, even make sacrifices that may not be advisable. On the one hand, passionate leaders are ruled by emotion, and this can drive them to neglect health, financial considerations, and other people. On the other hand, passionate people accomplish things. They tap into others' passions, and together they do the impossible.[5]

Passion is most powerful when coupled with rigor. Rigor is drive and commitment to a goal, but that drive is tempered by cool analysis of costs and benefits, risks and rewards. Rigor acts as a brake on passionate emotions. It inserts pragmatism into a leader's ambition. If you are a leader with passionate rigor, you may feel conflicted. You may believe that it's your passion that fuels creativity and that if it's cooled down, you'll lose that spark. If you are the kind of person who believes that the ends justify the means, you may cling to your passion regardless of the cost. As is true of these other paradoxical qualities, it becomes a balancing act to find the sweet spot between contradictory forces.

THE POWER OF CREATIVITY AND INNOVATION

What do Tony the Tiger from Kellogg's, birthday cards from Hallmark, McDonald's Big Mac, and Nintendo games all have in common?

They are brands produced by the creative minds of Leo Burnett, one of the premier creative advertising companies in the world. Tom Bernardin, chairman and CEO, leads this powerhouse of creativity that spans eighty-five countries. He is a master of combining the deep curiosity, adaptive mindset, and paradoxical thinking that nurtures his intellectual health. The result is creativity and innovation.

"Creativity is the most important asset in business today," claims Bernardin. "Our purpose as a company is to understand our client brands and work with them by using the power of creativity. It's a great time to be in our business because there's never been a higher value placed on creativity."[6]

Technology is the company's great accelerator. By combining traditional advertising with the power of the Internet, Leo Burnett has the power to transform human behavior. "Whether you are building your own site on flipboard, retouching photographs of your family, or creating global brands, creative technology can be taught and learned."

"I am a frustrated creative," admits Tom. "My father was a creative director, and I have it in my genes. But my job today is to create the right culture and leadership to help creativity flourish.

"Everything I do is transparent, so in a creative company you must realize you can't know everything. But you must be intelligent enough and risk-taking enough to surround yourself with creative people. My job is to help them reach their full potential. That means I have to be grounded in my own life.

"I am confident in who I am. I also need to like the people I work with. That is why I hire to the human being, to the person. Obviously they have to have talent. But beyond that I'm more concerned with what kind of human being they are. In our creative environment, I need to find people I like and who are good people."

THINGS TO CONSIDER

Healthy leaders must live in the present and future simultaneously. They must balance speed and urgency with discipline. Here are some ideas to consider.

Discover Your Core Paradox

Most of us have a central emotion or philosophy that underlies who we are and all that we value. It may be one of the paradoxes we've mentioned here or others, like pragmatic trust or reflective decisiveness. Or it may be about excellence, honesty, or duty and paired with an equally strong intellectual quality, such as a belief in reason, the importance of observation, or the necessity of conducting comprehensive research before taking action. Knowing your core paradox—the feelings and thoughts that create a vibrant tension within you—is the beginning of expanding your leadership repertoire.

Explore Other Facets of Your Creative Nature

Many leaders tend to stick with patterns they have used for years. It's human nature to stay with what's known and comfortable. Explore other ways of thinking by stepping back from your usual habits, taking time to detach yourself from work and the responsibilities of leading, and thinking about other ways to pursue your goals. This may include broadening your perspective, engaging more people for new viewpoints, changing your personal story, or seeing how other leaders handle similar situations.

Find Your Stretch Point

You naturally lean to one side of each these leadership paradoxes. Under stress, optimism can become unrealistic dreaming, confidence can turn into arrogance, and commitment can become obsession. This is the point at which your leadership is about to become imbalanced and is not a good place to be. Learn where your vulnerabilities are. The best way to handle this is to lean to the other side of the paradox. You have great capacity to monitor, assess, and modulate in the middle ground.

Try Lateral Thinking

A lateral thinker's thoughts jump the rails of straight, logical processing and come up with unusual, creative ideas. Those ideas may be appropriate or not, but that doesn't matter at first. It's the process that matters, being able to apply your intellect to fresh perspectives, novel ideas, and unlikely scenarios. Brainstorming helps, as do a variety of thinking puzzles.

View Life Through a Different Lens

Breakthrough thinking—it's one of the great talents of healthy leaders. This takes deep curiosity, an adaptive mind, and the ability to master paradoxical thinking. Think about a business issue from the perspective of a designer, mechanic, musician, or artist. Turn a problem upside down and look at it from all sides to get a new perspective. Look for patterns that might exist from the past or metaphors that might inform the future. Our experience is that the best leaders use a combination of these to innovate and think creativity.

Social Health

We have a radical proposition to make: all business is personal.

Whether you are calling a customer, running a meeting, presenting to your board, or having a performance discussion, the impact on yourself and others is a deeply personal one. In fact, everything you do in business affects who you are and your relationships with others. Executives who claim, "It's just business, nothing personal" are kidding themselves. Business is immensely personal, and the sooner we realize this the better we will be.

Why is this so important today? Because at a time when organizational life is screaming out for more transparency, intimacy, and collaboration in a networked world, many leaders underestimate these realities. Leading a great organization must be grounded in healthy relationships. Personal connections and all they entail are at the heart of a lasting enterprise. A company cannot function without strong social health.

When British poet John Donne wrote, "No man is an island entire of itself," he might as well have been writing about modern business. The leader who is not fully connected to his team cultivates distrust and discord in an organization. The result is a host of ailments, from disengagement and cynicism to lapses in integrity to stagnant earnings.

Every year, Edelman Consulting, a global public relations firm, conducts a trust and credibility survey of people around the world. Its 2013 Trust Barometer survey, which polled twenty-five thousand people, recorded a historic drop in people's trust of business and government. Less than one in five respondents believe that a business or government leader will actually tell the truth when confronted with a difficult issue, which represented the biggest decline since the survey began.[1]

Trust is built on transparency. Enlightened leaders strive to be as open and honest as possible within the confines of a competitive world. Starting with mastering their own social health, they know that personal identity and core principles are revealed in all they say and do.

Leadership follows an inside-outside progression. Social health starts with authenticity, advances to mutually rewarding relationships, and culminates in nourishing teams and communities.

The Edelman Trust Barometer asked what qualities make a leader trustworthy. Many respondents said, "A person like me." The most credible leaders were those with whom people could identify. If we believe that someone is similar to us, it's because we feel that we know her. Trustworthy leaders are genuine and sincere—in short, they are human. Ken Samet, CEO of MedStar Health, is such an individual.

WARNING SIGNS OF DECLINING SOCIAL HEALTH

- Inability to build and participate on strong teams
- Difficulty building peer relationships
- Inability to see other viewpoints
- Decreasing desire for productive collaboration
- Difficulty leading or following others
- Tendency to ostracize others with different perspectives

CHAPTER 13

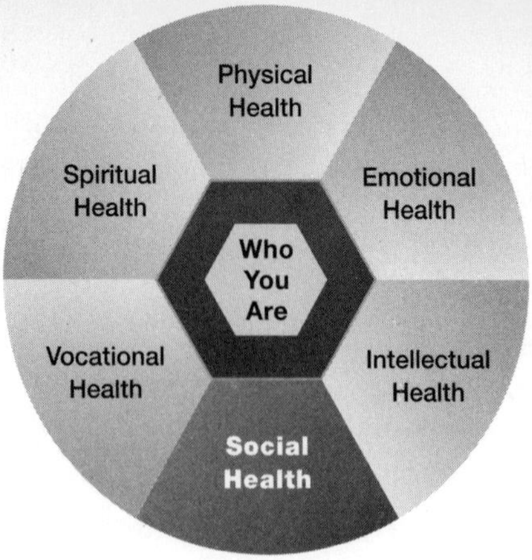

Authenticity

TOUCHING AND INSPIRING LIVES

As president and CEO of MedStar Health, a $4.1 billion nonprofit regional health care system, Ken Samet leads the largest system in the Washington DC and Baltimore region. In recent years, it has expanded in the market, upgraded facilities, and created more health care options. But Ken realizes that his primary job is to connect with twenty-seven thousand associates and fifty-six hundred affiliated physicians. Ken must make these connections count as the U.S. health care system is morphing from a bunch of independent, acute hospitals into a comprehensive distributed care delivery system.

Ken has thought a lot about authenticity, perhaps because much of what he does touches lives. We've been fortunate to witness up close and personal the effects of Samet's authenticity because we have been working with him and MedStar's executives for over seven years, helping them take the company to a new level of leadership and performance.

As part of MedStar's growth, Samet has been forging strategies and initiatives that emphasize MedStar 2020—a single comprehensive strategy for its future. Its powerful Good to Great culture strategy enables the organization to achieve high quality, patient service, and teamwork, while unifying the company's numerous hospitals and encouraging employees at all levels to work as one. To achieve these goals, one of Samet's best tools has been himself and his natural authenticity.

"You have to be real," he says. "You cannot fake it . . . so people have to actually believe that you're very sincere and real in what you're telling them. That they understand why you're committed to it."[1]

Samet strives to be consistent and transparent. He pays attention to the little things in daily life that matter. Courtesy and respect are part of his persona, as is an easy smile, an amusing one-liner, or a ready compliment. By doing his homework, he builds credibility. People know that he's informed. And he respects people's time, to the point of postponing a meeting if he's unprepared and answering every email he receives. All this shapes Ken as a leader whom people trust and respect.

"I think you have to be comfortable in your own skin. I'm privileged to have the opportunity to do this role. And, by the same token, I understand that it's not about me and there's a lot of smarter folks around me. For that reason it has to become a part of who you are. All of a sudden you stand up and you're not as real. And it doesn't take but a few times for folks to actually say, 'That was all bullshit'—just like that." Ken Samet's authenticity is grounded from the inside out.

DO YOU KNOW YOUR REAL SELF?

Self-acceptance is a huge part of knowing yourself, and for many people it's difficult. Denying certain facets of their personality, hiding emotions, refusing to admit mistakes, or running away from painful past experiences are just a few ways people avoid accepting themselves. A leader who grew up in a blue-collar family and has risen into the ranks of affluence may ignore the part of himself that knows what going without feels like. He may even compensate and be insensitive to those who "haven't worked hard enough." The executive who grew up in wealth may feel entitled or conversely ashamed of his unearned privilege.[2]

Being your real self is reflected in what you disclose and how you interact with others. It's sharing your thoughts and beliefs, and having the courage to expose yourself psychologically. Such a person is the business leader who feels comfortable telling personal stories to people she works with. This is a leader who can talk about a time when she made a mistake out of ignorance or embarrassed herself by being thoughtless. By sharing stories like these, a person shows self-awareness and an understanding of herself.

Only you can say who you are. We can't offer a definition. However, we can give you guidelines for self-examination: knowing yourself, being yourself, and sharing yourself. Here are some questions that can help you peel back the onion of your true self, identify who you are, and accept your inner self.

- Can you say you are comfortable in your own skin?
- Do you accept who you are, or are you always trying to change something about yourself?
- Do you have a "work personality" and another one for family and friends?
- Do you feel it's appropriate to talk about your "inner self" with others?
- Are you embarrassed about something about yourself that you do not share with others?

The unexamined life is not worth living.

—Socrates

BUILDING TRUST AND SHARING PRINCIPLES

Contemporary organizations often display a clash of principles. For example, they may espouse the importance of trust and transparency; yet at the same time, their actions show that other qualities, like obsessing over profits, promoting hidden agendas, or playing politics are more important. Personal core values are the bedrock of any trust. Some people call these values "principles," "beliefs," or "morals," but regardless of the label, they form a personal code of conduct.

Sometimes people's principles become compromised. No one starts out in business determined to lie, deceive, or manipulate himself to success. (We're not talking about the .5 percent who set out to perpetrate a fraud.) Lying to customers, screwing employees, bribing officials, spying on competitors, and taking unfair or unethical advantage in business relationships were probably not part of their original game plan. Even the most egregious business ethical failures, such as what happened at Enron or Madoff Investments, for instance, probably began as small transgressions. Corners cut, accounting rules ignored, a legal requirement bypassed—the lapses built up slowly. But over time they accumulated, and at some point, executives wake up in the middle of an ethical or legal storm. In the process, what they believed and stood for had evaporated, and their moral core was destroyed.

Knowing and examining your moral core by looking at your life and being aware of how your actions reveal what's really important to you is the beginning of building trust in an organization. Trust gets back to being self-aware and then sharing with others who you are and what is valuable to you. When you have a firm handle on your values, trust follows. There are various ways you can earn trust, and we have found that the following qualities can help strengthen your social health.[3]

Credibility. This comes down to being truthful: your written and spoken words are always believable, and your actions are consistent with your words. When you interact with people who have been taken advantage of in the past, you might have to work extra hard to develop credibility. If you are like most leaders, there will also be times when you may not know what's true or may be unable to fully disclose the facts. But if you tell lies or half-truths, instead of saying nothing or admitting what you don't know or cannot say at the time, you may find yourself spinning a web that you could be stuck in for the rest of your life.

Dependability. You must consistently make good on promises and commitments. Your word is your bond, even in the most difficult or trying situations. People expect leaders, especially executives, to be dependable and mature—to demonstrate an executive presence. If you don't, others are less likely to trust who you really are.

Predictability. This is expressed as consistency in your values and temperament. The predictable leader does not spring unpleasant surprises on people, does not engage in emotional outbursts, and does not constantly change policies or opinions without explanation or shared thinking.

Valuing the common good. Your words and deeds are driven not solely by self-interest but also by a desire for everyone to benefit from an organization's success. We are always balancing our self-interest with the collective interests of the group. It requires wisdom and self-awareness for a leader to understand that the two are not mutually exclusive and to craft a way to encompass both.

Emotional safety. You do not abuse people's health, feelings, self-image, or principles. You take their concerns and interests to heart. People who feel emotionally safe at work know that they will not be humiliated by a mistake or criticized unfairly or out of proportion to the situation.

HOW TRUSTWORTHY ARE YOU?

In business, trust is one of the most valuable coins of the realm. You can lose it in a moment's thoughtlessness, and you must keep earning it every day. You can never have too much. All of us like to believe that we are trustworthy. We've never heard anyone admit to being dishonest or duplicitous. But while everyone talks the talk, it's the walking the talk—showing that you can be trusted and that you trust others—that reveals the truth. These questions offer a way for you to assess whether or not your beliefs about trustworthiness are more than words.

- Do you keep your promises, even the small ones, or do you let some commitments slide?
- Do you guard against the "Big Boss Disease," that tendency to isolate yourself and cut off criticism, or do you shoot the messenger when you get bad news?
- Do you avoid hidden agendas, or do you share your intentions only on a "need to know" basis?
- Do you discount materialistic values, or do you like showing off your power, influence, money, or status?
- Can you make fun of yourself and admit mistakes so that others can see you as a complete person, or do you try to keep a faultless façade?

CLASSIC, HONEST

"I grew up as a kid with a poor self-image. I internalized my beliefs about myself—what I was and wasn't capable of doing. But I soon learned that life is all about being authentic and expressing all of who you are. You have the opportunity to become the champion of your own cause."[4]

These are the words of Mitch Kosh, senior vice president of human resources at Polo Ralph Lauren, one of the great corporate success stories of the last hundred years.

Today, Mitch is a trained psychologist, a steward of Ralph Lauren's special corporate culture, and one of the most authentic people you would ever want to meet. After a bumpy early start in his career, Kosh joined Ralph Lauren twelve years ago. At about that time, the company went public, and since then the company's rise in the world of fashion has been meteoric. It has grown from thirty-five hundred employees to thirty thousand, from revenues around $1 billion to $7.5 billion, and to a market cap of $17 billion. Despite this explosive growth, the company has remained its authentic self and strengthened its reputation and brand for high quality and classic elegance.

Mitch's success has been fueled by authenticity. "These last dozen years, I've been firing on all cylinders and integrating all the pieces and parts of who I am. One thing I learned early in my life is that you can preach authenticity all day long, but if it's not there, if it isn't anchored to the truth, if it doesn't come from within, it's just a veneer," says Mitch.

Mitch shares his wisdom: "Business is full of complex challenges, commercial realities, human dynamics, and ethical dilemmas. If you're not grounded in who you are, the more disconnected you are from yourself, the more unmoored you can become. And that's a very dangerous place to be."

Being a caretaker of the company culture with a brand famous throughout the world presents challenges. When Kosh started, the company was small and highly creative. Kosh says that the foundation of this fashion giant is authenticity, both personal and corporate. Authenticity is not something you buy off the rack. "If you've got above-average intellect and a good heart and you surround yourself with people who are authentic in these ways, you'll figure it out."

Kosh's own authenticity is rooted in plain speaking, a passion for what he's doing, and personal integrity. He's steady and consistent and true to himself. "The way this company has exploded and grown, for me, has a lot to do with authenticity and leading courageously. We pride ourselves, from a design perspective, in having a very clean aesthetic—nothing trendy." Indeed, to Mitch, "authenticity is the new international currency."

To illustrate, he tells this story: "The chairman of our Japanese business, a gentleman who is in his sixties and a dear friend, recently retired. His English is about as good as my Japanese, and we've used interpreters for the last ten years to talk to each other. But there is such affection and understanding that gets communicated right here, eye to eye, heart to heart, head to head. The trust that we developed got us through very complicated organizational challenges as we began to develop our business in Japan."

When this gentleman retired from the company, Kosh flew across the globe to make a surprise appearance at his retirement party.

"And when we saw each other, we embraced, on a stage with three hundred mostly Japanese employees, and we talked about our story—he did, and I did—to three hundred people who were watching. You can preach authenticity all day long, but if it's not there; if it really isn't coming from within, everyone knows it, most importantly yourself."

An essential thread in a person's authenticity is being openly vulnerable. Kosh readily admits to being imperfect—"If I had to look in the mirror and grade myself on where I think I am, I'm a work in progress." By airing personal weaknesses, you reveal your common humanity. In this way, your authenticity becomes a way of bonding and bringing people together. Paradoxically, admitting weakness makes you stronger: you reveal yourself to be honest and humane—powerful qualities in any leader.

MASTERING THE POWER OF VULNERABILITY: LET THEM SEE YOU SWEAT

You might remember a popular TV commercial that featured someone in a high-pressure situation, such as a female executive making a big presentation. It carried the tagline, "Don't let them see you sweat." The commercial was for a deodorant, so it was being literal. There was also the subtext that showing weakness or vulnerability could hurt a person's standing. That tagline has become a mantra for many in the business world, a motto people use when they want to appear invincible and powerful.

Contrary to that commercial, letting people see you work hard, truly care, and even have a bout of nerves makes you not only genuine but trustworthy. You're not hiding anything, but instead are showing who you are.

Business leaders find showing vulnerability difficult, understandably so. They need to project confidence and competence. Both employees and investors need to feel that a company leader can handle the pressures of managing an enterprise. So before we go any further, we want to make clear that we don't think that you are obligated to expose all your weak spots and shortcomings. You do not need to always reveal your entire self, warts and all, in order to be an authentic, vulnerable person.[5]

Too often, however, leaders equate vulnerability with weakness. Vulnerability is not weakness, but rather showing yourself to be human with the same flaws and imperfections as everyone else. People don't want leaders to be weak, but do want them to be real.

Being emotional, impetuous, a bad negotiator, sensitive to criticism, impatient; not being good at math or not being very verbal; avoiding confrontation; taking antidepressants; or having a short attention span, a checkered youth, or a chronic disease—the leader who reveals a vulnerability like one of these demonstrates not only his humanity but also the capacity to manage and triumph over his personal flaws.

TURNING REJECTION INTO RENEWAL

Health care executive Nancy Schlichting learned early in her career that being vulnerable could have a price. Sometimes a leader is forced into authenticity. The question then becomes, What do you do with it? Does your newly revealed vulnerability become an authentic asset?

For the past nine years, Schlichting has been president and CEO of the Henry Ford Health System, an organization of twenty-three thousand employees and a network of hospitals and care centers throughout Michigan. She also serves on numerous community and professional boards and is frequently on "Top Women Executives" lists. In short, she's at the pinnacle of her career. What's more noteworthy is that she got there by being honest about herself as a person, even though it cost her early on.

Schlichting has always been an exceptional health care professional. She was still in her thirties and an executive at the Riverside Methodist Hospital in Ohio when she was nominated and accepted the job as CEO of the hospital. Since her teen years, Schlichting had known that she was gay, but had kept this part of herself hidden.

When the CEO of the parent company, Ohio Health, resigned, Nancy was the logical choice to succeed him. But this time, when her nomination was announced, someone anonymously outed her by sending letters to every hospital board member.

Schlichting was certain that her career was over. When the chairman of the board came to her home to ask about the revelation, she offered to resign. She recounts that conversation: "Jack and I were very close, and he decided that this was not an issue. And he said, 'Nancy, what do you want me to do?' I said, 'Whatever you think you should do.' He called every board member and spoke candidly with each. In the end, all but one decided it was fine."[6]

Schlichting still marvels at the chairman's decency and fairness. For a time, it looked as though the hospital was going to do the right thing. But it fell apart when the one board member who could not accept Schlichting threatened to withhold his substantial donation if her nomination was confirmed. Six months later, she left the hospital.

She does not sugarcoat the difficult times. As she struggled with her own disappointments and career crisis, her mother was dying of cancer. It was years before she got back on track, this time as an openly gay woman. The next time she was approached about a job, she knew she would handle it honestly and tell anyone who asked who she was.

"Gail Warden called from Henry Ford—he was very interested in my coming here. And so I said to him, 'Gail, you know there's something before I accept that I want you to know.' And I told him I was gay. He said, 'Oh, I know that, Nancy.' I said, 'You do?'

Then I said, 'Well, how is it at Henry Ford? Is this going to be okay?' And he said, 'Nancy, it's the nineties.' "

Schlichting still laughs about that conversation, at her amazement and pleasure at finding that her sexual orientation, instead of being cause for rejection, was a nonissue. It was no longer news; it was just who she was.

In hindsight, she says that being forced to go public with her most personal self has made her a better business leader. "It strikes me that what we stand for as individuals and as people is incredibly important in how we function as leaders, either organizationally or even within families or communities . . . Every person brings gifts to work that we hope we can learn more about, so that we see ourselves as whole persons instead of just a job."

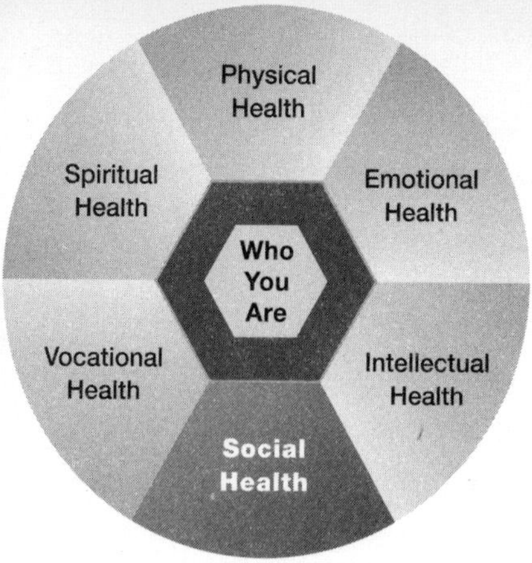

CHAPTER 14

Mutually Rewarding Relationships

Humans are social animals and depend on interaction to survive.

In his book *The Social Animal,* journalist and social scientist David Brooks captures the importance of our social bonds with a vivid metaphor: "We are like spiritual Grand Central Stations. We are junctions where millions of sensations, emotions and signals interpenetrate every second. We are communication centers . . . We seek, more than anything else, to establish deeper and more complete connections."[1]

Our intrinsically social nature is apparent in all facets of our lives, especially in business, as Per-Olof Loof, the Swedish-born CEO of KEMET, knows firsthand.

REACHING OUT AND BUILDING CONNECTION

Per Loof has a natural ability to connect with people, perhaps the inevitable result of growing up in the Nordic countries and the larger European community. Speaking four languages probably also enhanced his already well-developed communication skills. Each summer in the years when Loof was seven to fifteen, the family drove around Europe, traveling around forty thousand miles. Loof is very much a global citizen and as such readily relates to diverse coworkers and competitors around the world.

KEMET is the world's largest manufacturer of capacitors, producing fifty billion units per year. These devices store, filter, and regulate electrical energy and are used on almost all electronic equipment to help us stay connected. It has facilities around the world, and with its recent acquisition of NEC Token in Japan, recent revenues approach $2 billion. As a virtual CEO, Per's ability to engage with others and to project outward with confidence and empathy is apparent in many of his business dealings.

"It's more than being able to speak English and Chinese," says Per. "It's about trying to understand how you truly communicate with people in different parts of the world. When I'm in Italy and having a conversation with a union leader, of course I'm speaking English and of course he's speaking Italian. But I'm trying to calibrate how I talk about things in ways that he would relate to, always trying to think of what would it be like if I put myself in his shoes, what would I think or say."[2]

Loof cultivates his empathetic outlook in other ways. Through his daily Ask Per blog, he communicates about the company and solicits feedback on how he is doing as its leader. "Looking at yourself through other people's lenses often provides a great starting point for understanding each other," shares Per.

"I worry that I can be too emotional at times and too persuasive, and that might shut others down. So when something goes wrong, I try to avoid any personal criticism and instead talk about the situation, not individual actions."

Per is also adamant about challenging people intellectually, monitoring the level of anxiety inside the company; and, unlike other leaders who either participate or stand by as onlookers, Per is nonnegotiable about one thing: "NO POLITICS. Civility is the name of the game."

One story captures the essence of Per Loof and the importance of mutually rewarding relationships. It was 2008, and KEMET faced a crisis as banks were shutting down in the midst of a financial meltdown. So Per leveraged his social health to help the company during this difficult period An insurance policy covenant had been tripped by KEMET's debt-to-equity ratio, and the CEO had to raise $50 million immediately. Because the financial climate had eliminated the usual sources of money, he used his intuition and relationships and sought out a novel source of funding, namely Vishay Company, a direct KEMET competitor.

Although Vishay was a "fierce" competitor, its CEO, Felix Zandman, and Per Loof were more than cordial—they liked and respected each other. Loof knew that Vishay wanted to buy a small KEMET division, but Per had so far resisted the overtures because the division was a good performer. Now he needed money, so he went to his friend Zandman with a unique proposition: he offered to sell Vishay the division, plus he added a special request.

"So we had a conversation, and we agreed on a yellow piece of paper how this would work," the KEMET leader recalls. "And he said I'm willing . . . The business was like $16 million revenue, and he was willing to pay $35 million for it. And then I said, 'Well, Felix, I need fifty.' He said, 'I can't get the board to do it.' I said, 'Well, can you lend me $15 million?' " And the deal went down as they agreed, despite interjections by teams of lawyers who wanted caveats and riders and all sorts of conditions. KEMET was rescued from its insurance companies.

"So I think he thought it was the right thing to do to help his competitor stay alive," Loof says. What made the deal happen, its essential grease, was the mutual respect and empathy they had for each other. They understood each other at a fundamental, human level. Zandman could have waited on the sidelines for KEMET to fold and picked up the division for less, but he chose not to. For both men, doing business was not about crushing the other guy but about helping each other so both could prosper.

Although Per Loof's experience is unusual, his use of his social health to help his business is not uncommon. Knowledgeable businesspeople have found that leaders across the globe are reaching out to each other to strengthen their organizations.

The 2012 IBM Global Chief Executive Officer Study confirms this. The study surveyed 1,709 CEOs in sixty-four countries and eighteen industries on the role of "collaborative cultures" and how they are fueling the world's connected economy.[3] Nearly 70 percent of the CEOs said that they intended to partner "extensively" with other enterprises. "We tend to see everyone as a competitor, but we need to see them as partners . . . This is a cultural shift; but it's hard to change," commented a banking executive in Vietnam.

Intentions are a good start, but changing relationships is a whole other matter. Adam Grant, a professor at the Wharton School of Business, may be on to something. He's been studying relationships at work and sees two kinds of people: givers and takers.

Givers are more likely to share knowledge and help out others. Takers hoard information, take personal credit for their work, and manage by "kissing up and kicking down." Grant concludes that the single greatest predictor of group performance is the help people give to each other. Givers fill knowledge gaps, get work done faster, and show higher sales revenue, productivity, and profits. This is all very interesting, but where does this behavior come from?[4]

THE BIOLOGY OF BUSINESS CONNECTIONS

You and those you connect with are closer than you might know. Human beings are biologically programmed not only to form social bonds but to connect in deep, more personal ways—with empathy and laughter and trust.

A new field of study called "neuroleadership" has emerged from the combined fields of neuroscience and leadership development. It may sound like an odd marriage, yet there is much about the brain's activities that contributes to a person's success or failure as a leader. It appears that leaders who are adept at reading other people's moods and connecting on an emotional level can also stimulate feelings of shared bonds in those around them. There is literally a meeting of the minds.

Our brains are built to seek out connections with others. For instance, discoveries about the functions of mirror neurons and spindle cells, which are found in most regions of the brain, are helping explain the neurological basis of certain emotions vital to leadership. Italian researchers first identified mirror neurons when they observed that when one monkey watched another move its arm, the same area in both animals' brains became active.[5] The researchers initially thought that mirror neurons enable us to experience sensations involved with movement when watching someone else move.

Researchers now believe that these neurons enable us also to share certain emotions. For instance, when you see someone in the dentist's chair about to get drilled, you may wince in pain at the sight. This "shared pain" is triggered by your mirror neurons.[6] Even more remarkable, scientists have noted a rich presence of mirror neurons in the brain's insula, a key structure in generating empathy.[7] The insula is very involved in emotions such as happiness (especially pleasure and reward) and disgust.

Mirror neurons may be involved in feelings of happiness. These become especially active when you laugh or smile and make others react the same way. This may explain why lighthearted, upbeat feelings are often contagious. As a leader, surely you have noticed that when you are happy and joking around with others, they, too, lighten up and join in.

This science is hugely significant for leaders. It indicates that you are neurologically programmed to feel empathy (individuals known for a lack of empathy, like psychopaths, appear to have less-developed insulas). Furthermore, acting on feelings of empathy—engaging others because you "know" what they are feeling—creates a neurochemical loop within yourself between your emotions and behavior such that they reinforce each other. You can stimulate positive feelings in those around you so that everyone is more eager to work together to create something good.

Spindle cells also appear to be instrumental in making you a socially adroit leader. They fire more quickly than other types of neurons and are believed to send signals throughout the brain about your social emotions. A study involving how people react to a performance evaluation shows how this works. One group of people received a negative evaluation, but it was delivered with positive emotions, like smiles and nods. A second group got positive evaluations, but the evaluations came with negative emotional signals, like frowns and stern expressions.[8] In interviews of participants afterwards, those who received the positive signals with the negative evaluation felt better about themselves and presumably performed better afterward. The tenor of the emotions, rather than the substance of the evaluation, made the difference in people's attitudes toward this work.

Imagine a real-life company full of positive mirror neurons and spindle cells in action. "As a child my nickname was Smiley. Although I've always been a socially anxious guy, I learned early on that I was starting to smile out of social discomfort."[9] Phil grew up in Appalachia, a poor mountain area in the eastern United States. With "average intelligence" and "never taking a business course," Phil became one of the most successful CEOs in the pharmaceutical management business, leading several thousand employees competing against the industry giants, while his company became one of the most predictable performers on the NASDAQ stock exchange for over ten years.

Over time, Phil became what his smile represented—optimistic, confident, and affable. And it was the power of his smile that made the difference. The smile not only helped him manage his social anxiety but was infectious to everyone. "My smile communicated optimism and a can-do spirit. I hired people who smiled, and together we created the most friendly, positive, empowered culture that differentiated us from our competition. No matter how negative or tense a situation became, our smiles—inside and out—gave us this special sense of hope and confidence, and everything seemed to work out at the end." Whether we know it or not, we are all connected by our mirror neurons, and a simple smile can go a long way if we use our social health to inspire us.

Here's the good news: leadership is contagious. The truth is, every healthy leader inspires others to become healthy leaders. One healthy leader begets, let's say, ten healthy leaders, and so on—you do the math. We truly can transform the world one leader at a time.

FOUR PILLARS OF HEALTHY RELATIONSHIPS

The leadership literature is full of stories of executives who possess great analytical, strategic, or organizational skills yet fail in their jobs. It's the CEO who berates and humiliates people in public. It's the government executive who makes sexual comments about women on the staff. It's the nonprofit director who favors a chosen few with special perks. It's the business unit leader who stays behind closed doors all day doing who-knows-what. It's the manager who never thanks or compliments others. What brings them down is a glaring lack of social health.

A leader needs a repertoire of social skills to foster healthy, productive relationships. In our experience, the most powerful tools are empathy, fairness, communication, and appreciation. Here's how they enhance your influence as a healthy leader, and we offer some suggestions for putting them into practice.

Empathy: Don't Leave Home Without It

Empathy is deep understanding on an emotional and cognitive level about the fears, frustrations, aspirations, and concerns of people. The leader who viscerally understands what other people are feeling and experiencing is someone others want to follow. These leaders attract talent, and people are loyal to them. Being empathetic is not always easy. You may need to understand someone who is fundamentally different from you, confront negative feelings you have about that person, or address your fear that your empathy will send false signals. The secret is to understand what is influencing your reactions, work hard to put yourself in the other's shoes, and interact with her as a whole person. Don't forget to share something personal about yourself. It's amazing how good you will feel.

Fairness: It's Genetic and Fundamental

Human beings are intrinsically fair. Consciously or unconsciously, we will monitor a situation and do all we can—actively or passively—to remedy any unfairness we may witness. Healthy leaders fundamentally understand this unspoken principle. If you take advantage of people, they will feel it and will retaliate in one form or another. Leaders who are evenhanded and fair generate trust and cooperation. This sense of fair play is part of our genetic makeup. On a primitive level, it enables us to form mutually rewarding relationships and nurturing communities.

Psychological studies have shown that people are fundamentally fair. One such study involved an "Ultimatum Game," with individuals negotiating to share small sums of money.[10] Most of the players agreed to split the money evenly and punished those who wanted to keep most of the money. The leader who plays favorites, makes decisions that unjustly reward or punish, or does not reciprocate cooperative efforts will generate resentment. As human beings, we feel, analyze, monitor, and fight back when it hurts. Fortunately, we also are genetically hardwired to be fair and to work in community with others.

Communication: Conscious, Clear, Courageous

This social skill is at the heart of healthy leadership—it's the ability, in spoken and written word and deed, to express yourself and understand what others are trying to communicate. Good communication is *conscious*: you are aware of your intentions, the situation, your psychology and theirs. Deep listening to other people, without interruption and without preparing for your comeback, is a great gift you can give to yourself and others. Good communication is *clear*: you know exactly what you want to communicate—generally and specifically—and on the basis of the data you receive, you are prepared to pursue a variety of tributaries to reach mutual understanding. And good communication is *courageous*: you are honest and straightforward, you tell the truth about reality (how you see the world), and you are courageous inside yourself to let the other person own his view of the truth. His truth may be fundamentally different from your own, and fundamentally flawed. But he has the right to his truth, and it is your responsibility to listen. And you have every right to make a decision independent of him. The goal is for everyone to be heard and respected and for you not to get hijacked in the conversation.

Appreciation: Recognition Trumps Money

In many organizations, true appreciation is more noticeable in its absence. If our associates were to write a Bill of Rights, this is what it would contain:

- Respect our thoughts, feelings, values, and fears.
- Respect our desire to lead and follow.
- Respect our unique strengths and differences.
- Respect our desire to learn and develop.
- Respect our need to feel like a winner.
- Respect our need to be recognized for our accomplishments.
- Respect our personal and family life as we define it.

Studies confirm that appreciation is at least as important as money, if not more.[11] Say thank you, write a note, give a compliment or some time off, apologize, or ask a question about the weekend. At Intel, employees are eligible for sabbaticals every seven years. And at Google, employees can give any colleague a $150 bonus, but they must write a note of appreciation to go with it.[12]

• • •

Taken together, empathy, fairness, communication, and appreciation really matter. When leaders exhibit these attributes of social health, they shed light on everyone; when they don't, they are quick to cast shadows on the people around them.

BUILDING RELATIONSHIPS THAT MATTER

For years, Michael Ramirez felt like a fish out of water. After spending some "less than personally fulfilling" years at several large companies, he finally realized that his leadership style was out of sync with the companies he was working for. Fortunately, he stumbled across Herman Miller, designer and manufacturer of contemporary interior furnishings. The company is famous in the business world for its creative, people-friendly culture. It has maintained its admired culture while growing to nearly six thousand employees worldwide and sales topping $1.6 billion. It is often cited as one of *Fortune*'s 100 Best Companies to Work For and has become a fixture on *Fortune*'s Most Admired list.

Michael is the first to admit that Herman Miller gave him the opportunity to express what he values most in himself today: his capacity to build relationships and practice "servant leadership." But his personal leadership wasn't always that way. Some of his early challenges were due in part to his own lack of development. "Early in my career, I was young and full of piss and vinegar. I wasn't a real great listener. When somebody was trying to help me, I would often become defensive and negative. It has been growth for me to become self-aware and to admit I am not the smartest person in the room."[13]

Ramirez joined Herman Miller in the late 1990s as director of purchasing and over the years has risen higher in the company. Along the way, he has been both a witness to the company's remarkable growth and a participant in it. Today, Michael is senior vice president for people, places, and administration at Herman Miller and the steward of its corporate culture.

When he took over as vice president of sales operations at Herman Miller, Ramirez saw what happens when people ignore the personal side of business relationships and discount the importance of their social health.

"When I was asked to lead that organization, their previous leader had just died due to illness and had really been absent for about two years," he says. "In his absence, they had created little silos between the individual leaders who were left. There was infighting. They had no vision. Quite frankly, it was a train wreck."

It was Ramirez's job to change the toxic atmosphere and find ways to forge connections and get people to pull together. He improved communication by prompting people to share ideas rather than provide only negative feedback. He showed respect for people's efforts by giving them more authority and power to make decisions; he let them lead their renaissance and create a new identity for the group. He got all the group members talking about their mission and how the group was perceived by others in the company. Gradually the group went from being the "Department of Sales Prevention" to the organization that the sales team relied on to drive sales forward.

To develop his own relationship skills, Michael relied on his inherent need for connection and desire to belong and tapped into his natural abilities to empower others. He kept lines of communication open and cultivated a more familial atmosphere.

One of the reasons this story is so relevant is that Herman Miller and Michael Ramirez are leaders in their own right, but by their own admission are not perfect. None of us are. We are all on a journey to become healthy leaders.

DO YOU BUILD MUTUALLY REWARDING RELATIONSHIPS?

Imagine yourself in Michael Ramirez's shoes, faced with a dysfunctional department and warring factions. Here are questions to help you discover whether you have the self-awareness and insight needed to forge strong bonds.

- Do you know what people are afraid of? Do you know what they talk about when you leave the room?

- Do you give people chances to take the initiative, or do you like to keep a tight hand on the reins?
- Do people pick up on your moods, and do you pick up on theirs?
- Are you practicing empathy, deep communication, fairness, and appreciation?
- Do you recognize and reward "givers" and confront and council "takers"?

One final thought. Great relationships are built on courageous conversations. So start by telling the truth to yourself. Then be emotionally honest with others. Don't be afraid to speak up when others are avoiding the tough issues. By being direct and authentic, both you *and* they will be better leaders, colleagues, and human beings.

CHAPTER 15

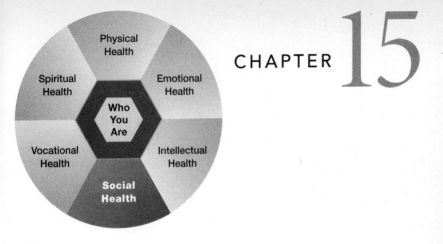

Nourishing Teams and Communities

Communities make us feel good—they support and rejuvenate us. We are happier when we are part of a group, be it a gang of coworkers involved in a big project, a team of board members governing a large corporation, a network of "friends" who share news via a Facebook page, or a group of tennis moms who get together to play every Wednesday night. And communities, particularly those created around a meaningful purpose, nourish us. Even communities of people dedicated to solitary, independent activities, like medical researchers, are finding that the quality of their lives and work improves when they join forces.

So what's the problem? Whether you work on the board, on the executive team, on a factory line, or as part of the network, these communities can be nourishing and high performing or depleting and de-energizing. And this has a huge impact on your health and performance.

BORN TO BELONG

We are born to bond into groups, and when we don't, we suffer physically and psychologically. Our bodies produce the hormone oxytocin to ensure that mothers nurture their children and that touching and caressing another person feels good, ensuring that we stay together. On the flip side, not coming together in social groups can be harmful. The physical damage that comes with being a loner can be considerable. Here's a sampling of research results showing what isolation can do to us:

- People who feel lonely and socially isolated are two to three times more likely to die from heart disease than people with strong connections.[1]
- People who use more "I" words (I, me, mine) in daily conversation have a higher risk of dying from heart disease. Such language is a better predictor of mortality than blood pressure or cholesterol.[2]
- British researchers found that the most significant predictor of people's health, better than their diet or exercise habits, is the number of strong groups they belong to.[3]
- Healthy people with strong support networks have lower cholesterol and better immune system function than those without.[4]
- A meta-analysis of 148 studies looking at how social interactions affect our health reveals that any kind of personal connection improves a person's survival chances by 50 percent.[5]

MOVING FROM ME TO WE

Christoph Lengauer is a dedicated cancer researcher who has followed his passion around the world. After receiving a doctorate in Germany and a postdoctorate in Austria, he traveled to Baltimore, Maryland, and the Johns Hopkins University School of Medicine. He then joined Novartis in Boston. From there he went to Sanofi in Paris, France, and recently returned to the United States to serve as chief scientific officer for a cancer drug start-up, Blueprint Medicines.

Although he has always been a member of the scientific community, he has devoted much of his efforts to solitary pursuits. Many researchers are lone-wolf types. Given the challenges of oncology and drug development, researchers can be wary of collaboration; they think it slows down their work or jeopardizes intellectual ownership in the discovery process. Lengauer began this way, particularly as a young postdoc from Europe eager to make his mark in the research world.

"First I thought I'd do it myself," Lengauer says about his research career.[6] But when he joined the molecular biology lab at Johns Hopkins, he found himself in a new world where his lone-wolf approach would be counterproductive.

"For the first time, I was submerged in a group where other people were better and smarter than me. And then working in isolation didn't get me anywhere. . . . And I felt the group worked so really well because the first thing that people were worried about was not their own success but the successes of others in the group," he says.

Forming a community of fellow researchers, as Lengauer did, is not easy. Some people have to be convinced and nudged toward collaboration and sharing the load. Others have to give up some ego to get something much larger. As Lengauer would learn, this can also apply to organizations.

When Lengauer joined Hopkins, it had gained fame for discovering HeLa cancer cells, a unique class of cells used by labs around the world. Hopkins had harvested HeLa cells from a single patient, Henrietta Lacks, who had died from ovarian cancer but whose cells continued to live in vitro and became the vehicle for virtually every new cancer drug that has been developed since her death.

While Lengauer and his colleagues were teaming together to discover how cancer works, the children of Henrietta Lacks contacted Hopkins to learn more about HeLa cells and their mother's contribution to medical science. But Hopkins repeatedly put up barriers. Organizations often resist connecting to larger communities because of their reluctance to share knowledge with outsiders or share their assets, or out of fear of legal or financial difficulties.

Lengauer felt strongly that the Lacks family deserved to know about their mother and her special cells. So he reached out to Rebecca Skloot, a journalist who was chronicling Henrietta's story. (It later became a bestseller, *The Immortal Life of Henrietta Lacks*.) He even went so far as to apologize for his employer's treatment of them and to bring them into his lab to answer questions, show them their mother's cells, and explain her incredible contribution to cancer research everywhere.

Lengauer has never forgotten what he learned about doing the right thing and the value of communities. In his current position with Blueprint Medicines, he is creating an atmosphere that emphasizes collaborative effort over organizational hierarchy. The company has a flat and fluid structure. Instead of layers of responsibility and reporting, people belong to groups distinguished not by status or power but by purpose.

"I want to help shift the whole organization from that very me-oriented thing toward a team atmosphere." As a result, any researcher at Blueprint who develops targeted cancer therapies can take the lead on a project but must insist on creating a collaborative learning community.

LEADING HEALTHY TEAMS

Teams have a special place in all organizations. However, the shape and function of teams have shifted as business trends and the nature of work have fundamentally changed how people connect and work together. Our research shows that flatter organizations foster shared information, authority, and decision making, and this changes how leaders and teams must relate to each other.

Visual to virtual. Team members may be spread out across a state, a country, or the globe. As a result, people have little face-to-face time and must create other avenues of communication. Virtual meetings have much to recommend them: they can be efficient and reduce a company's travel expenses. The challenge is that the absence of face-to-face time also means that people have to find new ways to build trust and influence among coworkers. Once the virtual team is up and running, leaders also have to monitor more closely any indications of dysfunction—for instance, clashes between people, disagreements over schedules, or miscommunication about trust, culture, and contributions.

Insular to boundary-free. On yesterday's team, members had well-defined roles and responsibilities, and there was a clear hierarchy for making decisions and solving problems. Boundary-free teams are much more amorphous, with people taking over or handing off tasks, responsibilities, and leadership as work progresses. People quickly get a sense of each other's strengths and weaknesses. People join and drop off a team as they are needed or redeployed. Leading such a team, particularly over cyberspace, requires someone well versed in articulating purpose, setting expectations, defining capabilities, and influencing others.

Static to flexible. A static team is typically assembled to tackle a time-limited, well-defined project. A flexible team, as its name suggests, is able to adapt to fast-changing conditions and adjust to moving targets. The flexible team anticipates problems and modifies its approach accordingly. Members have to be comfortable with ambiguity and must possess a better understanding of the risks and twists and turns of business. Because there is more freedom, it is easier to respond to evolving customer needs and to turn up or down the heat as the situation arises.

• • •

Social health is the guiding force for these twenty-first-century teams, whether they are intact or always changing. The healthy leader sets the tone and creates the conditions for success.

THE POWER OF SOCIAL NETWORKS

Rob Cross is a professor of commerce at the University of Virginia and has been fascinated with how work *actually* gets done inside organizations. "In today's flatter organizations work occurs through informal networks of people." The social networks are not on your formal org chart, but are critical to how your company executes its strategy. In one MIT study, for example, engineers and scientists were roughly five times as likely to turn to a person for information rather than to an impersonal source like a database.[7]

After examining thousands of social networks in a variety of organizations, Cross discovered three interesting findings.[8] First, people with larger and more diversified personal networks were higher performers; they were promoted earlier and were considered better leaders.

Second—and most significant—was their ability to energize rather than de-energize people in their networks. Rather than hog the show and drain the life out of a group, these leaders energized others, garnered support for initiatives, and attracted other high performers, which raised the performance of the entire group.

Last, companies with well-managed network connectivity simply outperformed their competitors. They created more knowledge, promoted innovation, developed communities of practice, improved decision making, and created more alliances and partnerships. Here are a few questions to ask yourself:

- Am I an energizer or de-energizer of people?
- Do I make an effort to weave relationship development into my work and day-to-day actions?
- How would I rate the quality of my personal networks inside my organization?
- How mentally and physically engaged am I in meetings and conversations?
- Do I look for possibilities or identify only constraints in team discussions?
- Do I sit in meetings glued to my emails rather than people's faces?

FACE-TO-FACE MEETS THE DIGITAL WORLD

The whole notion of community has exploded in recent years. The usual idea of a group of people, be it a work team or a neighborhood organization, meeting physically together in a space dedicated to a single function, is out the window. The biggest shift is away from face-to-face gatherings to digital or web-based communities. These are places like Facebook, Twitter, LinkedIn, individual websites, blogs, and chat rooms.

The "third place" community has also gotten a lot of attention. This may be a local coffee shop, library, or business conference center where people come together to link up either in person or via the Internet. We all have a "third place," if you think about it. It may be the gym, a café at the bookstore, or your living room.

A central element of social media and virtual communities is the dissemination of information. These are places where people learn things, ask questions, and explore unknowns. Want to know about someone's background or review the financial results of a venture? Go to the Internet. The World Wide Web is not known for keeping secrets. Inaccurate, even inflammatory information can cause legal nightmares and public relations disasters. It is very difficult for a leader to control the flow of information in the digital universe, and this makes people uneasy.

The best protection is to be smart about the digital community—staying up-to-date on what's being circulated and understanding the power and permanence of most email traffic. It also helps to realize that cases of egregious behavior are actually quite rare. These are like plane crashes—they don't happen often, so when they do, they get lots of press.

Perhaps the biggest objection we hear from leaders can be summed up in a phrase: "a sinkhole of my time." Leaders often assume that monitoring or managing digital communities will add hours to their workweek without tangible benefits. They hear about people spending great chunks of time blogging or logged on to social websites or sending out Tweets, and don't see the efficiencies that digital communities can add to their day.

Yet experience has shown that just the opposite can happen. As one executive commented, "Having this broadcast channel puts hours back in my week. It doesn't take hours away because I have to spend so much less time repeating myself and getting the story straight and saying the same thing to twelve different people."[9]

Trying to circumscribe the multitude of communities that pop up around your organization is a losing strategy. To do so is like trying to win at Whack-a-Mole. Rather than fight these communities, use and nurture them. Make an effort to become savvy enough to foster connections that nourish people. The possibilities for communities are almost endless. Departments, teams, partnerships, professional groups, neighborhoods, learning circles, communities of interest, affinity groups, educational associations, and religious or sports groups are just some of the communities you can encourage.

By harnessing Internet communities, you help those in your organization feel more connected and be more productive. But let's be clear: face-to-face connections are not going anywhere, nor should they. Your real opportunities are in leveraging face-to-face conversations and digital connections.

Think about how this is playing out in your life already: checking in for airline flights, buying groceries, choosing movies, interacting with your bank, or checking into hotels. Just imagine the near future and your changing desires—healthy relationships that combine high tech and personal touch, and are easy to do business with.

UNLOCKING THE VALUE OF SOCIAL TECHNOLOGIES

Social technologies are doing to business what decades of management consultants, flow charts, and interior space designers could not: they are bringing together people eager to collaborate. Leaders who encourage the use of these technologies have the potential of boosting high-skill knowledge workers' productivity by 20 to 25 percent. This is what the McKinsey Global Institute learned when it surveyed executives at forty-two hundred companies around the world.[10]

The McKinsey finding that 70 percent of companies and 80 percent of Internet users engage with a social network probably does not surprise you. However, you may well be wondering how you can tap into this and harness it to benefit you and your team and organization.

The biggest change in the world today is that the young don't learn from the old, they teach the old about the world today.

—Klaus Schwab, founder and chairman, World Economic Forum[11]

By creating a free-flow of ideas and open communications, social technologies are useful in managing logistics, procurement, and collaboration among functional groups of workers. In addition, they can help generate sales leads and be used for marketing by providing data for forecasting and monitoring. Companies use these technologies to gather new ideas, find solutions to problems, collect customer feedback about services and products, and generate reviews that can stimulate innovations. And they do this with minimal expense. The McKinsey study estimates that by enabling workers to share knowledge and information, social technologies can reduce time spent searching for information by 35 percent and free up about 6 percent of a person's workweek for other tasks.

To build up your digital skill set, expand your leadership thinking. Here are some ideas to help:

- Make peace with your inner fears about the Internet—for example, the question of trust and of people not being visible, the fragility of your reputation, or the fear of loss of control over people and information. But also be careful: don't lose the sense of human community and accountability.
- Stay attuned to what people are saying and writing. By listening, via online tools or by logging on to digital communities, you can stay in touch with how people are thinking and feeling about your team or organization.

- Monitor the content of community discussions and activities. Whatever information you glean can become a source of ideas for other parts of your organization and may enhance your own development.
- Get online and talk to people. Learning the language of the Internet will make you a better digital communicator.
- Look for opportunities to collaborate. Be more than just an observer—participate. Join forums, create your own blog or personal video, and use online communities and social networks to gather ideas and bring people together.

BUILDING AND LEADING A HEALTHY COMMUNITY

When Lieutenant General Eric Schoomaker served as the Army's forty-second surgeon general and commanding general of the U.S. Army Medical Command, he functioned very much like the CEO of a large corporation with offices and personnel around the world. Although he naturally had to work with the higher-ups at the Pentagon, much of Schoomaker's effort was directed at building a healthy community within the Army, for its seventy-five thousand soldiers and the three million members of their extended families.

What makes Schoomaker unique is his ability to combine broad notions of health, leadership, and community into a large-scale, multiyear organizational transformation. Let's step back and take a look.

In contrast to many who view health in a narrow way, Schoomaker understands the holistic nature of health. "Top performance in the military is much more than being physically fit. It's about focusing on all aspects of health, for both soldiers and their families. It's a fusion of physical health, emotional well-being, mental health, spiritual health, and family health."[12]

One way of doing this was to first "demedicalize" the Army's health care, meaning expanding the force's care beyond hospitals and doctors to a "comprehensive soldier fitness" program that eventually was expanded by Admiral Mullen of the Joint Chiefs of Staff as Total

Force Fitness. It included many of the dimensions of health we discuss in this book.[13]

An outcome of this effort was the Army's response to the growing concerns about posttraumatic stress syndrome and family divorces when soldiers returned from active duty. Schoomaker tells the story: "Your ability to reintegrate in society and reconnect with your family is driven by events that occurred while you were in the combat zone, and how totally fit you are in the broad sense of the word 'health.' For us, we discovered that the length of deployment and time between deployments (twenty-four to thirty-six months) were more important than the frequency of deployment. Soldiers needed time to reestablish social connections and regain their social and emotional grounding."

Schoomaker also sought to forge twenty-first-century communities by extending the Army "family" beyond soldiers and family members to include the millions of civilians who support and interact with them. It's a huge community, with upwards of three million people looking to the Army for leadership and direction. By reshaping people's notions of health and getting everyone to pull together, Schoomaker used the power of the Army hierarchy to cascade his efforts.

The general is a savvy leader with years of rich experience. The Army has a 236-year tradition of investing in leadership development. "So how do you get this unity of mission delivered over time and space without eroding it? The secret is developing the next generation of leaders." Schoomaker continues, "there's no substitute for actual leadership experience. We must expose soldiers to good leaders who are nourishing their willingness to be uncomfortable, rewarding them when they do things successfully, and not overly punishing them when that risk doesn't pay off."

Yet don't be deceived. Not everything in the Army is about command and control. Just ask Eric Schoomaker, who remembers pulling rank only a handful of times in his thirty-two-year career while knowing full well each time that he had "already lost." As he explains it, "You can never underestimate the power of what I call 'organizational elastic recoil.' It will snap back to whatever. . . . If you can't get at the fundamentals of how the system works and what is measured, treasured, and rewarded, then it doesn't matter whether you have authority to order or not." So he spent much of his time mentoring, influencing, teaching, and coaching people close to him and supporting them as they went forth with the message.

Using the power of health, leadership, and community, General Schoomaker is a great example of a healthy leader building a healthy community.

SOCIAL CONNECTIONS BUILD HEALTHY COMMUNITIES: THINGS TO CONSIDER

Social health is clearly about using our relationships with others to accomplish what we want in the world. Regardless of your mission and goals, developing your social health should include an inside-outside approach. This starts with an inward assessment of your personal character and authenticity; you then turn outward to develop mutually rewarding relationships and pull people together into nourishing teams and communities. Ask yourself these questions to think about which sphere of your social health needs attention:

- Am I the same person (my personality and principles) at work as I am outside of work?
- Do I share with people my full self—my views, thoughts, and feelings?
- In my relationships, do I naturally judge the person or the situation?
- How do I react when people give me bad news or criticize something I have said or done?
- What efforts do I make to nurture and promote our organization's learning and community networks?
- What do I do to create trust and loyalty in my teams?

- Is social health one of my personal assets or one of my vulnerabilities?

Let us make two final points to underscore the power of nourishing communities.

First, organizations of tomorrow will be concentric circles of interconnected relationships, starting with full-time people in the core and moving outward to part-timers, contingent workers, and alliances and strategic partners. Healthy relationships will be the glue to hold this community together.

The second point is to remember the power of customers. Peter Drucker once said that the purpose of an organization is to create a customer. Finding, developing, and keeping customers depend on our social health. So listen deeply to your customers' problems and concerns. Ask them what's working and what's not working. Brand your customer experience and then walk your talk. Be their partner and their friend.

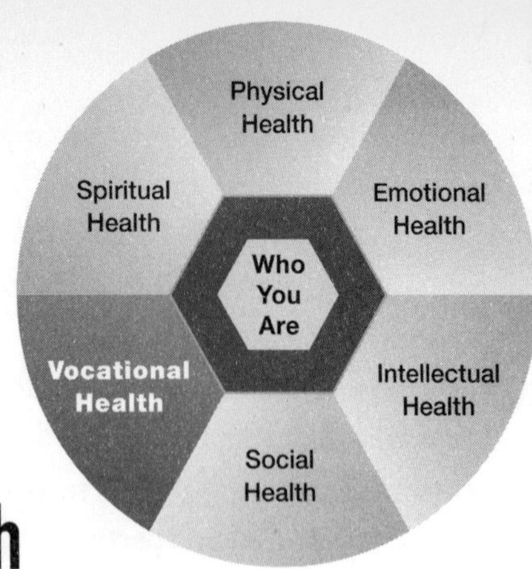

Vocational Health

When Steve Jobs was at the pinnacle of his career, having created Apple, NeXT, and Pixar and then rebuilt Apple, he delivered the commencement address at Stanford and told two stories about what mattered to him. Remarkably, these personal stories were also about his pursuit of vocational health.

The first story was about dropping out of college without a plan, wanting only to follow his curiosity and trusting that all would work out. "You can't connect the dots looking forward," he said. "You can only connect them looking backwards. So you have to trust that the dots will somehow connect to your future. You have to trust in something—your gut, destiny, life karma, whatever."[1] His belief that he would find a meaningful calling was clearly not misplaced.

In his second story, he talked about what he learned from being fired from Apple. "Sometimes life hits you in the head with a brick. Don't lose faith. I'm convinced that the only thing that kept me going was that I loved what I did. You've got to find what you love," he told the graduates. The humiliation of being fired opened the door to some of his most amazing achievements. It gave him the freedom to become a great entrepreneur and fueled an uncompromising drive toward excellence.

Steve Jobs used his mastery of technology and design to produce numerous vocational accomplishments. He obviously also possessed enormous intellectual health and spiritual health. But, given his neglected physical, social, and emotional health, he was by no means the perfect healthy leader. His imperfections, however, did not diminish those facets of himself that were so extraordinary. He transformed seven different industries, from personal computers and animated movies to telephones and music to tablet computers, digital publishing, and retail stores. Possessing extraordinary vocational health enabled him to change the world.

Vocational health is a leadership quality that is becoming increasingly vital because, as Jobs's life vividly shows, it is directly linked to results and performance. Without strong vocational health, you lose the ability to keep up in a competitive world. You become eclipsed by more competent, knowledgeable individuals and organizations going after the same thing. Many businesses today are not prepared for this global competition.

When leaders neglect vocational health, failing to pursue meaningful work and career well-being or to engage and develop people, their companies suffer, too. It sounds counterintuitive, but someone who focuses on short-term results and micromanages for quick profits ends up neglecting what is important to a healthy company: a leader with purpose and drive. A company led by an ill-equipped leader soon falls behind in the race for talent and productivity. Now more than ever, people are yearning for leaders to create the conditions that enable others to excel and to reach their full potential.

Vocational health enables you to convert dedication and hard work into tangible success. A direct benefit of being vocationally adept is that you become more successful and fulfilled, and your company becomes a much more attractive place to work. Unfortunately, in today's world, many leaders don't understand the power of vocational health inside themselves, don't appreciate it in others, don't see the connection to making money, and lack the skills or motivation to solve it.

To develop your vocational health, you need to cultivate three elements:

- Find a meaningful calling. Do what matters to you and then help others discover their purpose.

- Develop personal mastery. Know what you're good at, work on your weak spots, and teach others how to become healthy leaders themselves.
- Drive to succeed. Keep pushing to perform even better, and help others tap into their highest performance.

WARNING SIGNS OF DECLINING VOCATIONAL HEALTH

- Increasing loss of energy at work
- Growing disengagement and boredom
- Reticence to work with others to achieve common goals
- Decreasing ability to learn and master new ideas
- Lack of long-term vision and purpose
- Declining performance at work

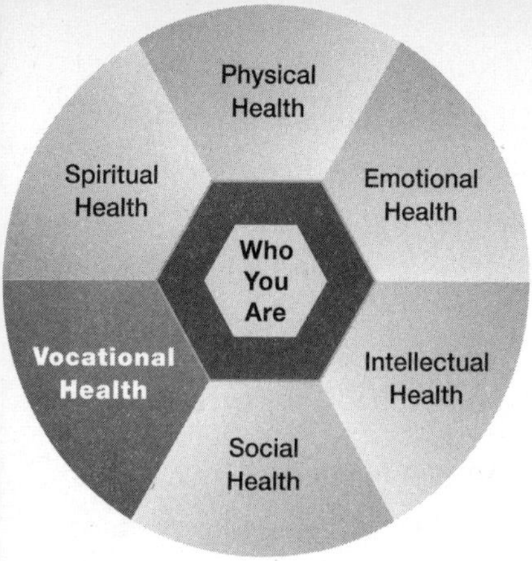

Physical Health
Emotional Health
Intellectual Health
Social Health
Vocational Health
Spiritual Health
Who You Are

CHAPTER 16

Meaningful Calling

THE CALLING INSIDE YOU

As a young man, Jack Stack tried the military, was fired from General Motors, and then landed an assembly-line supervisor job at International Harvester. Eventually, he would become CEO of the engine construction firm Springfield Remanufacturing Corporation, and an extraordinary motivator and leader. But in his early years, his most valuable asset was the insight that everyone, himself included, needed a feeling of purpose beyond his or her immediate, selfish needs.

The supervisor job was no plum assignment. The line was performing terribly, with about a 50 percent defect rate. In talking to the line workers, Stack realized that all of them regarded their job as only a paycheck. They didn't realize that their engines were part of farm tractors that produced food that ended up on dinner tables. Stack decided to show them what their work meant: he parked trucks and tractors at the end of the line and covered the factory walls with posters of tractors on farms and in fields. Gradually the rate of line defects declined.

The day a worker told a story about his son, Stack understood the power of having a sense of meaning and purpose. The man and his son were out driving, and while they were idling at a stoplight, a big International Harvester truck pulled up beside them. The worker tapped his kid on the shoulder and pointed at the truck. "Do you know who built that engine? Your daddy did," he declared.[1]

THE POWER OF MEANINGFUL WORK

Ever wonder why we work, aside from the obvious, mundane stuff like needing money and wanting to eat? What explains the countless people in the world who have all the money and food they will ever desire yet keep working? The answer we've found is both simple and complicated. The simple part is about people being motivated not by physical need but by necessities closer to the heart. The complicated part explains the power of our unique, individual passions.

As workers, people fall into three groups. There are those who feel that what they do is solely a job, those who feel that their work reflects who they are, and those who feel that their work is a personal calling. This third group—people whose daily efforts are a merging of talent and passion, people like Steve Jobs and Jack Stack—are the leaders whose companies are consistent overachievers.

Discovering what inspires you is fundamental to meaningful work. For each of us, the discovery is a personal journey. Some get inspired by historical figures like South Africa's Nelson Mandela or Singapore's Lee Kuan Yew, the father of modern Singapore. Others are inspired by a parent, a coach, or a great boss. Whatever the path, those lucky enough to find that perfect combination of talent and passion known as the "flow state" are the ones who achieve harmony in their work. A person's meaningful calling may be more internal, such as becoming a good person, or external, such as making a difference in the world or contributing by creating jobs and a robust economy. Some acknowledge that their job is not meaningful at all and use it simply to generate cash so that they can enjoy the rest of their lives. Surprisingly, though, many of us have similar ideas about what moves us.

Employees, especially young people, want more than a paycheck.

—Marissa Mayer, CEO, Yahoo[2]

Our research into different generations of workers, Baby Boomers, Gen X, and Gen Y, has found that they possess universal desires about what they want from work, namely:

- A sense of purpose and meaning
- Belief that they are making a contribution
- An opportunity to use their skills and talents
- An opportunity to learn and grow
- A significant amount of autonomy
- Respect

Unfortunately, many of us have fallen into a Faustian trap by taking a job with lots of power or salary and ending up in a job that we dislike. Or we conform to what others think we ought to do in life and ignore who we really aspire to be. Stepping back and giving this part of your life attention is critical to your overall leadership health. One study of a thousand people by York University School of Human Resource Management yielded these findings:[3]

- Of thirty-three separate work characteristics, all categories of respondents said "meaningful work" was the most important.
- There was a strong correlation between meaningful work and job satisfaction. Those with meaningful work were more committed; they intended to stay in their jobs and had less burnout.
- Meaningful work had four components: it was self-actualizing, it had social impact, it instilled feelings of personal accomplishment, and it created a belief in being able to reach career goals.

FINDING WHAT MATTERS

Kelly Services, the international outsourcing and counseling services firm, conducts an annual survey of workers' attitudes. In a recent survey, the Kelly Global Workforce Index polled an estimated 170,000 employees around the world to hear why two-thirds of them intended to leave their current companies within the year.[4] What was making people want to leave their jobs, and how could their minds be changed? Kelly's findings tell us much about the need for people to have a meaningful calling in their work.

Only 44 percent of the people Kelly surveyed felt that they had job fulfillment. Most said that their work does not give them a sense of purpose. People found meaning at work when they felt valued, were happy with what they were doing, felt connected to coworkers and the organization's purpose, and were able to develop their skills. When the survey delved deeper into their attitudes, it found that what gave a job meaning was personal development. It seems many people are simply bored.

Responding honestly to thought-provoking questions is a good way to discover what is meaningful for you. Remember: if you are frustrated with your job, disengaged from work, or fearful of your own passion and success, your colleagues and subordinates will see right through you. Think about these questions and maybe talk with a coworker or friend to expand and sharpen your thoughts.

- What are you most proud of in your life?
- What would you do with a million dollars?
- What is your biggest regret, and why?
- If you had a year to live, how would you spend it?
- What do you like most about yourself?
- Is there something in your life about which you are passionate?
- When you have a completely free day, what do you most enjoy doing?
- How would you describe your ideal job?

MERGING A UNIVERSAL DESIRE WITH YOUR UNIQUE EXPRESSION

The desire for meaningful work is a universal drive, but people differ according to their generation, culture, time of life, and personal values. We can't detail all the qualities that give people meaning in their work, but we can offer a collage of examples of how others have found what matters to them. Perhaps their journeys of discovery will inspire your thinking.

People ask me all the time why I'm here. My objective isn't to make a ton of money. I'm not going to raise a big IPO or sell the company over to eBay. My objective from the start was to make a positive difference in the banking industry. When we lose our sense of greater purpose, we lose everything.

—Arkadi Kuhlmann, chairman and president, ING Direct USA[5]

You have to decide what your highest priorities are and have the courage—pleasantly, smilingly, non-apologetically—to say "No" to other things. And the way you do that is by having a bigger "Yes" burning inside. How different our lives are when we really know what is deeply important to us and keeping that picture in mind, we manage ourselves each day to do what really matters most.

—Stephen Covey, author and thought leader[6]

Our business operating system—think of the best set of assumptions and protocols beneath our businesses, how we move people and apply our human resources—is built entirely around extrinsic motivators, like carrots and sticks. That's actually fine for many kinds of twentieth-century tasks. But for twenty-first-century tasks, that mechanistic, reward-and-punishment approach doesn't work . . . and often does harm.

—Daniel Pink, author of *Drive*[7]

We found that when you give people a meaning to their work that goes beyond money, they buy into it and want to participate. Take a housekeeper cleaning a patient's hospital room. Her work must go beyond cleaning the floor and actually touch on patient care.

—William Pollard, retired chairman and CEO, ServiceMaster[8]

FOLLOW YOUR HEART

Sometimes people realize by accident that their work doesn't give them the purpose or meaning they need. A flash of insight can come anytime and from anywhere. For Ingrid Srinath, a top advertising executive based in Mumbai, India, the realization that her working life felt empty was slow in coming. This was because she had been schooled to believe that for women, work and personal drives were to be kept separate.

"If you're female," she says, "I think then the messages that business sends out to you is that we should bring a brain to work and leave the rest of the crap behind . . . they just hire your brain."[9]

Srinath was deep into her career managing advertising campaigns when she attended a professional development workshop. The workshop was like many others she had participated in, but then something changed. The moderator asked her and the other participants to list all the personal qualities that drove them. What values motivated them? Srinath had only a general idea and no specific answers. One thing she knew for certain: what mattered to her had no relationship to her current job. She realized that a core responsibility in her job—being accountable to shareholders—felt trivial and insignificant.

So the high-achieving executive quit. She recounts, "From that moment, I went into this huge malaise, and the next eighteen months I wasn't able to find any great motivation in what I was doing."

It took soul searching for Srinath to realize what would give meaning and purpose to her work life. She had to do something that involved working for justice and caring for others. So she turned her back on advertising and found a job in the nonprofit world with the organization Child Rights and You, an international effort that pushes for universal education. Later, she took over as CEO of Civicus, a global alliance for strengthening citizen action working toward justice and equality. Srinath had finally found something that moved her.

CREATE YOUR PERSONAL SHIELD

We don't know the exercise that sparked Ingrid Srinath's epiphany. It could have been a leadership exercise similar to what we call Creating Your Personal Shield. Its purpose is to help you discover moments in your life when you affirmed core beliefs or crystallized new ones.

Who you are and what matters emerge in how you think and feel, how you live, how you interact with others, and how you perform. If you understand your values, strengths, and vulnerabilities, you begin to know what gives you meaning. Time goes fast, and if you are to shape events instead of being shaped by them, you need to know what you want to achieve. What are you here to do? What higher purpose are you serving? What is your desired legacy?

Medieval knights wore armor that was emblazoned with a unique design. These shields announced the person's identity and served as a bridge between the individual inside the armor and the persona he wanted the world to see. The shield not only protected the individual but also announced his core values.

Imagine for a moment that you must design a shield for your armor. On a separate piece of paper, copy a larger version of the design shown in Figure 16.1, and use it to create a symbolic representation of your shield. Try to think in concrete images as well as words. Your shield is going to have four elements. These questions will help you craft a design that best expresses the inner and outer you.

Figure 16.1

- What matters the most to you in your life?
- What three words best describe you?
- What do you want your legacy to be?
- What is least known about you?
- What is your leadership motto?
- What leadership quality do you most admire?
- What is the value you bring to your organization?
- What special gift or talent do you have?
- What image do you most associate with leadership?
- What experiences have most influenced your leadership style?

FORGING A LEGACY OUT OF MEANING

Some people discover early in life what gives them meaning and fulfillment, yet that is not the end of their journey. You may know what is important for you but not how to express it in a life's work. Peter Bell, for instance, has had a long-standing commitment to making the world a better place. Figuring out how that might be accomplished and finding the perfect outlet for his drive have shaped his career.

Bell's working life has been dedicated to helping others. For him, making the world a better place has meant immersing himself in humanitarian organizations to end poverty, promote peace and social justice, and empower ordinary citizens. For five years, he served as the chairman of CARE USA and for ten years after that was president of the organization. CARE is a global organization that fights poverty, responds to humanitarian emergencies, and advocates for people in poor communities struggling to improve their lives. Before that, Bell worked for a foundation that fought poverty in the United States and for an international peace organization.

Bell's clear-eyed vision of what matters helped him shape the values that guided his leadership of CARE. As chief policymaker, administrator, and fundraiser for the organization, he helped the group achieve its goals by applying these principles:

- Know that change needs to begin with each of us
- Accept that excellence is its own reward
- Appreciate all contributions
- Give away credit for success
- Hold yourself accountable
- Be slow to blame others
- Speak out when silence is safer
- Define the boundaries of acceptable and unacceptable behavior

Although Bell has always known what matters to him, implementing programs to promote those values has taken effort. At CARE, he strove to help the organization align its explicit values—respect, integrity, commitment, and excellence—with the individual workers who were implementing its programs. He explains his approach and philosophy: "I tend to err on the side of trust and am rarely disappointed. People want to be trusted—in service of good values, to make people's lives better. It's part of our DNA, and we can tap into it."[10]

Bell is retired from CARE and, at seventy-one, more of a guiding spirit than frontline leader. Yet the values that have defined his life, beginning with "fulfillment is more important than money," are always at work and will never be retired.

TAPPING INTO THE PASSION OF OTHERS

If we don't put ourselves in other people's shoes and understand what inspires and motivates them, we can easily become frustrated and disappointed with the people we lead. Nothing is worse than trying to lead somebody you don't understand or respect, or simply don't like. Here are a few thoughts you might consider about tapping into the passion of others.

- Talk to people about what they love to do.
- Identify their unique talents and let them excel in that space.
- Ask people what they like and dislike about their jobs.
- Facilitate dialogues across the generations, looking for similarities and differences.
- Share your compelling story and guiding principles with others, and ask about theirs.

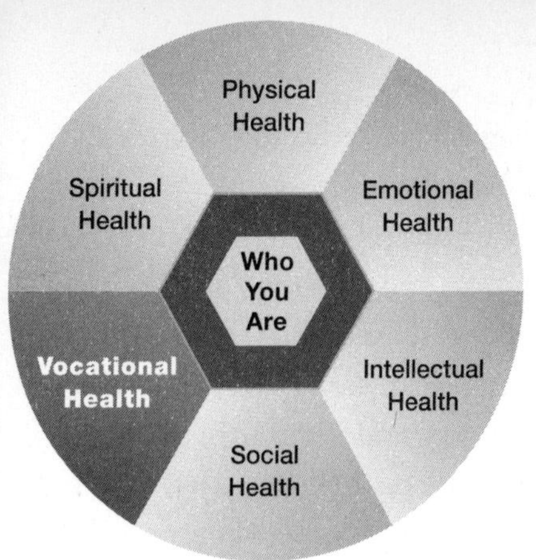

CHAPTER 17

Personal Mastery

Your vocational health demands personal mastery, which may sound like one of those talents possessed only by a Jedi knight—you know, like a phenomenal IQ or an amazing memory, something that you're either born with or not. The reality, however, is much more intriguing.

Everyone has the capacity for personal mastery, but what holds us back is not our genes but our attitude. Personal mastery is best summed up as an innate desire for growth, self-improvement, and the inner satisfaction that comes with being able to do or know something thoroughly. It's between our ears, not in a strand of DNA.

Personal mastery is not easy. It requires a firm commitment to a particular kind of effort—to learning. Your ability to master a skill or body of knowledge depends on a commitment to lifelong learning. Read what it's done for Brian Cornell.

A LIFELONG LEARNER

Brian Cornell has been leading companies for more than thirty years. His expertise in managing consumer products firms has put him in the executive suite at Safeway, Michaels Stores, Sam's Club, and twice at PepsiCo. He knows firsthand the benefits of dedicating himself to learning—along with what happens when he neglects it.

Part of that process is acknowledging that he doesn't know everything and being comfortable as a student and listener. For a leader, especially one in charge of a large public corporation, this can be humbling. It requires being self-aware, able to learn in real time, and comfortable on a public stage. Even when under the lights, such a leader has to be able to admit mistakes and ask questions that might reveal huge knowledge gaps. Cornell's learning curve was especially steep early in his time at Sam's Club.

When he took over the membership warehouse company, he had just successfully spearheaded a turnaround for the arts and crafts retailer Michaels Stores. Sam's Club presented numerous challenges, including lagging store sales, and Cornell was committed to learning why the warehouse club was slipping. Being a successful lifelong learner, he had a healthy set of skills to boost his education. For one, he was good at gathering information.

"When I traveled in clubs and stores, I was talking to our associates asking questions. I always framed the fact that this was a question, not direction. I wanted their input because I learn a lot more by asking questions . . . So I really try every day to wake up with that ratio in my head—to say you've got to ask more questions in meetings throughout the day than you're making statements."[1]

With his education about what was happening at Sam's Club in full bloom, Cornell drilled down into performance figures, talked to consumers, and conducted qualitative and quantitative research. He and an executive team crafted a thoughtful, far-reaching strategy for reversing the performance decline, road tested it in warehouses around the country, and gradually implemented it throughout the organization. Given all that Cornell had learned in his leadership education, it's reasonable to understand why this felt like a surefire strategy. But it wasn't.

As Cornell discovered, learning is not a sometime affair. It must be a constant throughout your working life. Cornell's graduate course, so to speak, began at a company town meeting.

"I started to do regular town hall sessions and small informal gatherings and asking our associates and some of our key leaders, 'Tell me about the strategy, how is it working, how do you explain it, what feedback can you give me.' Dead silence. Next group? Not a word," he recounts.

"Finally, someone raises their hand and says, 'Brian, you seem like a really smart guy, and this sounds really exciting. But I have no idea what you're talking about. You're using terminology and phrases that we've never heard before, and we have no idea how to explain it.'" Suddenly, Cornell did not feel so smart. But in the spirit of a lifelong learner, he turned that lesson into an opportunity. "We had to step back and retool not the strategy but how we talked about it. Put it into terms that could be easily cascaded and, importantly, embraced. And I learned how important it was to not prove how smart you are and how sophisticated your terminology, but how do you make sure you're relating to people in terms and thoughts and themes that they can comprehend and own."

Cornell has since left Sam's Club and is now CEO of PepsiCo Americas Foods, a $23 billion business, which includes brands like Frito-Lay, Quaker Foods, and all of PepsiCo's Latin American food business. Along with a rich trove of experience, he has brought with him a lesson that could well ensure his success both as a CEO and lifelong learner. He offers this primer: "Leaders that mature effectively recognize that they can't be perfect. I was criticized for it, wanting to be perfect at an early stage in my career. I wanted to make sure I was completely buttoned up. And my old boss sat me down one day and said, 'Brian, you do great work, you have an amazing work ethic, and you're always organized. Everything is perfect and every word's been thought out. But you should spend more time just being yourself, being genuine, and staying approachable.'"

THE JOURNEY OF SELF-IMPROVEMENT

Our desire to learn and improve is imbedded deep in our psyches. From the moment we come into the world, we are reaching out to learn all we can about our environment and how we fit in. Although we receive our basic education in our early and adolescent years, we learn throughout our lives. Especially for a business leader, always adding to your knowledge is critical.

The desire to learn is a psychological force that begins early in life. Erik Erikson, a pioneer in human development, identified eight stages of learning that we go through, from infancy to death.[2] The stages are fundamental landmarks. As we grow, we confront and master each new challenge, and the stages build on each other. We often forget that learning is a continuous process, but we retain our innate desire for mastery deep into old age.

Our need for self-improvement, which is what learning fulfills, confers a special quality that we cannot function without—autonomy. This is a fierce drive to define ourselves as individuals, to determine the course of our lives, and to choose how we live. Another term might be free will. Whatever you call it, it is the propellant that pushes us to learn, to conquer the unknown, and to master not just our fate but the world around us.

An insightful leader is aware of not only his own need for autonomy but that of others, too. By harnessing this quality, a leader helps those around him shape their goals, establish a purpose, and perform to the maximum of their potential.

It's natural to want to improve. The motivation for it is intrinsic, and the payoff is pride and satisfaction. Being able to improve and learn confirms that hard work matters more than pure intelligence, leveling the playing field for everyone. With lifelong learning, life becomes an adventure, giving us something to look forward to, a purpose and goal. It is a life with no regrets.

The drive toward self-improvement may not always be obvious in the working world, but it is pervasive. The success of Google as a search engine (and its truly crowning achievement, coinage of a new verb) has been underwritten by countless individuals eager to know more. Google, acclaimed as a great place to work, has shown the power of learning. Its stock has soared 700 percent since its public offering in August 2004. The rise of Wikipedia and all its permutations is an even more dramatic example because it's less commercial and more knowledge based. Just ask any quarterback at the start of a season, a teacher at the beginning of a semester, or an entrepreneur who starts a company: learning is the fuel for growth and performance.

Here's the interesting challenge. At a time when we need our leaders to be learning and relearning as the world changes so quickly, adults of working age (thirty to fifty) are often resistant to change. Their priorities of getting ahead, raising a family, and generating money often take precedence over their personal learning and development. Pressures to perform and a shortage of time get in the way. This is a challenge for our entire society—in business, politics, and nonprofit agencies. We simply need more willing adult learners.

By the age of 10, I'd read every book in the Omaha Public Library with the word finance in the title—some twice.

—Warren Buffett[3]

WHAT STOPS US FROM LEARNING

Many leaders don't seek out opportunities to learn, or they avoid exposing themselves to situations where they need to learn. On one level, this is understandable. Tough situations can be humbling. Learning is a great equalizer, and some people are not comfortable with temporarily handing over control and leadership to those who know more about a subject.

Signs of resistance are all around. It's clear in executives who are reluctant to hire people who have more experience or education than they. It shows in leaders who discourage question-and-answer exchanges as a way of sharing knowledge. It's obvious in executives who punish people for taking calculated risks when they don't perform as predicted. Yet another example is the leader who avoids operational challenges because of discomfort with uncertainty or the unpredictable. The executive who leads meetings with a "know-it-all" attitude and looks only for people to agree with him is exposing his resistance.

Other attitudes also get in the way. Fear of failure, a desire to avoid the pain of struggling to understand complicated information, or a lack of confidence can retard the process. Some people give up too easily or tend to take shortcuts, thinking they can master something without putting in the effort. There are no CliffsNotes for personal mastery.

Perfectionism can be a big obstacle. It can make you afraid of being a student again. With it, you limit yourself to situations or projects where you are already a master so that you don't have to admit ignorance or start anew. Your perfectionism can also prompt you to be too critical of yourself—it's not fast enough or thorough enough. In short, perfectionism provides reasons not to be an open learner.

Research now shows that the lack of natural talent is irrelevant to great success. The secret? Painful and demanding practice and hard work.

—Geoffrey Colvin[4]

WHAT'S YOUR LEARNING PATTERN?

Your upbringing, education, general knowledge, experiences, and, yes, even innate cognitive abilities all influence how you learn. Even though no two people learn the same way, there is an assortment of learning patterns that people use. Knowing what works best for you can be a huge advantage. It can save you wheel-spinning time and eliminate wasted trips down unproductive side roads. Valuing diverse learning styles can also help a team be more creative. To help you identify and refine how you best take in and retain information, here are a range of learning styles to consider:

- Learning on the public stage with others
- Learning in the privacy of your own mind at home, work, or library
- Learning by doing and practice
- Learning by reading about successful people and company best practices
- Learning by focusing on the big picture at forty thousand feet
- Mastering details before progressing to the bigger picture
- Learning from written, video, or audio sources
- Observing others and modeling their behavior
- Remembering by repetition
- Learning visually—using boxes, circles, bullets, mind maps, and the like

YOUR DRIVE FOR PERSONAL MASTERY

Although much of the research into mastering a skill or body of knowledge is focused on the fields of sports, music, and intellectual pursuits like chess, the working world offers numerous challenges to be mastered. As a leader, you may be eager to develop your ability to deliver speeches, master negotiations, conduct performance reviews, understand accounting and financial reporting, sell to and serve customers, run a meeting, or even search for a job.

In order to master something, you must invest time and commitment. You have to work at it, refusing to be deterred by slow going, setbacks, or doubts. Being committed means making a promise to yourself about being disciplined in your pursuit. Without discipline, nothing happens.

It's not unusual for people to question their motivation, to wonder if they truly have what it takes to stay the course to command a subject. The following questions can help you assess your own mental mettle before you plunge into something:

- Do you tend to learn things only when you know there is an external reward? How much does personal satisfaction matter to you?

- What is the last skill you mastered? What sacrifices did you make to do it, and are you willing to make them again?
- Are you easily discouraged? Are you someone who's enthusiastic at the outset of an activity but whose attention and dedication wane?
- When you receive feedback from 360 evaluations, do you work to understand and change your behavior?
- When you don't know something, do you push to understand it and find answers?
- Do you feel threatened by and envious of people who know more than you do?
- How do you feel when someone tells you how to do something as opposed to letting you discover what you can and can't do?

RAISING THE BAR ON YOURSELF

Ted Mathas works hard for his success. As the youngest person (age forty-one) to become CEO at New York Life, the 168-year-old, largest mutual life insurance company in the United States, being highly disciplined and self-motivating is ingrained in his genes. It's not about him winning and someone else losing—it's about being the best that he can be. By challenging himself, learning from others, and being thoroughly prepared, Ted pursues personal mastery.

He faced his most recent challenge on day one when he took over the job. Even though he had been working for the company for thirteen years and possessed a strong track record of accomplishments, when he took the corner office, the insurance industry along with other financial services firms were about to get slammed. It was 2008, and the subprime crisis was gaining momentum.

His challenge was to figure out how to prepare the company and its employees for the headwinds they were about to encounter. New York Life stood on a bedrock of financial strength and had assets of about $287 billion and triple-A ratings from everyone. But Ted believed that despite its financial strength, the company needed to be more agile and less hierarchical and bureaucratic. Leadership and decision making were concentrated in a few individuals, so change happened slowly and laboriously. This would not work in the new environment of speed, uncertainty, competition, and complexity.

Around this time, we at HCI began working with Mathas and his executive team on their leadership and culture strategy and on what Ted envisioned as the path forward to position the company for the future. And we had a front-row seat.

To many, Ted is a "man with a plan," positive and optimistic, self-driven with a real sense of responsibility for his people, his customers, and the business he is in. "Committed to leaving the company better than [he] found it," Ted found this to be the perfect time to start making a series of difficult but necessary decisions, while the winds were blowing outside and the company was grounded inside.

Mathas reflects on his early life: "I learned a great lesson from my father, who trusted me at age eighteen to borrow on his insurance policy so I could go to the college of my choice, but only with the promise that I would take care of my mother if my father died."[5] This sense of responsibility and personal mastery became embedded in Ted's character.

He describes his process for getting ready for the challenge. "Anything you're going to try, you need to study. You need to prepare. You need to ask people who have done it before how they did it. You need to observe. You're going to do all that because you want to do well."

Part of the process is asking questions, then standing back. "I'm not afraid of asking the same question in many different ways. I have enough confidence to speak up if I don't understand something." Ted believes that his job is to encourage others to do the same, and to bring forth the wisdom that may be lying dormant around the table.

Yet Ted openly admits that his personal vulnerability is the high standards he sets for himself. "I can be too hard on myself, too much of a perfectionist, and my challenge frankly is to be more patient, to give myself and the people around me more room to grow and learn." Like many leaders, Mathas finds that managing his own and others' anxiety and giving space for people to think and master themselves are his biggest areas of learning.

The proof of Mathas's change strategy was in how New York Life fared during the economic downturn. His deep confidence in his company, his colleagues, and himself allowed him to proclaim, "We are built for times like these." The message clearly got through. In 2012, New York Life generated record earnings of $1.6 billion, up from the $1.2 billion generated in 2008. And surplus, its primary measure of financial strength, now stood at $19.6 billion, up nearly $7 billion from just four years earlier. The company never needed stimulus money to survive the recession headwinds, and it continues to soar.

To some, pursuing personal mastery may seem like a self-absorbed process, focused solely on improving one's own skills and performance. But as Ted Mathas illustrates, finding the right balance between self-improvement and helping others is the secret to great leadership.

As New York Life's motto reminds us, "We aspire to greatness, but never at the expense of goodness."

LEADERS ARE GREAT COACHES

Healthy leaders are great coaches, and their impact is felt throughout an organization. Whether you are positive or negative in your approach, conscious or unconscious, you are continuously mentoring and modeling behavior for the people who work for you. People are hungry to learn, and they naturally look to you for values, vision, and direction. Some of your colleagues will be excited to learn and will even thank you. Others will never admit their appreciation, or will even resist your teaching because of their own need to demonstrate competence, power, or control. Whatever the situation, just remember that you are teaching others, whether you like it or not.

There are lots of ways of modeling behavior and mentoring others. Some people want their leaders to inspire, stretch, and challenge them. Then there are the people who want you to hold their hand as they navigate through the difficult obstacles in the marketplace or the political dynamics inside the organization. Some people like their leaders to be their coaches and mentors; others just want a North Star and clear expectations. Still others are scrutinizing who you are as person, want a friend after hours or a shoulder to lean on in difficult times. Everyone is different, and knowing who to be at the right time for the right person in the right way is the art and science of leadership.

Companies led by skilled, competent leaders outperform those that are not. A survey of 326 Canadian CEOs examined whether there was a connection between executive development and company performance, as measured by profit, market share, customer satisfaction, and costs. It found that those firms headed by "learning leaders" were more likely to achieve operational goals than the companies that did not have such leaders.[6]

Leaders passionate about teaching and modeling "who they are" send a message to people that they need to challenge themselves, adapt, and learn. When people are always learning, they are better able to anticipate problems, create solutions, turn mistakes into opportunities, and stretch themselves into better people and better leaders. As one CEO once said to us, "Leaders have one job, and that is to develop other leaders."

Companies whose leaders are dedicated to learning and teaching perform better. Research shows that they are 27 percent more productive, produce 40 percent more revenue, and have 50 percent greater net income growth.

—Jim Clemmer[7]

CHAPTER 18

Drive to Succeed

If by this point you're getting impatient, we understand. You may be thinking that all these healthy dimensions are fine and good for making you a better person, but what about making you a *successful business* leader? Where are those insights? Keep reading, because this chapter is all about how you merge personal success with your innate drive to be successful. As Kay Koplovitz demonstrates, the spirit that pushes you to improve your leadership health is the same force that helps you forge a successful business environment.

PLAYING TO WIN

In the male-dominated world of cable TV in the 1980s, Kay Koplovitz was one of the bolder female entrepreneurs. Fueled by a competitive spirit honed on tennis courts and ski slopes, and a knowledge of satellite technology, Koplovitz and a partner created the first national television professional sports network. The company—Madison Square Garden Sports, which later became USA Network—and its founder created a unique combination.

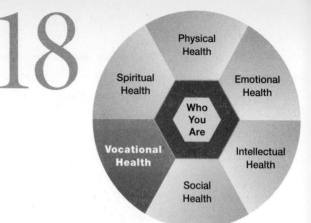

Koplovitz brought to her leadership of USA Network an array of skills and experience. She knew sports and was by nature a competitive person; it wasn't just the boys who could use phrases like "running interference" and "making a hat-trick" with authority. Along with her drive was a savvy understanding of the commercial possibilities of cable technology. One of her innovations was introducing the concept of two revenue streams, licensing and advertising. Her business acumen was accompanied by passion. She was propelled by this belief: "In this eat-or-be-eaten world, what doesn't kill you makes you stronger."[1] In the twenty years she led USA Network, her ambition was always tempered by a deep understanding of herself and business dynamics.

USA Network taught her numerous leadership lessons. A failure, the collapse of yearlong negotiations to buy another cable outlet, was especially instructive. She reflects, "I always like to cross the finish line first. But sometimes other people are better than you, and you have to recognize it or you're not going to cross the finish line at all. It's something you have to realize; it's a part of the process. And it's really important not to have personal grudges about it."

Her innate resilience strengthened with every obstacle she encountered. If a contract was cancelled, she used the setback as an opportunity to try something new. "Everything doesn't go in a straight line," she says. "Sometimes you have to go around a barrier, sometimes you have to go over a barrier, sometimes you have to go under a barrier, or sometimes you just have to change course."

After years building USA Network, the company was sold. Again, the experience brought lessons about business leadership, and an opportunity to spread her wings. The company was sold for $4.5 billion, yet Koplovitz, because she owned no equity, received none of the proceeds. She had zero funding for a new venture, and in her search for backing, she learned yet another lesson. Men controlled the bulk of the country's venture capital. Again, this realization became the impetus for her success.

She decided to share her knowledge and help other women as well as herself learn to be stronger entrepreneurs. Her vehicle was a venture capital forum, Springboard Enterprises, dedicated to helping women develop the contacts and skills needed to find investors to back them. Today, Springboard helps hundreds of female entrepreneurs learn how to compete in the business world.

Koplovitz has extended her leadership skills in yet a third direction, as chairwoman of the retail clothing conglomerate Fifth & Pacific Companies, which was formerly Liz Claiborne and includes such brands as Juicy Couture and Kate Spade. The role of chairwoman has brought Kay more chances to flex her drive to succeed.

As a nonexecutive chairwoman, she has acquired skills essential to leading other board members while at the same time taking a backseat. She calls this "leading from the middle."

"I had to learn how to engage people, think on my feet, be clear on our objectives, and not have to be the strongest voice at the table," she says. All told, Kay has mastered the drive to succeed. Her lessons are clear: stand up for what you believe, understand yourself and how others see you, be resilient, and balance your passion for winning with being meaningfully centered in your life.

SUCCESS—A JOURNEY AND A DESTINATION

We all want to be successful. Winning, getting ahead, achieving goals, making a positive difference—these make us feel better about ourselves, affirming our self-worth and humanity. This is a universal truth, of course, but no one has yet been able to answer the question of precisely how we achieve success.

Countless books, motivational speakers, gurus, coaches, and consultants have offered fads and formulas for finding the holy grail of success. For some people, the advice has worked, at least temporarily. The problem has always been that the "achieve success now" programs have employed one-size-fits-all approaches. And if there is one thing we know for certain about success, it's that everyone's idea of it is different. Each of us has a personal definition, forged from our values, upbringing, education, and experiences, of what success would look like in our lives.

While many people aim for the usual markers of money, status, or power, they often discover that these goals are inadequate. Success is more personal than a dollar figure or a title or the ability to command. It hinges on who you are, what you value, and what you do. For a businessperson, it could be making products, leading teams, developing people, or achieving profit goals—or simply enjoying her life with the money she already has. For someone with a career in public service, it may be solving social problems or protecting the country. An individual in the nonprofit world may consider success to be a drop in the incidence of a disease or having an effect on the climate change debate. An actor might strive for audience acclaim. Success to teachers is often reflected in how their students perform. And for a parent, success might simply be happy, healthy children.

Remember Mike Puzziferri, the New York Fire Department battalion chief? Success for him was a version of the public servant's "serve and protect." It was saving lives and keeping crews safe. Eric Schoomaker, the retired surgeon general, also strove to serve and protect, but in another way. Success meant keeping soldiers and the broader military community healthy in all senses of the word. Mike Petters, the shipbuilder CEO at Huntington Ingalls Industries, uses a couple of yardsticks for success: delivering ships on time and on budget, and instilling a higher purpose for protecting the country. The Lego chief, Jørgen Knudstorp, sees success when employees feel engaged and free to be innovative.

When you read about Bob McDonald, CEO of Procter & Gamble, in Part Three, you will encounter yet another definition of success. He wants to improve lives and make the world a better place in very practical ways. For Ford CEO Alan Mulally, success is about making a great product by creating a culture of pride and performance. The ex-CEO of REI, Sally Jewell, envisions success in terms of personal relationships, while aiming to improve the environment.

Of course, achieving goals is rewarding; but there's another element in the pursuit of success: the journey—all the work and thought and time you invest in that pursuit. It may sound strange, but we have seen many successful leaders derive great satisfaction from the struggle itself. "It's not fun if it isn't hard."

The easy achievements are not half as satisfying as those that demand persistence and hard work. The pursuit of success has even spawned a branch of scientific study. Researchers believe that to be an expert at something, you need to devote at least five hours a day to deliberate practice and to do this for about ten years.[2]

The takeaway of this research is clear: to be successful at something, you need to work long and hard; there are no shortcuts. Still, some of the most successful businesspeople we know have found their particular version of "deliberate practice" to be as fulfilling as achieving the goal. They relish the pursuit and are not deterred by personal limitations or hampering environments.

THE PUZZLE OF THE ZEBRA

Ideas about what defines success and how you get there are often split between two schools of thought. We think of this split as the puzzle of the zebra: Is it black with white stripes or white with black stripes? Put another way, what is its essential nature?

In the debate about success, these two schools can be labeled "capabilities" and "circumstances." Some believe that success turns on a person's innate abilities—talent, skills, or intellect. That's the capabilities argument. The other way of thinking is that a person's circumstances or environment is the primary force in success.

In *Outliers*, Malcolm Gladwell dug into this debate because of misconceptions about successful people. He sought to explain why someone like Bill Gates has been so successful while others who are equally ambitious and bright have not been. His answer falls squarely into the "circumstances" way of thinking.

"We vastly underestimate the extent to which success happens because of things the individual has nothing to do with," he says.[3] He explains that success is largely "a group project" that happens "because of the contributions of lots of different people and lots of different circumstances."

Gladwell makes a good point about success rarely being the result of only individual effort. However, research suggests that he's only half right, that "What causes success?" is not an either-or question.

People who believe that their success rides solely on circumstances or that it depends only on their capabilities can readily go off-course. Either way, they misjudge success, themselves, and the broader context. The zebra is black *and* white, not just one on top of the other. Its coloring reflects a balance in nature between light and dark, shadow and sun.

University of Texas researchers looked into the careers of successful U.S. presidents and found that what distinguished such notables as Abraham Lincoln and FDR was both their character *and* their circumstances.[4] They stand out as leaders not only because they had character but also because they happened to find themselves leading during a time whose circumstances allowed their exceptional leadership to emerge. Lincoln kept the Union together and freed the slaves. Roosevelt brought the country out of its worse depression and enabled the Allies to defeat Germany and Japan.

No one can say that Lincoln or FDR had an easy road to success. They had to overcome enormous hurdles and merge their drive with their talent. In many ways, their worlds conspired against their success. But they persevered. Similarly, a business leader pursuing success may encounter environments that impede progress. An environmental accident, a natural disaster, high unemployment, a product recall, the expiration of a patent, or the loss of key executives are just some of the circumstances that can impede a business leader's progress toward success.

What you believe about your organization's success has a strong influence on your actions and attitude. If you feel that your company's success is the direct result of your talent and drive, this will skew all that you do. Someone who thinks that he is the sole reason for a company doing well becomes more important than the organization or its people. When you assume that it is all because of you, arrogance and demands for greater power and financial reward are soon to follow.

The other extreme is equally disastrous. A business leader who credits luck and external circumstances for a company's success has rendered himself powerless, a fragile tree in the winds of fate. You cannot apply your talents and skills and help an organization pursue its vision unless you take responsibility for your role in its journey to success.

People who cling to either-or ideas about success get hijacked in a variety of ways:

- Feeling a sense of overconfidence, entitlement, or arrogance
- Aiming for goals that won't last or that conflict with their values
- Giving up when their luck turns bad or when circumstances are against them
- Aiming too low or too broadly, making achievement either insignificant or impossible
- Having a skewed sense of insecurity, doubt, and lack of confidence
- Obsessing over winning and competing at all costs
- Feeling overwhelmed and unable to function in the face of difficulties
- Becoming undermined by a fear of winning and of being powerful and successful

Success requires both personal talent and an environment that supports your efforts toward achievement. The critical quality for a leader is to be constantly pushing forward, making progress, eschewing the status quo, and seeking out new horizons. It's the love of pursuit that matters.

I missed more than nine thousand shots in my career. Twenty-six times I was trusted to take the game-winning shot and missed. I've failed over and over and over again in my life. And that is why I succeed.

—Michael Jordan[5]

A PASSION FOR SUCCESS OR AN OBSESSION WITH WINNING?

The business world is full of cautionary tales about what happens when a leader becomes obsessed with winning. A fixation on success can push people to violate personal ethics, deprive others of what is due to them, cheat, lie, commit fraud, and even jeopardize the health of an entire organization. This is what happened to Joe Nacchio.[6]

Nacchio was the CEO of a Denver telecom company, Qwest International, that had its sights set on becoming one of the big boys, like its competitors Bell, AT&T, and SBC. To win this coveted spot, Nacchio sought to boost revenue growth in a big way. He applied unremitting pressure on executives to meet astronomical targets. Winning in terms of revenue growth was more important than the company's service or product, the company culture, or the well-being of its employees. People at the company knew that if they didn't provide the numbers needed for Nacchio to win in the revenue game, there would be hell to pay.

The executives became complicit in Nacchio's drive for revenue by booking one-time sales as recurring sales. This became a pattern, and ultimately the company was charged with fraudulently reporting $3 billion in revenues. Nevertheless, Nacchio continued to push for inflated revenue figures even when the company's credit rating dropped because of its exorbitant debt, and it had to write off $20 to $30 billion in goodwill.

Nacchio's pursuit of winning eventually drew the attention of regulatory and criminal justice officials. He was forced out of the company, which had to restate its revenue downward by $2.2 billion. Then the courts found that Nacchio had been profiting from the company's bogus revenue reports by selling his company stock when he knew Qwest was sinking. He was sentenced to more than five years in prison.

Admittedly, Nacchio is an extreme. But in our culture, it is not unusual to encounter people who are obsessed with winning. There is no denying that our society places a high premium on financial success and power. It is possible that you may be infected by the winning-is-everything bug and not be aware of it. Ask yourself:

- What am I trying to prove to myself, and could it be hijacking my life and business success?
- Will I do anything to avoid losing?
- In order to win, do I believe that the ends justify the means?
- Am I always worrying about my next promotion and success in life, or do I allow myself the luxury of enjoying my daily life?
- How do I define success? Do I set my own standards and compete against myself, or do I try to achieve goals set by others?

Let's face it: there will always be winners and losers. And there are real limitations to what we can do. A five-foot guy cannot be a champion shot putter, and an introverted scientist is unlikely to be a dynamic motivational speaker. But introverts and extroverts, men and women, people of all colors, gay and straight, young and old—all can become healthy leaders.

So go after what you want; be comfortable with success *and* failure; don't feel the need to prove anything to others; don't be afraid to win or lose; keep getting better and raise the bar; and enjoy the journey and the destination.

But keep in mind that people who report the greatest interest in attaining money, fame, or beauty are consistently found to be less happy than those who pursue less materialistic goals.[7] As the wealth doubled and tripled in the last fifty years in many industrial nations, the levels of happiness and satisfaction with life have not changed, and in fact depression has become more common.[8]

For the Type A's among us, it's fine to drive for success. But if you add too much cynicism, hostility, and selfishness to that intensity, you're heading quickly toward a premature heart attack.

In a global survey of social values, Americans scored higher than any other industrialized country in approval of competition. A separate study of values in forty-two countries found that a person's happiness decreases as the level of competition increases.

—"Why Do We Have an Obsession with Winning?"[9]

START WITH SUCCESS IN MIND

Being a politician is rarely an easy occupation, and if you happen to be mayor of a historic borough in Mexico City, achieving success can be a constant uphill battle. Citizens tend to be cynical about what government can do, and problems feel eternal. Raul Flores, a career politician with a business degree, and one of the founding members of the Democratic Revolution party, knew the challenges when he assumed the leadership of Coyoacan.

Before taking the top spot in this vibrant neighborhood, he was the police chief in the historic center of Mexico City. You can imagine that was not an easy job. To Raul, success was making the streets safe and turning around the city's dangerous reputation. Flores tackled it wholeheartedly and instituted a number of programs that addressed the problem. He relocated merchants, publically attacked the issue of gang violence, installed security and traffic cameras, and pushed for a facelift to the downtown area.

When public safety is your goal, measuring success can be difficult. Nevertheless, Flores points to a number of indicators that his efforts paid off. "Now it's a beautiful place, which is crowded with tourists, people going to work, meeting friends at restaurants, in the evening for a drink . . . It's the most safe place in all the country," he says.[10]

As mayor of Coyoacan, a borough with a population of six hundred thousand, Flores had to redefine success. The needs of the community, an educated enclave with a large student population, were more subtle and less obvious than those of the streets of downtown Mexico City. Flores zeroed in on a more specific goal: improving women's safety and reducing domestic violence. To confront this problem, he applied a fresh perspective and enlisted help from inside and outside the borough. The first step was understanding this kind of violence.

"We put most of the effort of the administration into this—to understand the problem, and why many women were being beaten by their husbands," he explains. "We faced the problem from different viewpoints—the gender view, the woman's view, the man's view, the child's view, the injured people's view."

Once he grasped the scope of the problem, he instituted changes both to the environment and to people's attitudes. This entailed such actions as installing extensive street lighting and educating the police force.

"Now the policemen in Coyoacan know that if they see a woman, if they see an older person, if they see a child alone, they have to ask if they need help or watch them to see they are safe."

In his pursuit of success as a public servant, Flores went beyond protecting and serving the more vulnerable members of the community. He achieved another goal: "Life gave me an opportunity to change things inside our community. I don't know if many people have this opportunity for change, so I am not going to lose it."

CREATING A LEGACY

Healthy leaders are crystal clear on the leadership legacy they want to create. It's common for leaders to spend their first days and months, even years, focused on learning about the job, developing key relationships, and making sure they survive the difficult transition into the job. They defer thinking about their legacy until they contemplate moving on. Yet some leaders start thinking about legacy before they step into the office. "Legacy" can be an intimidating concept, especially if you tend toward being realistic and tactical. But without the driving force of legacy, your efforts can be dissipated into a series of worthy but loosely joined initiatives.

By starting with the end in mind and thinking about your legacy before you break new ground, you can visualize the big change you'd like to make, and create a blueprint for the future that gives form to your values and goals.

To successfully build a legacy, you must answer three critical questions:

- *Who am I?* What are my core values, and what are the experiences that formed them?
- *What do I want?* What do I want to achieve, who do I aspire to be, and what higher purpose am I serving?
- *How do I show up in my role?* How do I shape my environment and deploy my strengths, what do I need from my work, and what is my desired impact?

Andrew Demetriou is a former football star and currently the CEO of the Australian Football League, managing the biggest sports league in Australia. He reflects on the value of legacy: "When I was appointed to the job, the chairman called me into his office. Then he said something I will always remember: 'In this role you are a custodian of the game. You get to borrow the game for a few years, but you can't own the game. You want to leave the game in better shape than how you found it, and that's the challenge you face as the leader. So you need to think about what your legacy is going to be. What will you be remembered for?' "[11]

Says Andrew, "That was a very profound comment. He was absolutely right. The game is 150 years old and rich in history. It's been served by many wonderful people over the years. And now I only get to borrow it. It's not mine."

That's the power of legacy. Here are a few questions to ask yourself about your desired legacy.

- What kind of leader does my company need me to be?
- What kind of leader do I aspire to be?
- How would I describe my leadership style, and what would others say?
- What leadership qualities and skills do I want to acquire?
- How will I act when I have fully embodied them?
- Who are my role models?
- How do I want people to think of me when I leave this job?

THE POWER OF ENGAGING OTHERS

Here's the dangerous reality: the majority of workers are not engaged and fully succeeding in their jobs, according to a recent poll by the Gallup Organization. It found that more than 70 percent of workers feel emotionally disconnected from their employers and, as a result, are less productive than they could be.[12] Their disengagement affected most elements of their jobs, namely customer service, quality control, commitment to staying with a company, safety, and activities related directly to profits. If we could figure out how to change these numbers, amazing things would happen.

Healthy leaders must create the conditions for success. For a leader to engage workers, he must first be fully engaged himself. The problem is that some leaders don't take the time to understand engagement inside themselves. Consequently, they don't fully appreciate the psychology of engagement in others; they don't believe people are disengaged, don't feel they have the time to figure out the problem, or simply don't understand how to change it.

Researchers studying engagement have identified three essential elements:[13]

- First, employees need to believe that their company is committed to helping them grow and advance. It must offer them opportunities within their job.
- Second, it's also vital that a company be more than just profit vehicle and be dedicated to making a difference in the world.

Employees want to feel that they are not cogs in a financial machine but contributing to bettering society.

- Last, company leaders have to show that their values are worthy of people joining in and following them. When these needs are met, engaged employees work together, enjoy what they do, exhibit passion, and use their initiative to further a group's vision.

The benefits of employee engagement are quantifiable. A study by Towers Watson shows that when company employees are highly engaged, operating income improves by up to 19 percent in just a year. Conversely, when employees are not engaged, operating income quickly sinks by as much as 33 percent.[14]

WHAT TO DO MONDAY MORNING: GET INSPIRED

Perhaps one of the biggest obstacles to developing vocational health is lack of attention. Even though people pay lip service to developing a meaningful calling or personal mastery, and many admit to their drive to succeed, other "more pressing" things tend to get in the way. It's understandable—you're busy, and this takes hard work, deep reflection, and dedication, not just for weeks or months, but years. So in the spirit of recognizing that many of us lack a willingness to devote attention or motivation, we offer these five steps to get you started, along with red flags signaling where you can get sidetracked.

Step 1: Dedicate yourself to learning. Demonstrate that learning is vital for you and everyone else in the company. Talk about what you are trying to learn; create opportunities for others to learn. *Red flag:* Don't let your efforts stagnate with a single program or announcement. Keep revitalizing the spirit of learning.

Step 2: Create a shared vision. Move your thinking from your personal vision or idea of success to a common one—from "me" to "we." Weave individual visions into a collective vision and share it throughout the organization. Use tangible symbols for what the company stands for. *Red flag:* Disengaged employees are a sign of a lack of shared vision. Constantly seek feedback to ensure a shared sense of purpose.

Step 3: Promote outcome thinking. Make sure that you and the company have concrete goals and that they are attainable, not just ideals. Don't tackle too many missions at once, and emphasize execution. *Red flag:* Beware of people becoming obsessed with winning and triumphing over others. Don't lose sight of why everyone is striving so hard.

Step 4: Build a high-performance culture. Push yourself and the entire company to high standards of excellence and competence. Let people know what's expected of them and eliminate systems, processes, and bureaucracies that keep people from doing their best. Set quantifiable goals and link them to performance standards. *Red flag:* Watch out for too much focus on activity and busyness and not enough on results.

Step 5: Celebrate success and find a balance. You can't keep pushing at a breakneck pace forever. At some point, you need to back off, evaluate your progress, and set new goals. Your company will go through cycles; learn to recognize them and to find the balance that helps everyone stay energized. Finding balance means celebrating success, catching your breath, then resetting for the next push. *Red flag:* Burnout indicates that you or others are pushing too hard and are under constant stress. If you see signs of burnout, step back and reevaluate how you are progressing toward your goal.

Spiritual Health

What is spiritual health, and what does it have to do with business?

Spirituality can be an amorphous concept. Some say spirituality is a belief in a higher purpose, belief in a personal God, or being true to one's inner self. Others feel that it is being a moral person, having a deep sense of inner peace and happiness, or experiencing the fullness of life in a world much bigger than ourselves. Spirituality is all these and more. It's about connection at the macro level.

The world is growing smaller every day, brought closer together by communications, technologies, transportation, and education that foster a global-village mindset. A consequence of this smaller world is the unmistakable sign that spirituality is on the rise. Ours is a time of sharing values and traditions across cultures. With Eastern and Western cultures cross-pollinating, spiritual practices can be seen in every corner of life. People are engaging in yoga and meditation, exploring religions other than those they were raised with, and discovering a life of contemplation.

The impact of spirituality on your business and working life is reflected in a worldview that values each individual and embraces our global community. Spirituality connects you to people you work with every day and to those in distant cultures. It is a recognition that you are a strand in the fabric of the world and that what you believe and do affects the texture of countless lives.

In the absence of spiritual health, you and your business suffer. On a personal level, individuals become alienated, rootless, and self-destructive. A business devoid of spiritual health promotes selfish, parochial, and narrow financial interests above humanity and social responsibility. In the process, trust deteriorates, the environment is neglected and destroyed, people starve, epidemic diseases topple populations, civil wars erupt, and economies collapse. The Haves rule the world, and the Have-Nots battle for survival.

Spiritual health is not a panacea for all that ails us. Of course it has its limits, and some people will never understand how vital it is to their enterprises. However, leaders with a clear vision of their connection with all of humanity—where they fit in, what they can do to relieve suffering and improve lives, what they can do to make the world a better place—find that their lives have joy and their companies have meaning and make money.

Some people say they are religious or spiritual, but don't act that way. They may go to church, synagogue, or the mosque on the weekend, but then become a different person at work on Monday morning. Others are spiritually healthy but do not think of themselves in that context. From our experience, the essence of spiritual health comprises these three qualities:

- Believing in a higher purpose that gives you a mission in life
- Feeling a global connectedness that transcends cultures as well as borders
- Showing a generosity infused with kindness and gratitude

WARNING SIGNS OF DECLINING SPIRITUAL HEALTH

- Inability to handle adversity and life's ups and downs
- Difficulty feeling empathy and compassion for others
- Distrusting self and others
- Feeling ethnocentric and ignoring cultural differences
- Having little or no alignment between beliefs and actions
- Preoccupation with oneself and one's needs

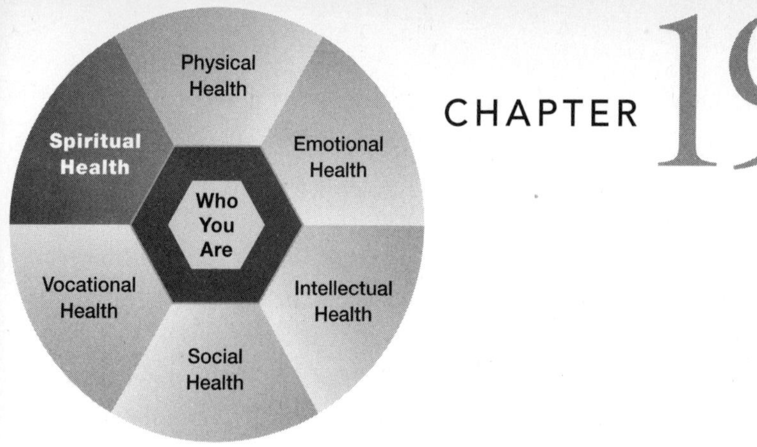

CHAPTER 19

Higher Purpose

WHO I AM INSPIRES WHAT I DO

Dr. Jack Stephenson is one of those rare leaders whose focus is totally on others, not himself. He's the kind of leader who, when confronted by a situation that could threaten his reputation or his organization, asks first what he can do to help others.

As the senior pastor of Anona, one of the country's oldest and largest Methodist churches, in Largo, Florida; the national head of Natural Church Development International; and a professor of world religions, Jack is truly a leader and mentor of spiritual health for both his congregation and the larger community.

What's striking is his emphasis on leadership as much as spirituality. In word and deed, he demonstrates his belief that his job is to help others be "all that God has created you to be." Translated into everyday terms, this means that he lives a life of selflessness. "I really try not to do anything that doesn't raise up other people. I try to put people in places where they are set up for success, where a person can thrive and blossom."[1]

This is his higher purpose—to be a good person, to lead an open, relevant church with contemporary values, and to put others before himself. Such selflessness is not always easy. His dedication to this higher purpose was sorely tested a few years back when he and his church were thrust into the public eye and became the subject of law enforcement attention in a sexual abuse scandal.

Stephenson had learned that a member of his staff had been sexually molesting boys and girls, and alerted the police to have him arrested. When Stephenson was questioned by church officials and law enforcement, he was advised not to make any public statements. They thought it best to keep quiet. There was fear that both his reputation and that of the church would suffer if the community knew about the abuse.

Stephenson knew what he had to do. "I remember facing the cameras, and in a moment that was Zen-like in its clarity, I simply said, 'This happened here. It was one of my staff members. We want to reach your child, we want to get him or her to a pediatrician. This is real. Talk to your children, talk to me. Let's find the kids who are damaged, and let's bring them healing.'"

There was no doubt in Stephenson's mind about what was the right thing to do. He had to take care of the children first. This is central to his higher purpose—dedicating his life to others and speaking to people's higher inner voice. He offers this explanation of why this is fundamental to him: "The more your life is all about you, toward your success, toward you looking good, toward other people looking at you and giving you the credit, the less you are able to truly lead healthy people to become healthy leaders."

You may be saying to yourself, "Of course it's Jack's job to be a spiritually healthy leader. He's a pastor." But we have found that great business leaders are spiritually healthy just as Jack Stephenson is.

Your true passion should feel like breathing; it's that natural.

—Oprah Winfrey[2]

THE POWER OF A HIGHER PURPOSE

An irony of human life is that we all possess a higher purpose, yet many of us have no idea what it is. Our minds and bodies are intended for more than mere survival—they are vessels for deep social and emotional drives that give us meaning. For whatever reason, many people have never asked themselves, "What is my purpose here? Am I meant to do more with my life than take care of myself?"

Finding the answer begins with the knowledge that this is not like coming up with a New Year's resolution. The answer is not a program you throw yourself into for a year and then abandon. It is not a formula like a weight-loss plan with a series of concrete steps. Instead, it is like a long journey to a country that is both familiar and quite foreign.

You are on a journey of discovery as you look for ways to use your unique gifts while also helping others, improving the world as you go along. What you discover will also have as profound an impact on others as it does on you. The journey will help you understand who you are and how best to touch other lives.

Discovering your higher purpose changes you. You think about yourself and others differently, and the world around you takes on new qualities. It is a little like reinventing yourself. It gives you a new persona or definition, one more closely aligned with what you value and what you are passionate about. Here are some questions for deep reflection as you clarify your higher purpose. Ask yourself:

- What do I love doing, and what am I passionate about?
- When do I feel most alive? What are my natural talents and skills?
- What do others say are my special abilities and qualities?
- What values am I most committed to? When do I feel best about myself?
- What would I change in the world if I could?
- How can I make my life a service to others?

WHAT IS YOUR MISSION?

Your journey is unique, and we cannot predict what you will discover. We can perhaps help you recognize possibilities by sharing the higher purposes others have discovered: Some people internalize their missions, committing to realizing their full potential or being an authentic person. Others focus on their relationships with others—spreading kindness, being honest and trustworthy, or helping others be better people. Still others extend well beyond themselves, working to empower women, create jobs, or promote freedom and equity in the world.

Organizations and businesses also have higher purposes. This is what a company wants to achieve other than self-perpetuation and profits. It may be a company's mission or an ideal it strives to reach, and like a personal higher purpose, it redefines its owner. Here are examples:

- Ending hunger
- Improving people's daily lives
- Guarding public safety
- Caring for the environment
- Helping people fulfill their dreams

PURPOSEFUL LEADERS IN ACTION

Leaders and organizations realize meaningful benefits when they care about how their activities and products affect their employees, the lives of their customers, and the communities and environment in which they operate.

Research into the power of product brands has identified a cause-and-effect relationship between a brand's power to convey a company's higher purpose and that company's financial performance. Brand consultants Millward Brown and Jim Stengel examined the impact of fifty brands, names like Stonyfield Farm,

Chipotle, Starbucks, and L'Occitane.[3] They chose these brands because they have strong connections with customers. What makes these brands especially compelling is their ability to inspire spiritual values, such as

- Experiencing joy by creating feelings of happiness and wonder
- Establishing connections by helping people relate to each other
- Encouraging exploration by revealing new horizons and experiences
- Evoking pride by giving people confidence, security, and vitality
- Improving society by challenging the status quo

Brown and Stengel compared the financial performances of companies with strong brands to those of companies without such brand power. The companies with values-based brands showed much faster financial growth in a ten-year period. They outperformed a larger group of companies by 400 percent. Their financial growth came from every facet of their companies, including marketing, R&D, finance and human resources.

By presenting its products and services within the context of a higher purpose, an organization actively demonstrates what it is doing for others, for the global community, or for the environment. This aspect of its spiritual health becomes part of its identity and encourages others to connect to a higher purpose. Here is how some top brands connect to a higher purpose:

- Red Bull shows that it seeks to uplift minds and bodies.
- Zappos promotes the ideal of delivering happiness in its boxes.
- P&G uses Pampers to show that it cares about the happy, healthy development of babies.
- JetBlue emphasizes its belief that success comes from playing by the rules.
- Nokia strives to connect people.

- Lego conveys its commitment to developing creativity and logic skills in children.
- Whole Foods educates people about personal health and the health of the community and global environment.

LEAD FROM YOUR DEEPEST NATURE

Wai-Kwong Seck has devoted his professional life to the financial services industry, earning an MBA from Wharton, working as an investment banker for Lehman Brothers, and serving as the CFO for the Singapore Exchange. Yet even though his working life revolves around finance and international investing, making money is not his higher purpose. Quite the contrary. What moves and motivates Seck is enabling those around him to succeed, to find their own inner purpose.

Currently the executive vice president of State Street Bank in Hong Kong, which serves institutional investors largely in the Asia Pacific region, Seck manages thirty-six hundred employees, who in turn help administer over $2 trillion in client assets.

"I've got a large responsibility; the platform is a big one," he explains. "You can get carried away with the size of the job, but there's a higher purpose here. I think at the end of the day you've got to remember that it's about people."[4]

Seck tells a story to illustrate how he works not only to do the right thing himself but also to help others pursue values beyond personal gain. While CFO of the Singapore Exchange, he attended a board compensation committee meeting to discuss compensation packages. Among the items under discussion was the options pricing for the new CEO, who happened to be in the room. Seck was uncomfortable with the talk for two reasons: the CEO's being there and that the options were not due to be granted for another five months. With the company's underlying stock rising, fixing the price at that time would have created a windfall for the CEO.

Seck could not remain silent: he spoke up, reminding the board of the actual options' schedule. As a result, the pricing was postponed. Seck was embarrassed about speaking up in front of the CEO and apologized to him the next time they met. To his surprise, the CEO responded, "If something like this happens again, I want you to do the same thing."

Seck was moved, realizing that others in the company shared his appreciation of integrity over money. "If the CEO is willing to be personally penalized because one of his staff does the right thing, this is the way we ought to act. It sets the tone. It must be right from the very top . . . Forget about spreadsheets, forget about all those wonderful analyses. If the management is not right, you can forget about these numbers."

Seck understands the irony of a banker who believes that profit is measured by the people he helps along the way, not by the size of a bank account. He notes, "Outlandish rewards may attract the wrong crowd." At the same time, he reminds us that decency and humanity can be found all around. "There are still very many good and decent bankers who do the right thing. They enjoy the work and believe what they are doing is positive."

HOW TO LEAD WITH HIGHER PURPOSE

Leading according to your higher purpose can be difficult. It can mean holding firm to values even in times of doubt and economic uncertainty. You may need to be public and vocal, even offering yourself as a role model in order to show people the rightness of having a bigger purpose. With a higher purpose as your driving force, you inspire others to make a difference. You also imbue your organization with a spirit of authenticity and meaning that helps people get through tough times. Use these questions to reflect on whether your actions are aligned with your higher purpose. Ask yourself:

- Are my personal conduct and ethics consistent with a leader who pursues a higher purpose?
- Do I regularly refer to our higher purpose to inspire and motivate people?

- Do I tell the truth about today's realities while trying to inspire hope for the future?
- Do I maintain a clear view of what our work means above and beyond business success?
- Do I help people see that what they do can make the world better?

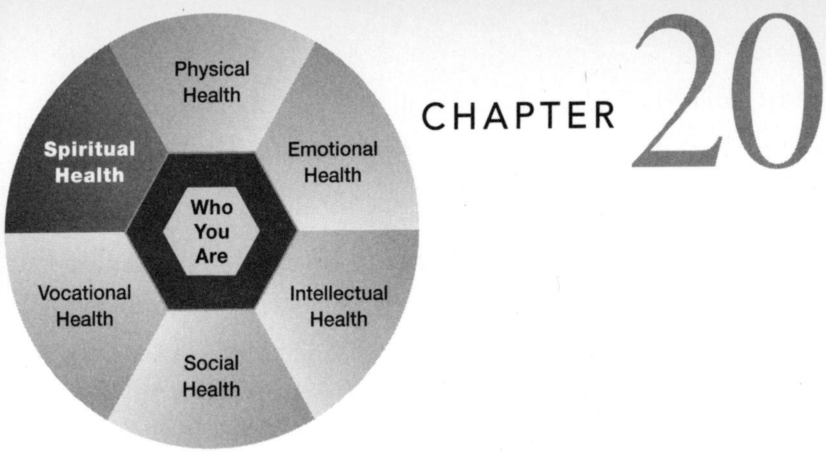

Global Connectedness

TOUCHING THE WORLD

Christoph Kurowski was born in Germany and has lived in Latin America and Africa. He also spent time in Lebanon and Sri Lanka with Doctors Without Borders. Today he is a global citizen and views the world as a single community. His role, he feels, is to bring this community closer together through a shared global vision and mutually rewarding cross-cultural relationships. What strikes you most is his deep sensitivity to other nationalities.

Christoph is working on the challenge of a lifetime: helping rebuild the social fabric in a region of the world torn apart by centuries of ethnic violence, the western Balkan countries. He is doing this under the auspices of the World Bank, where he works as a human development and sector leader for programs in Serbia, Bosnia and Herzegovina, Macedonia, Montenegro, Kosovo, and Albania. His focus is on health, education, social protection, and labor markets. His mission is making sure the countries' and people's needs take priority over the governments' wishes.

He explains, "We have to bring much more than just peace, investments, and monitoring. We have to really rebuild the social fabric so that people can learn to pull together."[1] Ethnic divides still run deep in this region. Poverty and unemployment are high; for example, in Kosovo, unemployment is a rampant 40 percent and, among the country's youth, close to 70 percent.

Christoph is facing a huge job, especially because it has so many components. He's well suited for it because he understands that despite cultural disparities, everything depends on people finding commonalities. "Making it work between the people and their governments across countries, within the bank, and with other partners such as the European Commission—that's the management challenge. The challenge is to have relationships that are authentic," he says.

Kurowski envisions a world in which narrow, nationalistic perspectives are abandoned for a wider one. It is beginning to happen, he says, as people realize that Cold War institutions have outlived their usefulness and that the actors on this world stage have changed as a result of social media, as demonstrated by the Arab Spring, among other things. In this global village, he sees a new generation of leaders who can bring everyone together.

"True global leaders will leave this kind of baggage behind, not thinking of nation states and national interest. That is the fundamental change that we have to see over the next thirty years," he declares.

NAVIGATING IN A WORLD WITHOUT BORDERS

No matter where you live, each morning you may well brew coffee from Brazil in a pot from Germany, watch the news on a TV from Korea, shower with soap from France, wear a shirt made in Cambodia, eat butter shipped from New Zealand on toast from America's heartland, and drive to work in a car made in Japan. At work, you use computers made in Malaysia to send emails to friends in the Philippines, get tech help from a person in India, eat a lunch of Mediterranean-style food, make calls on a cell phone assembled in China, and write with a pen made in Mexico. At the end of the day, we may be residents of a particular country, but our lives have no borders.

Cultural forces have a huge impact on an organization, regardless of whether your business has dozens of overseas offices or is strictly a local enterprise. Every country thrives on a steady stream of diverse and talented immigrants; your employees undoubtedly represent a melting pot of cultures.

Although many businesses are global, most markets are local. Whether you run a retail chain from Bangor, Maine, or a seafood company from Bangkok, your customers and competitors have certain needs and desires that are culturally based. It's vital to understand these diverse cultures. Leaders especially need to understand and master the cultural forces that affect their business.

Let's face it: we are all different, and valuing these differences is critical to business success.

This fact is unsettling to unhealthy leaders. They harbor strong biases and resentments. Generally arrogant, they feel superior to others and believe that people are born different and unequal. Not surprisingly, they tend to be dogmatic and unable to take another's perspective, and typically demand conformity.

In contrast, healthy leaders have a much deeper appreciation for what makes people unique. They believe that people are created equal and different and that each person has a special contribution to make. To them, we are all extensions of everyone we know, and have the right to be accepted for who we are. As leaders, they understand their own biases, know how to tap into diverse talents, and build cultures of mutual respect.

[W]e have this notion of free speech that we really love and support at Facebook . . . But different countries have their different standards around that . . . My view on this is that you want to be really culturally sensitive and understand the way that people actually think.

—Mark Zuckerberg, founder, Facebook[2]

A survey of two hundred global business leaders found that the overwhelming majority believe it is imperative to understand cultural forces. Conducted by the United Kingdom's Ashridge Business School, the survey stated, "The global leader of tomorrow needs to understand the changing business context—82% of those polled say senior executives need to understand the business risks and opportunities of social, political, cultural and environmental trends."[3]

Ask yourself:

- What are my biases and prejudices that influence my leadership actions?
- What leadership qualities and business practices are fundamental to my own national culture?
- How can I create a business culture that mobilizes diverse people?
- How does a business in another country operate in culturally unique ways?
- What lessons and innovations can I learn from other national cultures?

In 1955, of the hundred largest industrial businesses in the world, seventy-five were American. By 1996, that number had dropped to twenty-four. By 2037, predicts the *Harvard Business Review*, only eight U.S. industrials will be in the top one hundred.

—***Race for the World***[4]

CULTURAL LITERACY: THE LANGUAGE OF GLOBAL CONNECTIONS

If you were asked to describe your cultural background, what would you say? Of course you'd mention the country you grew up in and maybe the region, especially if it has a distinctive identity, like the American South or Northern China. Other major forces have molded who you are, too. There's history, geography, religion, economics, language, politics, psychology, and upbringing, and each of these has personal and national dimensions.

How we think about and conduct business also reflects our cultural identities. As you develop cultural literacy, it is useful to recognize distinctive qualities of various cultures. For our book *Global Literacies,* Healthy Companies conducted a study of top leaders around the world. We began to see the power of these national personalities. Here are a few examples to illustrate not only how national cultures can influence our identity but also how each country has something special to teach the world.[5]

- **India:** Serving Merchants
- **Japan:** Contextual Harmonizers
- **China:** Ancient Modernizers
- **Netherlands:** Tolerant Traders
- **Brazil:** Affable Humanists
- **United States:** Optimistic Entrepreneurs

Becoming culturally literate is a complicated and ever-evolving process. Our work finds that people go through phases in their cultural education. The developmental path of a global leader typically begins within oneself and one's family, then gradually radiates outward. Think about how you are evolving as a global leader. Here's a brief description of these phases:[6]

Proud Ancestor. You honor your national background and learn to overcome any feelings of cultural superiority or inferiority.

Inquisitive Internationalist. You look beyond your business to the bigger world for solutions to pressing problems. You encourage cultural diversity and debate within your company.

Respectful Modernizer. You are aware of your own cultural strengths and weaknesses, and constantly seek out the global community for ideas to enhance, upgrade, and modernize your business and country.

Culture Builder. You establish strong working relationships with people from other cultures. You are always learning and making cross-cultural connections, one person at a time.

Global Steward. You are a student of the global marketplace and the world, scanning it for customers, capital, ideas, suppliers, and talent. In the process, you and your business take responsibility for contributing to the well-being of your immediate community and the larger, more worldly one.

The World in a Village

If we could shrink the world to a village of 100 people, there would be 56 Asians, 21 Europeans, 9 Africans, 8 South Americans, and 6 North Americans. Of these 100 people, 30 would be Christian, 18 Muslim, 13 Hindu, 6 Buddhists, 5 animists, and 21 without religion. Also, 80 would live in substandard housing, 70 would be illiterate, 50 would be malnourished, and 6 would possess 60 percent of the world's wealth; 1 would have a college education, and 1 would own a computer.

—***Global Literacies***[7]

PUTTING YOUR GLOBAL LITERACY INTO ACTION

You need an assortment of personal qualities in order to create global connections. These attitudes and behaviors will enable you to build on your cultural literacy and give you the means to lead your company in a global economy.

Use global awareness to broaden your worldview. Recognize how the world is changing. Stay informed about world events. Anticipate and recognize trends and changes in public opinion abroad. Keep up with global politics. Cultivate a sense of social responsibility across the globe. Understand how your organization affects the world.

Employ business acumen to tap into the global marketplace. Everything is interrelated. Customers, suppliers, employees, and competitors are linked via technology and communications. Realize that your business can change overnight as a result of natural disasters, terrorism, new trade agreements, war, or an economic crisis. Constantly scan international markets for new opportunities. Assess your global competitors and what you can do to stay ahead. Look for ways to customize your goods and services to meet the needs of individual countries or cultures. Share with other people in your company what you know about cultural norms in areas where you do business. Prepare a cultural "Dos and Don'ts" list for particular countries.

Practice cross-cultural respect. Think about what motivates other people from different lands. Acknowledge awkward situations and use them to learn. Make an effort to learn about the cultural traditions of individuals you work with. Take steps at work to celebrate cultural diversity. Find opportunities to work with people who are culturally different. Expand your network of business contacts to include such people. Constant exposure and understanding are the best antidotes to discomfort.

Travel internationally. One of the best ways to learn cultural literacy is through personal experience. A practice among international companies is to transfer high-performing individuals to assignments in regions far beyond their comfort zone. Living in another culture is not always practical, but you can expose yourself in other ways: traveling, reading, listening to music from other countries, even learning the basics of a foreign language.

Cultural Illiteracies

- McDonald's took thirteen months to realize that Hindus in India don't eat beef.
- Kentucky Fried Chicken's slogan "Finger-Lickin' Good" translates to "eat your fingers" in Chinese.
- In Africa, companies show pictures of what's inside bottles so that illiterate customers know what they're buying. When a baby food company showed a picture of a child on its label, it's little wonder the product sold poorly.
- A Swiss restaurant sign declared, "Our wines leave you nothing to hope for."
- A bathroom sign in Finland read, "To stop the drip, turn cock to right."
- A Swedish vacuum cleaner maker claimed, "Electrolux sucks."

—***Global Literacies***[8]

DO YOU HAVE A GLOBAL MINDSET?

One of the most authoritative sources of insight on the relationship between social cultures and business leadership is the Global Leadership and Organizational Behavior Effectiveness research project, also known as the GLOBE study. With the help of 170 social scientists, it has collected data from seventeen thousand middle managers and eight hundred CEOs in fifty-eight countries.[9]

While gathering information about specific country cultures, the study has focused on how leaders acquire an international perspective and apply it to their organizations.

The quality that made a difference among leaders was a "global mindset." Leaders possessing such a mindset were most successful in companies operating around the world and with executives from many cultural backgrounds. Particular leadership qualities formed the bedrock of their global mindset. These were integrity, honesty, and being collaborative. The qualities that were destructive to a global mindset were being irritable, asocial, or self-centered.

Ask yourself:

- Am I always on the lookout for new opportunities in the context of global trends?
- Do I make an effort to understand how cultural differences influence what people do?
- Am I alert to how people from other cultures might interpret my actions or attitudes?
- Do I make an effort to learn about other cultures and what makes them unique?
- Do I keep up with international competitors?

SHARING YOUR LESSONS WITH THE WORLD

Music is a universal language, and as Armand Diangienda has shown, it is also a powerful cohesive among people of widely divergent backgrounds and cultures. The story of how this former commercial pilot created Central Africa's only symphony orchestra and the only all-black orchestra in the world demonstrates how the vision of a single individual transformed a community and morphed into a global movement.

Diangienda is the founder of the Kinshasa Symphony Orchestra (KSO) in the Democratic Republic of the Congo. As a young man, he was a commercial airline pilot for twenty years, until his employer went out of business. At loose ends, without any other career opportunities, Diangienda decided to pursue his love of music. As a child, he had taught himself how to play the piano, but had never received any musical education or training. Nevertheless, with a few friends who also loved music, he created the KSO.

The odds against Diangienda's succeeding were astronomical. The Congo is the world's poorest country and has been at war for sixty years. The music the KSO played was largely classical—Western

European, not African. And he himself had no experience in leading such an organization. Nevertheless, growing one musician at a time, many of whom sometimes shared instruments or salvaged them from scrap heaps, the KSO expanded. A choir was formed, and even more people joined.

The orchestra became a community that stretched beyond Central Africa. Members discovered that when they played their music, their hearts and spirits reached outside the Congo and harmonized with people across the globe. German filmmakers made a documentary about the KSO, inspiring music lovers everywhere to donate instruments and offer master classes. A feature on the TV news program *60 Minutes* established bonds with America's music community.

Music is the language that Diangienda has used to create a community larger than the Congo, a global family of music lovers dedicated to spreading joy and shared humanity. "Our collaboration with musicians from Europe and other parts of the world is important to our own development as musicians, and for the growth of opportunities here at home," he says. He adds, "In the end, music is music and is something we all share. There really are no borders."[10]

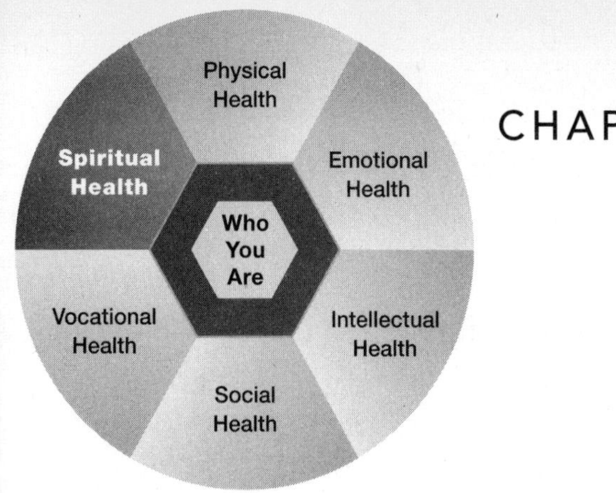

CHAPTER 21

Generosity of Spirit

GRATITUDE

Gratitude is the lifeblood of spiritual health. In its simplest form, it's saying "Thank you." When we show appreciation, we are saying that we care.

Showing gratitude is highly personal: you have to accept who you are and what is both good and not so good about yourself. It reflects a humility which recognizes that you are human like everyone else on this planet. Although it begins inside yourself, gratitude radiates outward and touches the lives of everyone close to you. Once you open your heart to expressing gratitude, the benefits accrue. Others respond in kind, and entire communities and cultures are uplifted when people encourage what is best about them.

Some people fear that showing gratitude will open the door to someone else's greed. Other leaders assume that showing gratitude means giving money. In truth, gratitude is more sincere when it consists of other kinds of currency, such as giving praise or offering greater responsibility.

Expressing gratitude in the workplace is critical. Not only does it create an atmosphere of loyalty and engagement, but it also has bottom-line effects. A study by Bersin & Associates, a research and advisory group, examined companies known for their strong expressions of appreciation. Bersin found that these companies are twelve times more likely to show better results than companies less generous with their gratitude.[1]

An explanation for the multiplying effects of gratitude is that leaders know that gratitude begets gratitude. When a leader shows, through praise, credit, or increased responsibility, that she appreciates and values what someone has done, she inspires people to reciprocate. It comes back tenfold as everyone under its umbrella wants to do better and create even more appreciation and positive feelings. One of the most generous businesspeople today, David Rubenstein, is a profound example.

A LIFE OF THANKFULNESS

We often read about the generosity of billionaires, people like Bill Gates, Warren Buffett, and David Rubenstein, and perhaps think, "Of course they're generous. It's easy for them—they have so much."

David Rubenstein now has stratospheric wealth, but that wasn't always the case. He was raised in modest circumstances, his father a mail clerk and his mother a saleswoman. A voracious reader as a child, he earned full scholarships to Duke University and the University of Chicago Law School. In 1987, he founded the Carlyle Group, one of the world's most successful global alternative asset management firms. Today it has more than $170 billion in assets under management. Rubenstein and several partners started Carlyle when Rubenstein was a young man with a resume distinguished by a position in the Carter White House.

When he left public service, he wanted to do something that he could succeed at. He liked the idea of making money, although he had little interest in the things it could buy. He tried law and politics, but eventually chose the investment world. Bright and well connected, he readily admits that luck played a large role in his success.

"Every single person who's started a company, they had a breakthrough. In my case, I met somebody who introduced me to the people I'm still partners with today. I had a couple early successes and deals. Had those deals collapsed, we would've ended," he explains.[2]

The deals did not collapse and were quite profitable for his group. Carlyle began to grow, and Rubenstein's personal worth began to rise. (Eventually it would be about $2 billion.) Rubenstein had been leading Carlyle for twenty years when he had an epiphany.

"I read that an average white Jewish male will live to be eighty-one, so when I turned fifty-four, I realized that I'd lived two-thirds of my life," he recounts. "I thought I'd better do something with the other third."

Rubenstein chose to start giving back. His philanthropy has a special quality: much of it is an expression of his gratitude to the individuals and institutions that have made his success possible. "I enjoy giving things back to the government or the country, like museums, the National Archives or National Gallery of Art, because it's a way of saying thank you to the country that enabled me to do this." The scope of his generosity often makes headlines; for instance, he loaned a copy of the Emancipation Proclamation signed by President Lincoln to the Obama White House and partnered with the federal government to repair the earthquake-damaged Washington Monument.

Rubenstein gives away about $100 million a year and intends to keep doing so until the end. "I'm giving away basically most of my money. I want to do it while I'm alive and do it in ways that I think will help other people," he says, then adds, "I don't want to spend my life trying to be the richest guy in the cemetery."

Rubenstein's philanthropy is a reflection not only of gratitude but also of love. He muses, "Philanthropy is an ancient Greek word for loving other people. It doesn't mean billionaires giving away money, so I tell people give away your time, your energy, your ideas. That's philanthropy."

DEEP IN OUR MINDS, DEEP IN OUR BODIES

Research shows that the emotion behind generosity, kindness, is neurologically wired and part of our sophisticated survival arsenal.

The hormone in our brain that stirs feelings of kindness is oxytocin, which we also mentioned in the section on social health. The brain produces oxytocin when a person acts generously toward another, such as by showing kindness or physically caring for someone. Increased oxytocin levels make a person feel more trusting and closer to someone else.

Oxytocin may well explain the idea of "reciprocal altruism." Many acts of kindness are returned with equal or greater kindness. By doing for others, you do for yourself. There is an abundance of research showing that behaving this way can enhance a person's happiness.[3] Scientific studies have found that people who spend on others instead of themselves report being happier. Spontaneous acts of kindness and ones that are out of the ordinary also boost a person's happiness.

Trust, too, has a neurological component. A feeling of trust stimulates areas of the brain that makes decision making easier and reduces fear. This may explain why so-called high-trust corporations have been found to do better than companies driven more by fear. One study found that these trusting companies outperformed the fear-driven corporations by 286 percent.[4]

Our brains appear also to be wired for fairness.[5] Acts of fairness stimulate the reward network, a vital player in our survival instincts. When your reward system is active, you feel better. Dopamine is released, and unpleasant stress chemicals diminish.

Psychologists have noted that acts of charity, whether a person is participating or observing others showing kindness, also appear to quiet the stress system. Volunteering and other ways of giving create physical changes in the body known as "elevation." These changes, which are regulated by the parasympathetic nervous system, lower stress and generate both physiological and emotional feelings of calmness. The heart beats less rapidly, breathing slows, and blood vessels dilate, helping circulation.[6]

Kindness makes a person feel better in other ways. Being kind stirs compassion in people, helping them recognize good qualities that were unnoticed. Kindness creates a connection between the giver and recipient as well as the giver and the larger community. A person feels like a part of something bigger, more meaningful. When you are generous, you think better of yourself and are grateful for your own good fortune.

Michael Norton, a professor at Harvard Business School, has explored how people's belief that "it's better to give than to receive" affects their attitudes at work. He looked at how money influences a person's attitude and whether earning more made people happier. Another part of his study focused on how people spent their money. He discovered that what made the difference in a person's happiness was not income but spending. People were asked how much they earned and how they spent it, and to rate their degree of happiness. The results showed that the income levels were irrelevant to happiness. What made people happy was spending money *on others rather than themselves.*[7]

When you are grateful for what you have in life, you are likelier to feel happy and more willing to give to others. By sharing what you have, you contribute to the well-being of others and give back to the community.

MAKING GENEROSITY YOUR BUSINESS

Bringing heart and mind together for the greater good comes naturally to Debbie Shore. When she was a young woman, her strong convictions prompted her to volunteer to work on a presidential campaign. Even though her candidate was knocked out early, this dedication to a cause bigger than herself snowballed. During the campaign, Ethiopia was experiencing a horrific famine, and images of starving children on the nightly news had a profound effect on Debbie and her brother Billy Shore. After her foray into politics, she teamed up with her brother to establish a nonprofit organization, Share Our Strength, dedicated to fighting hunger and poverty.

Shore's motivation was reciprocal altruism, giving her a feeling she was making a difference, and helping others, especially the most vulnerable. She reflects, "I didn't know how fun it would be, how rewarding it would be, or how successful it would be. But I knew it would be meaningful, and that was enough at that moment in time."[8]

Shore and her brother used a $2,000 advance on a personal credit card to start the organization. They threw themselves into the arduous task of fundraising while also building programs to get meals to as many children as possible. That was in 1984, and since then, the group has raised and invested more than $360 million.

People sometimes assume that volunteering or nonprofit organizations are just for emotionally driven, softheaded types. Like most stereotypes, this is off the mark. Shore is a good example. She took lessons learned from political campaigning and tailored them to her organization. Her experiences in fundraising, financing, hiring, staff development, communications, and long-term sustainability have been the engine behind the group's success.

Initially, she says, "We didn't have a plan. But when we changed our message from 'fighting' hunger to 'ending' child hunger, that was transformational and made all the difference in our success."

Shore has kept her eye on the business and the bigger picture.

"You're not going to end something as big as child hunger in America with people who aren't talented. And you're not going to get talent without buying it. To wipe out child hunger—I'd pay anything for that. Why is that not every bit as valuable as Wall Street?"

HOW GENEROUS IS YOUR COMPANY?

Here are some inspirational examples of how business leaders show gratitude and appreciation in their companies:

- Southwest Airlines shows that it appreciates people for their values above all else by hiring based on attitudes, then later providing training for specific skills.[9]

- Aaron Feurenstein, the CEO of Malden Mills, which makes Polartec fabric, showed how much he appreciates the company's three thousand employees by keeping everyone on the payroll even after a fire destroyed three of the four company factories.[10]
- The founder of the Body Shop, Anita Roddick, reached out to help a community near Glasgow, Scotland, a region suffering from high unemployment and urban decay, by building a soap factory there. She also pledged to return 25 percent of net profits back to the community.[11]
- Marriott International encouraged its ten thousand employees to dedicate a day to serving local communities through a Spirit to Serve program.[12]
- SAS, a computer software company, thanked its employees through a no-layoff policy coupled with thirty-five-hour workweeks, flextime, and numerous worksite amenities, including a medical clinic and massage therapists.[13]

THE SOCIAL RESPONSIBILITY FORMULA

Many business leaders are putting muscle behind their gratitude and kindness with a commitment to corporate social responsibility (CSR). At its heart, CSR means that a company does well by doing good.

Businesses for Social Responsibility, an international network of socially responsible leaders and organizations, says that CSR is "achieving commercial success in ways that honor ethical values and respect people, communities and the natural environment."[14] This concept is best expressed as a formula:

Social responsibility = Higher purpose + Global connectedness + Generosity of spirit

---

My personal vision statement is to expand the world's collective wisdom and compassion.

—Jeff Weiner, CEO, LinkedIn[15]

Leaders who embrace this formula bring to their work a sense of personal purpose, a genuine wish to help others, and a desire to contribute to the world. When the leader's values interact with the company's higher purpose, something special happens:

- Stonyfield Farm CEO Gary Hirshberg has translated his commitment to building a successful business that benefits the environment into the largest organic yogurt producer in the world, with revenues of $330 million and powerful customer loyalty.[16]
- Herman Miller is pledged to protecting environmental resources. It is now powered with 100 percent renewable energy.[17]
- Coca-Cola has been teaming up with the environmental organization Greenpeace.[18]
- UPS is working with its energy providers to reduce carbon emissions.[19]
- Tom's of Maine uses all natural ingredients, and packaging from 100 percent recycled cardboard.[20]
- Levi Strauss has been very vocal about its attention to and concern for human and civil rights in countries where its jeans are manufactured.[21]
- Toms Shoes is pledged to match every pair of shoes sold with a donation of one pair to a child in need. Its sister company, Toms Eyewear, has a similar program for donating glasses.[22]
- Interface Carpets trained eight thousand employees in environmental sustainability in order to reduce pollution.[23]

Spiritual health is critical to a leader's success and is becoming more relevant every day. The role of business in society is much broader than simply to maximize financial performance and profit. Reestablishing trust in business, government, and the financial markets and rethinking the role of business in society are more critical than ever. Just look into the future:

- *Shifting to a global perspective.* Leaders are becoming especially cognizant of their responsibility along the entire supply chain, which often involves operations in different parts of the world.

- *Attention to human rights.* This, too, is considered a vital concern for leaders as they interact with local communities.
- *Increasing transparency.* Healthy leaders are realizing that they are under increasing scrutiny, and are responding in kind.
- *Reaching out to younger workers.* Leaders are discovering that spiritual health and social responsibility are talent magnets for young, passionate workers.
- *Rising influence of sustainability consumers.* Socially responsible leaders are responding to consumers' demanding products that are green and sustainable.

SPIRITUALITY AND THE BOTTOM LINE

[W]e hope to achieve a more sustainable form of capitalism: one where business sees itself as part of society, not separate from it; where the focus is on the long term, not on quarterly earnings; where the needs of citizens and communities carry the same weight as those of shareholders.

—Paul Polman, chairman and CEO, Unilever[24]

There is a "triple bottom line" boost for companies that commit to social responsibility. The payoff is better engagement and performance of company employees, stronger financial results, and a bigger commitment to communities and the environment. Numerous research organizations have quantified the benefits. Here are just a few:

- A report on CSR and its consequences looked at thirty years' worth of data and found a strong connection between socially responsible business practices and a company's financial performance.[25]
- *The Trends Report* polled consumers to find that 75 percent said they would switch to a company dedicated to a good cause, assuming that price and quality were the same.[26]

- Companies that pursue a kind of social responsibility initiative known as "conscious capitalism" are outperforming their overall industry at a rate of nine to one. Such an approach creates a culture of trust, authenticity, caring, transparency, integrity, learning, and empowerment.[27]

The challenge for socially responsible businesspeople is that employees and customers like their policies, but analysts on Wall Street often penalize them for making wise long-term decisions and being responsible citizens in society.

A MASTER OF "RESPONSIBLE ENTREPRENEURSHIP"

Klaus Kleinfeld grew up in a tough, working-class West German neighborhood, the son of refugees from East Germany. The death of his father when Klaus was only ten years old and his living with his relatives in East Germany were two major experiences that influenced his life.

After his father died, he had no choice but to "grow up fast." He and his mother were determined to survive on their own wits and hard work. By the age of twelve, Kleinfeld took his first paying job to help support their household, stacking the supermarket shelves after school and on weekends. He learned to take on family responsibilities and help his mother navigate through the difficulties that the sudden death of his father had brought—from managing the finances, to accommodating her way back into a full-time job, to taking care of his own education. "Coping with the enormous grief made me connect to my inner strength, much aided by my local pastor," Klaus recalls.[28] As a beneficiary of the church's youth outreach, he was motivated to work with troubled youth later in his twenties.

Most of Kleinfeld's relatives lived in East Germany, and he was sent there by his mother to spend his school vacations. Her decision was driven as much by her desire to maintain close family ties as by pure economics. Spending his summers with relatives in a small rural village there gave him a strong appreciation for the rewards and responsibilities of freedom. He saw firsthand how bleak life can be when the human spirit is repressed. Yet he also saw the power of hope in keeping that spirit alive under harsh conditions. He learned how important it is to form one's own beliefs and not to be swayed by the masses. He came to understand how one's values fundamentally define who you are, and that actions speak louder than words. Observing people standing up for their beliefs, fully aware of the risks of repression, forged Kleinfeld's great respect for people of character and his view of personal responsibility and accountability.

Years later as a business leader, he participated in the miracle of a reunified Germany, eventually witnessing a woman from the former East Germany rise to become chancellor of the thriving nation. Seeing how German citizens and businesses worked together to modernize the crumbling industry of the East showed him the power of freedom, self-determination, and hope.

Generosity and hope—Kleinfeld never lost those values, and as he grew into the world of business leadership, he made sure they were reflected in his actions. Today he is the CEO of Alcoa, the leading aluminum company in the world. Through the Alcoa Foundation, one of the largest corporate foundations in the United States with assets of $446 million, he is translating his values into action-oriented programs.

He describes an initiative that is close to his heart. "Alcoa's headquarters is in New York, a city that treats us very well. So it's no surprise that our employees here want to give back to the people of New York. And one of the most critical issues where we can make an impact is education," he says. Alcoa Foundation gives financial support to City Year New York, an organization that provides academic tutoring and mentoring to underserved students at two schools in the South Bronx, the poorest district in New York City. Kleinfeld also joins Alcoa employees who volunteer in that community with the students and their college-age City Year tutors.

"In 2012, thirty-four thousand Alcoa employees—60 percent of the worldwide employee population—volunteered in schools and communities around the globe, from the Bronx to Brazil and from Beijing to Belaya Kalitva, Russia," Kleinfeld notes. They also gave their energies and more than $9 million in donations to a wide variety of environmental causes, from planting trees in remote areas of the Amazon to supplying recycling bins in busy New York's Times Square.

Reflecting on the $21.5 million that Alcoa donated in its communities around the world in 2012, Kleinfeld describes a strategy he calls "responsible entrepreneurship"—combining his German-bred passion for excellent execution with his commitment to social responsibility. He likes to say that strong values are Alcoa's true north, the fundamental reason the company is still thriving after 125 years. And he applies those values to every facet of Alcoa's operations, from the work the foundation does to ensuring that the company's leaders are socially committed.

"It's important for me and all of Alcoa's leaders to be generous with our time and resources so we can ensure sustainable communities and a company that has long-term success," he declares. "Maybe that's why I connect most with people who demonstrate depth, passion, and generosity."

THE SPIRITUALLY HEALTHY LEADER: THINGS TO CONSIDER

- **Define and articulate your higher purpose.** What moves you, what you value, and what you believe are the essence of your higher purpose. Take some quiet, reflective time to think about yourself and your place in the larger world of humanity. Once you feel comfortable that you know what you're all about, share it with others and make it part of your life. Let your actions and words show what you believe.
- **Explore your company's cultures.** It is quite possible that the people you work with come from strikingly different cultures and have roots in other parts of the world. Often people are reluctant to talk about their cultural heritage, wanting to blend in. Go out

of your way to ask people about their backgrounds and distinctive cultural, national, ethnic, and racial values. Educate yourself and others as you go along.

- **Be kind.** Research indicates that people who are kind or grateful are happier than those who are not. Acts of kindness that are spontaneous, that are not intended to illicit a response, and that are committed regularly make everyone feel better. The same is true for people who are kind to themselves and gratefully count their blessings.
- **Show generosity of spirit.** Apply the leadership skills that are directly related to your spiritual health. These include showing respect for others, demonstrating fair treatment, expressing care and concern, listening responsively, recognizing the contributions of others, and engaging in reflection.
- **Volunteer to help others.** The evidence is clear: people who do volunteer work not only report greater happiness but are healthier and live longer. Altruism is as good for the body as it is for the soul. So volunteer and join a for-profit or nonprofit board.
- **Hire spiritually healthy colleagues.** Klaus Kleinfeld uses the "T-bar formula" for guiding him at Alcoa. The top of the T refers to a person's breadth of experience. But the vertical bar describes someone's depth of character and the inner sense of the person. That truly differentiates people.

So there you have it: the six dimensions of leadership health. All six are meant to be ideals and aspirations. Make a personal commitment to live them every day.

Yet remember we are all imperfect human beings, and some days will be easier or harder than others. Challenge yourself to be the best person and leader you can be, and be gentle and forgiving when you make a bad choice.

Tomorrow is another day!

CHAPTER 22

On Becoming a Healthy Leader

Many leadership books and consultants believe that business success is attributable to what you *do*. They insist that it's all about actions, as they lay out deliverables, performance indicators, and all the data you need to track your activities. We shake our heads at this approach because it is not in tune with reality. Twenty-plus years in the business suites of the world have taught us that behavior is only a part of the story.

At the beginning of this book, we explained why it's called *Grounded* and the implications of this for leaders. We hope by now that the meaning is clear: as a leader, you need to understand what sparks your actions. Your well-being, success, and organization depend, first and foremost, on who you are. You need to examine the internal stuff—what goes on in your mind and heart—before doing anything.

The roots of healthy leadership form the core of who you are. They are integral to your leadership. Putting them into practice, however, may look a bit daunting. You may be wondering how to cultivate a full complement of robust, healthy roots. What do you do to make them grow?

The answer lies in what we call the four channels of learning (illustrated in Figure 22.1). In practical terms, these are tools you already possess that you apply in order to learn about yourself, those around you, and your environment. We call these tools "channels" because, like the channels of a television or radio, each is a gateway to a larger, broader world. They reflect parts of yourself and all the ways you interact with others. The channels are deceptively simple. They are

See: your sense of yourself, others, and situations
Think: your assumptions, opinions, beliefs, and internal dialogue
Feel: your negative and positive emotions, whether expressed or only felt
Act: your behavior as an individual and leader

We say "deceptively" because putting the channels into play requires both attention and intention, difficult feats that demand discipline. The *attention* part is a matter not only of self-awareness and insight into others but also of focused mental repetition. By *intention*, we mean a dedicated commitment to activating your four channels. It's a belief in yourself and an unwavering confidence in your ability to change and improve.

Harry Kraemer, former CEO of the health care giant Baxter International, a professor at the Kellogg School of Management, and an executive partner in Madison Dearborn, intuitively understands how attention and intention mobilize the channels: "If I'm not being self-reflective," he says, "I don't think I can really know myself. And if I can't know myself, how can I lead others? So you have to start up front by asking a lot of questions: Why am I here? What's important? What is it really all about? It takes a lot of self-discipline to be open enough to ask these kinds of questions."[1]

Some people are naturals at mastering the four channels, with their conscious mind always engaged and instantly seeing clearly, thinking with an open mind, feeling positive, and acting constructively. Yet most people wrestle with one or more of the channels.

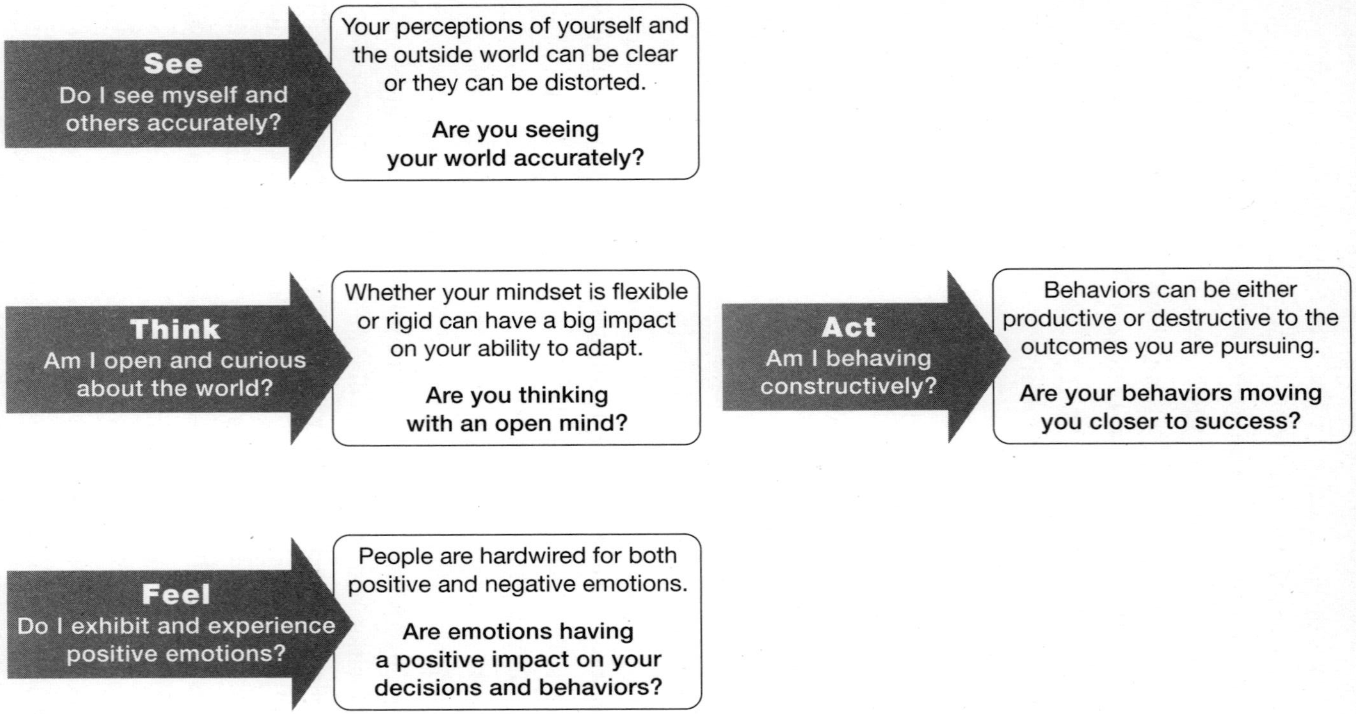

See
Do I see myself and others accurately?
Your perceptions of yourself and the outside world can be clear or they can be distorted.
Are you seeing your world accurately?
Think
Am I open and curious about the world?
Whether your mindset is flexible or rigid can have a big impact on your ability to adapt.
Are you thinking with an open mind?
Act
Am I behaving constructively?
Behaviors can be either productive or destructive to the outcomes you are pursuing.
Are your behaviors moving you closer to success?
Feel
Do I exhibit and experience positive emotions?
People are hardwired for both positive and negative emotions.
Are emotions having a positive impact on your decisions and behaviors?

Figure 22.1 The Four Channels of Learning

THE CHANNELS AT WORK

Perhaps the easiest way to understand how these channels affect business leadership is to tell you about two leaders, Joe and Josephine. Both are middle managers and going through the feedback phase of their annual 360 performance assessment.

Joe is self-assured and highly vocal about his accomplishments and abilities. He's a talker and always has an opinion. In any discussion, he often interrupts to interject his take on events. In his assessment, he gives himself high ratings, thinking of himself as a top performer. He believes this distortion because he always takes credit for others' accomplishments and over time has come to think they are his. If he makes a mistake or misses a target, he blames others.

In his dealings with employees, he says he's "spirited and spontaneous." However, colleagues say he's mercurial and unpredictable. He doesn't like to collaborate, fearing that someone will steal his thunder or that he'll lose control of a project. He attributes his lack of team involvement to the short-sightedness of others. When learning about areas he needs to improve on, he becomes angry over some points and glum about others. He argues or challenges the source of the evaluation with the declaration, "That person doesn't know me."

Joe's learning channels are severely flawed. His perceptions are blurred, his mind closed, his emotions negative, and his actions destructive.

The other manager, Josephine, reacts to her 360 assessment much differently. Tending to be quiet where Joe is flashy, Josephine listens more than she talks. She avoids calling attention to herself and often underestimates her abilities. As a result, many of her assessment scores are higher than she expects. She is grateful that others share her belief in long-term planning and the notion that productivity does not happen overnight. She has a broad perspective on success, makes adjustments when events go against her, and is not discouraged by small setbacks. Having a clear picture of herself, she realizes that she's a perfectionist and so does not know how effective she is.

Throughout the assessment, she is open to what her peers say. Many cite her as a great team player. She enjoys teamwork—bouncing ideas around and working with others to pool their talents and find help for what they can't do. Frequently, she deflects compliments and is generous in her praise of others' good work. The assessment process does not fluster her. Emotionally secure and stable, she's not easily riled or discouraged. Rather, she often laughs at herself. When she hears specific criticisms, she nods in understanding and shows a determination to make changes. At the end, she's appreciative and grateful for the feedback. And although she feels encouraged about her contribution so far, she resolves to redouble her efforts to keep improving.

Josephine's channels are strong and vibrant. Even though her perceptions may be slightly askew or her analysis of situations not always spot-on, she has enough insight to continually sharpen her learning channels.

A PSYCHOLOGICAL MRI

If you are wondering where you might fall between Joe and Josephine, these question will help you tease out the strengths and weaknesses of how you see, think, feel, and act. Ask yourself:

- Which dimension of the Healthy Leader Model do I want to focus on?
- What perceptions about myself and others may be hindering my ability to change?
- What regular thoughts or assumptions might be dysfunctional or erroneous and getting in my way?
- What persistent feelings might be interfering with my ability to change?
- What automatic responses or actions do I resort to that may be counterproductive and impeding efforts to change?
- Which specific perceptions, ways of thinking, feelings, and behavior patterns do I want to change?

INSIDE YOUR LEARNING CHANNELS

Leaders have various ways they can approach their personal learning. It does not have to begin with any one channel or proceed in a certain order. We have seen executives who start with their actions and then unpack the ways they see, think, and feel; others dive into the middle. Regardless, you need to believe that you can change the way you think of yourself and how you interact with the world around you.

The mental patterns you have created over a lifetime can be altered. The human brain has the ability to neurologically rewire certain processes. Scientists have seen it happen in musicians, athletes, amputees, stroke victims, trauma patients, and even ordinary people committed to altering how their brains work. Researchers have discovered that repetition, practice, and concentration can, over time, produce significant neurological changes.[2] Even seemingly simple activities like daily meditation, memory exercises, or just deciding to smile every morning can not only alter neural connections but create new ones.[3] So let's drill down on these four channels of change to discuss how each one can strengthen or undermine your leadership.

Seeing: Acquiring Clear Perceptions

This channel is dedicated to self-awareness, perceptions, and a level of consciousness that enables a person to see himself and others clearly and honestly. This channel is manifested in various ways. It is a perspective that is free of bias and prejudice, and one that recognizes stereotypes. A leader with a strong seeing channel understands the reality and distortions of personal memories and fantasies. She does not let a rich internal life, be it an active imagination or a tendency to daydream, undermine her understanding of herself and others.

Many people have difficulty with this learning channel. They do not have an accurate sense of what they are communicating and how they are perceived. Blind spots; ingrained ideas about others; self-absorption; and ancient, immature ego boosts all get in the way. These people hear and see what they want to or what they expect—not what is in front of them. When they get constructive criticism, they become defensive. They stubbornly cling to misperceptions about others despite contradictory facts or evidence.

Removing the distortions from your perceptions requires looking inside yourself and talking to others. You need both an internal and an external reality check. Here's a collection of suggestions to get the process started. As you can see, some ideas are general and others specific; some will ring a bell, and others will not. That's our intention—people do not all respond to the same ideas, particularly in the realm of personal perception. Go through and find what's meaningful and relevant to you.

- Look closely at yourself in the mirror. What do your expressions convey?
- Check your BS meter: Do you know when you are kidding yourself?
- Envision what you want to be and imagine your ideal self.
- Ask others about your image and how you are perceived.
- Examine your biases, prejudices, and stereotypes.
- Shed old skin—outdated ideas about yourself.
- Experiment with seeing yourself and others in a new light.
- Pay attention to the first words or first thoughts that pop into your mind when you are asked a question. Do they reveal something about your conscious mind that needs adjusting?

Thinking: Developing an Open Mind

Your thoughts, an endless stream of words and images, often produce the material that becomes a life script. Conscious and unconscious thoughts swirl together to generate ideas, help you interpret people and events, and fuel the internal dialogue you constantly have with yourself. Tapping into your thinking channel allows you to expand this dialogue and give it more material to work with, enabling it to become deeper, more diverse, and more useful.

Your thinking channel reveals deep-seated assumptions, mental models, and beliefs. It functions on a continuum that ranges from a closed mind—one that refuses to consider new ideas, new information, or contradictory impressions—to an open mind that is constantly expanding as it absorbs the unfamiliar and the novel.

All of us like to think that we have an open mind, but frequently our reactions belie this belief. A closed mind is obvious in someone who's stubbornly clings to old ideas, often expressed with the line, "We've always done it this way." Another red flag is a resistance to change or experimenting. This is reflected in someone who avoids taking in new information, saying it will just confuse him. A closed mind wants only predictability despite an environment of uncertainty. It holds fast to outdated mental models. Someone with a closed mind clings to the past, to absolute control, to perfection, or to an idealized version of the future. In short, his thinking is mired in exhausted ideas and old habits.

An open mind is vital for learning because it enables you to add to knowledge, recognize new patterns and trends, analyze problems, and craft innovative solutions. Leaders with an open mind avoid the thinking errors that trap the less astute. They are alert to the dangers of overgeneralizing and jumping to conclusions. Striving not to dwell on problems, they are sensitive to either magnifying or minimizing issues.

An open mind is most apparent during times of stress. How you think when under pressure or when things are going wrong or when exhaustion has drained you says much about your thinking channel. It's times like these when the ability to consider new avenues, seek out more information, or just pause and reflect, all the hallmarks of an open mind, are vital.

Typically, most of us move somewhere along the continuum between a closed and open mind. Knee-jerk reactions are a hard mental habit to break, but these suggestions will get you started:

- Carve out time in your schedule for quiet reflection.
- Let go of unexamined attachments to control, perfection, success, and ego.
- Engage in mental workouts, like puzzles or problems.

- Pay attention to your memory and practice ways of strengthening it.
- Experiment with asking different kinds of questions.
- Look for new sources of information.
- Strengthen your ability to concentrate by gradually extending the amount of time you focus, then testing yourself.
- Use your imagination in solving problems. Learn to brainstorm correctly.

Feeling: Creating Positive Emotions

Your emotions are directly tied into your neurological survival system. They are essential for helping you form bonds and survive threats to your life and well-being. Negative and positive emotions both have a place in your life. There are times when anger is the right response or when compassion is best. However, for a leader, it is vital to recognize when negative emotions obscure reality, damage relationships, and threaten your personal health. Feelings such as fear, anger, greed, envy, pessimism, frustration, and shame can sap your energy and distract you from consciously engaging those around you and focusing on what's truly important. Negative emotions are notorious for hijacking the feelings that make you healthy.

In your role as a leader, your positive emotions are an invaluable tool. Feelings of love, hope, faith, forgiveness, compassion, and enthusiasm are the gist of creative ideas, a steady moral compass, tolerance, and understanding. They don't just make you a better person; they make you a stronger leader. Our research has shown that a company led by someone defined by positive emotions not only has inspiring vision and direction but also has employees who are committed to everyone's success.

Activating your positive emotions requires first understanding the wellspring of your negative emotions. It means getting to know yourself and the myriad experiences, memories, instincts, and thoughts that fuel them. Many people resort to negative emotions as their default mode. This approach is destructive and insidious, and needs to be exposed and discarded before you can shift your emotions from negative to positive. These suggestions can help you in the process:

- Get some perspective and remember that "it's not fatal." Most of what happens isn't going to kill you or your company.
- Know the downside, but focus on the upside.
- Practice applying both positive and negative emotions to a situation.
- Face your fears and talk about them.
- Express gratitude and be kind whenever possible.
- Practice saying "I'm sorry" or "I was wrong" more often.
- Try to understand the emotions of others.
- Get comfortable with being emotionally open and vulnerable.
- Identify which negative emotion you feel most often and learn to control it.
- Use the power of love and compassion to form stronger bonds.

Acting: Behaving Constructively

Acting with your behavior is a critical learning tool, as we mentioned at the beginning of the chapter. But it's important to keep in mind that actions come after you have explored your other learning channels. The acting channel is the visible expression of what you see, think, and feel. There are numerous ways for you to activate this channel: it comes alive through verbal and nonverbal communications; in your decisions, interactions, and habits; and in how you conduct yourself on a day-to-day basis.

As a learning channel, your most valuable actions are constructive. They contribute something, be it information or support, rather than detract. They build things up and make people feel better instead of tearing down and leaving a void. They use influence and persuasion instead of dominating. There is no single way of doing things or reacting. In every situation, you have a choice as to whether you react constructively or destructively. How you respond—your actions—will define you as a person and will affect the health of your company. The suggestions here will help you focus on taking action that produces healthy results that in turn profit individuals as well as organizations.

- Imagine the best outcome, then walk it backwards to figure out how to get there.
- Practice, practice, practice.
- Make commitments to others and be good to your word.
- Set short-term and long-term goals and regularly monitor your progress.
- Act as if the "new, improved you" is already in place.
- Examine past and present actions to understand your constructive and destructive behavior.
- Speak the truth to yourself and others. Be known as an honest person.
- Try to be always dependable. Say what you do; do what you say.
- Learn to read nonverbal signs.

WHO KNOWS YOU BEST?

These four channels are at the heart of self-development. So why is it so hard for people to create deep self-awareness and sustainable behavior change? Psychologists have been studying this subject for decades. In the workplace, most people have avoided these deeper conversations and have stayed focused on what they can see and measure, namely behaviors. The problem is that behaviors are just the tip of the iceberg and not always good reflections of who a person is.

Many of us are not very good at assessing our real selves. Two obstacles stand in the way. First, we consciously try to fake or distort the impressions we want to leave on others, and delude ourselves in believing that we are successful. The second obstacle is self-denial. This kind of self-deception blinds us until someone points it out to us or we have a fresh insight about ourselves. By strengthening our healthy roots, we can deepen our understanding of ourselves and accelerate our development.

Here's the fascinating twist. We are all much better judges of other people's character and performance than we are of our own. Although some aspects of ourselves can seem invisible, such as our inner thoughts and feelings, research says convincingly that other people are better skilled at assessing us and our performance than we are ourselves.[4] This includes our perceptions, thoughts, feelings, and behavior.

Nothing in the world is more dangerous than sincere ignorance and conscientious stupidity.

—Martin Luther King[5]

The implication for leadership is profound. The more we share our true selves and interact with people in authentic relationships, the more accurate we will be about our self-perceptions and the psychology and performance of others.

Here's the challenging news: research says that leadership cannot be taught. Leadership is not simply the transfer of knowledge or information from one person to another. The good news is, leadership can be learned. Leadership is rooted in your self-awareness and personal development, and the responsibility is yours to take what you see, think, feel, and observe, and make something of it inside yourself. These opportunities are what stretch your leadership muscles and influence how you show up in the world.[6]

Leaders produce results! This is probably the most common message you have heard over the course of your career. Make and keep commitments. Challenge the status quo. Make bold decisions and take calculated risks. Hold yourself and others accountable. Deliver on goals and make your plan. Take ownership and drive for results.

You have been told that these behaviors define what great leaders do.

We at HCI agree. But all of us have also underestimated how difficult it is to consistently create these results. You need to remember that who you are as a healthy person is the most powerful driver of your success at the job.

PART III

Putting Leadership into Action

How Healthy Leaders Build Healthy Organizations

At Healthy Companies, we have spent the past twenty-five years helping leaders build healthy, high-performing organizations. Regardless of the industry, sector, or country, the leader's job always seems to be the same: to take people to a place they've never been before, develop other leaders, build great solutions and reputations, and leave the world a better place than she found it.

For-profit leaders achieve this by pursuing profitable growth and long-term value creation. Government leaders create healthier, sustainable communities. Nonprofit leaders help improve the lives of people and the environment. In organizations of all sizes and sectors, people are the nerve center of the business.

One thing we have learned in all our consulting and research is this: *who you are* influences *what you do,* and that determines *how you perform.* As Figure Part 3.1 illustrates, business success emanates from developing the roots of healthy leadership and then mastering the leadership actions by mobilizing people around you. Many of us have a sense of what success looks like. Our problem is that we lack the full set of leadership insights and capabilities to achieve these outcomes.

When who you are is translated into what you do—your behaviors, actions, decisions, and practices—you create an environment

Physical Health
Emotional Health
Intellectual Health
Social Health
Vocational Health
Spiritual Health
Who You Are
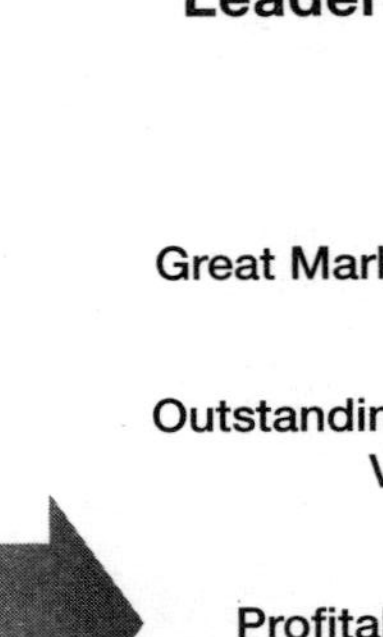
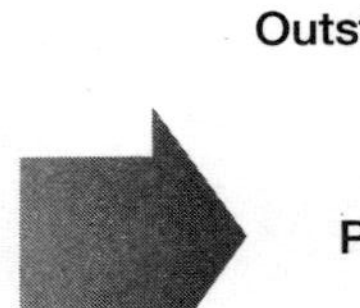

Who the Healthy Leader Is
What the Healthy Leader Does
Taps into a Higher Purpose
Awakens people's passions and sense of meaning
Forges a Shared Direction
Paints a compelling future and enlists people's commitment and ownership
Fosters Productive Relationships
Models and teaches authenticity, connectivity, and reciprocity
Unleashes Human Potential
Challenges people's minds and engages their hearts
Seizes New Opportunities
Embraces uncertainty and cultivates optimism, curiosity, and learning
Drives High Performance
Promotes a culture of excellence and accountability
How the Healthy Leader Performs
Great Market Reputation
Outstanding Shareholder Value
Profitable Growth
Renowned Talent Magnet
Positive Societal Impact

Figure Part 3.1 Healthy Leaders Build Healthy Organizations

that makes all the difference. Leaders shed light or cast darkness on their organizations. This is the most profound power they have.

This is the theme of Part Three—how the personal roots of healthy leadership become the fuel for what you do and how you perform. We have chosen six healthy leaders to illustrate how "who they are" influences how they lead their organizations. These are the leadership actions that build healthy, successful, and sustainable enterprises:

- Tapping into a higher purpose
- Forging a shared direction
- Fostering productive relationships
- Unleashing human potential
- Seizing new opportunities
- Driving high performance

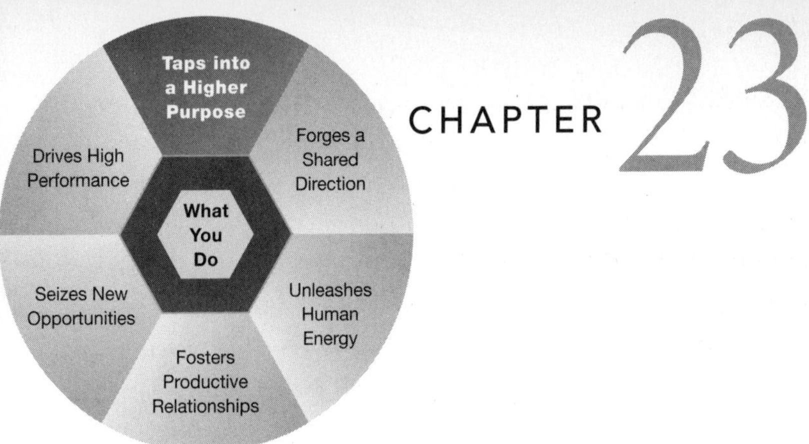

CHAPTER 23

Tapping into a Higher Purpose

Healthy leaders first must tap into the higher purpose of their organization. The grounded leader understands that everyone is rooted and enriched when people pull together for something greater than themselves. When individuals pursue more than simply a livelihood, they fulfill a quintessential human need to contribute to the community of their fellow man.

As we discussed earlier in the book, long before this gets turned into actions, you as a healthy leader cultivate a combination of positive emotions, meaningful calling, and higher purpose inside yourself. This powerful process helps define who you are. Only then does your personal philosophy about life and business get coupled with action and translated into your company's vision and higher purpose.

Leaders who do this well, like Bob McDonald of Procter & Gamble, understand the importance of others' believing in a higher purpose. They realize that ultimately most people are motivated less by external rewards than by deep personal values. People want to feel that they matter and that what they do adds to a greater good. They work to earn a living, but they also realize that their toil must do more than put food on the table and clothe them. It must feed their spirit.

To tap into this intrinsic motivation, a leader must inspire. And inspiration arises from what gives people hope—hope that they can make a difference and hope that they are helping others. To enable people to embrace this vision, a leader creates a context and opportunities. This means not letting the day-to-day work environment obscure the importance of broader dreams and goals.

The challenge for a leader seeking to instill a higher purpose is twofold: creating the vision and inspiring people to pursue it. It is one of both concept and execution. This may sound difficult as well as complicated, and it is, as Bob McDonald has found out during his term as CEO at P&G.

For four years, Bob led the company through some challenging times. On May 23, 2013, he resigned for slower than desired growth and was replaced by his predecessor A. G. Lafley. Over the years, we have spent time with Bob and A.G. discussing their leadership philosophies. Both are healthy leaders.

In Bob's case, he was grounded before his departure and grounded after, and likely got caught in the winds of change. Outstanding leaders get eased out of their jobs all the time for legitimate reasons and for factors beyond their control. Bob's departing message says it all: "When we get to a point where too much attention becomes a distraction, it's time to change that dynamic."[1]

The Payoff of a Higher Purpose

- Increased energy across the organization
- Greater sense of pride among employees
- Less conflict from competing goals
- Higher morale, better teamwork, and more camaraderie
- Stronger alignment between the company mission and performance

---

TOUCHING AND IMPROVING LIVES

Bob McDonald led the world's largest consumer products company, Procter & Gamble, known for such products as Crest, Gillette, Charmin, Pampers, and Tide. More than adding convenience, P&G's products have improved the hygiene and bettered the lives of countless individuals. And Bob McDonald was at the center of the company's vision and mission. His values and those of the company are one.

He declares, "Who we are drives what we do. It starts with touching and improving lives, which is our highest purpose. This influences our objectives, goals, strategies, and metrics."[2]

From the time he joined the company in 1980, McDonald was driven by positive emotions and an authenticity that people can relate to. He harnessed teamwork and pride to produce solid results, while never losing sight of the bigger picture. P&G's mission is to make people's lives better.

"We've been doing this for 175 years, and the purpose and values haven't changed. If you keep the purpose and values the same, they become pervasive in everything you do, be it attracting people from college campuses, developing people, or moving people from one geography to another. We promote from within, which provides a bedrock for character development. That is immutable. We keep the values and purpose the same, but are willing to change everything else to grow."

An example of this is how the company has handled one of its flagship brands, Pampers. McDonald describes how P&G recognized that it needed to make a change in managing the brand in order to continue supporting its employees while also serving its customers.

"We recently moved our leadership of our baby care operation, which makes Pampers, from Cincinnati, Ohio, to Singapore. Why? Seventy percent of the babies being born today are in Asia. So we're creating a globally dispersed organization, an agile organization that's networked and can make decisions in real time. All while they're grounded in their purpose and values—that's what we're trying to do."

During his career at P&G, McDonald had developed other healthy roots. His authenticity had made him an effective communicator. It gave him credibility and a down-to-earth quality people relate to. He sees himself as the hub of a grand wheel. He sets things in motion and is connected to others, but progress comes from everyone moving together in the same direction.

"Becoming CEO is not success," he states. "Doing something with the job as CEO and improving others' lives, that's success."

Just as a hub ties spokes together, McDonald's self-described role as "chief ethics officer" set a tone and standard that everyone can follow. He did all this with constant communication throughout the company. He reached out around the world to its 126,000 employees working in seventy-five countries. P&G employees heard his message in many ways—global webcasts, Internet notes, face-to-face meetings, working lunches, Facebook posts, and YouTube clips.

By using an array of digital technologies, McDonald and the company are able to make real-time decisions, never losing sight of its purpose and values. During a recent running of the Daytona 500, a race car's transmission blew, and it plowed into a truck that was drying the track. The truck exploded, spewing jet fuel across the track. Immediately, workers swarmed the track with boxes of Tide to clean the mess.

P&G people watching the race on TV contacted the network immediately to get copies of the news clip of the Tide cleaning incident. Within twenty-four hours, the Tide team had launched a social media campaign, acquired the rights to the video, and aired a commercial with the video during the NASCAR race the next week. McDonald says that staying focused on how P&G products help people is why the company has been so successful while also maintaining its vision.

P&G's "Thanks, Mom" campaign shows how its values and vision cascade throughout the company. The concept, part of P&G's

sponsorship of the London Olympic Games, was relatively straightforward. Using its marketing muscle to widely distribute a video, it showed its belief in the values of sacrifice coupled with gratitude. The "Thanks, Mom" tagline put a smile on everyone's face, bringing together the common appreciation of family and hard work.

A quality McDonald often applies in his efforts to realize a higher purpose is empathy tied to building nourishing communities. P&G's approach toward its operations in Japan is a good illustration. P&G is committed to diversity, and in Japan this entails a strong program for hiring women. Difficulties arose, however, because the Japanese culture is not always supportive of working women.

"Our women were highly stressed," McDonald recounts. "They'd come to the office, and they'd be treated exactly like the men, but then they'd leave the office and go home and have expectations on them that were killing them. So we created a family day and said bring your family to the office."

When the husbands and children saw that working women were treated with respect at work, attitudes began to shift. "You know, if you don't take care of the family, you're not going to succeed," McDonald says.

The benefits of P&G's dedication to its vision radiate throughout the organization. Individuals are proud to work for the company and see that their contribution connects them with people across the globe. At the same time, their work enhances the company's reputation and boosts financial results. The company's experience marketing a razor to Indian men offers a vivid example.

McDonald explains that a Gillette executive in England was trying to devise an effective razor for Indian men's difficult beards. His first approach was to assemble a focus group of Indian men in England to learn what worked and what didn't. However, P&G executives in the States suggested another approach—that he go to India, live with the people, and see firsthand the problems men there encountered when shaving. The results changed lives.

"He designed a fantastic razor, which today is booming in India," McDonald says. "The exec went there thinking he was going to help them. He came back knowing that by helping them, he helped himself. The exec said the experience changed his life."

By engaging all of his healthy roots, McDonald clears away the clutter and confusion about what's possible. He not only motivated people to join the P&G cause but also energized people to do their best. Along the way, he demonstrated that they are all connected and that when they come together, not only does the company benefit, but millions of lives are made better, too.

WARNING SIGNS	WINNING SIGNS
• People putting their own agendas first • People getting sidetracked by short-term fixes • Low morale and energy • High employee turnover • Turf wars, with people protecting information, time, and resources	• People operate with a shared set of values. • People enjoy working together toward something bigger than quarterly earnings. • People show passion for the company's success. • People are proud to work for the organization. • People willingly share expertise, resources, and time.

WHERE DOES YOUR HIGHER PURPOSE FIT IN?

Look around you to see whether you have tapped into higher purpose and made it part of a larger whole. It should define your leadership and be the centerpiece of your values. Consider these actions to review your progress:

- **Unite people around a higher purpose and enduring values.** Invite the entire organization into a conversation about the higher purpose. Help people see that what they do makes the world a better place. Articulate a connection that is meaningful and bigger than themselves.

- **Be the role model of your company's higher purpose.** Show people how your higher purpose is connected to the company's higher purpose. Make sure your ethics and behavior are consistent with the higher purpose. As Gandhi says, be the change you want to see in the world.
- **Drive the higher purpose into the strategy, goals, tactics, and metrics.** Don't just let the higher purpose be a sign on the wall. Make sure it guides the business strategy, informs goals and tactics, integrates into performance plans, and becomes part of the metrics of the business.

CHAPTER 24

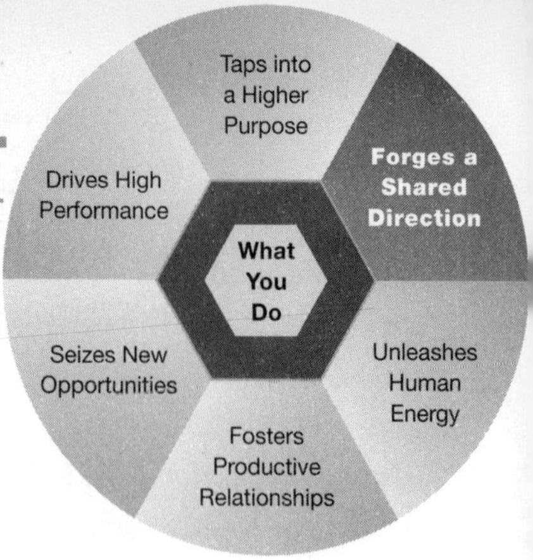

Forging a Shared Direction

If a leader's higher purpose answers "why" people and companies are in business, then the question of "where" they are going is answered with a shared direction. A shared direction gives people a goal to shoot for and offers a path for hitting that target. A healthy leader brings people together to push for a common goal, something everyone can commit to—an inspirational objective that is bold enough to challenge people and bring out the best in them.

There are an endless number of directions an organization can pursue—from the tangible, like market share or profitability, to the intangible, like reputation or impact. As you will discover in the profile of Alan Mulally, sometimes the direction is vital to a company's survival. Regardless of the direction, getting to the goal line entails change for both a company and the people making it happen. Priorities are reconsidered and realigned, and people learn new ways of doing things. All this creates uncertainty within a company, which makes personal ownership and commitment critical to the process. A leader cannot pursue a bright, new future without the support and dedication of others.

The second step for the healthy leader is to design a clear road map. This is a blueprint for success and includes strategies for moving ahead, metrics for measuring progress, and an always-humming communication network binding people together and renewing their commitment. For Alan Mulally, developing this road map entailed facing hard truths and new realities.

The Rewards of a Shared Direction

- Increased operational efficiency
- Less strategic drift
- Fewer missteps and less rework
- Greater momentum
- Greater return on investment

AT ONE WITH THE WORLD

Sometimes the right leader shows up at the right time to forge a shared direction, and ends up saving the day. This is what happened when Alan Mulally stepped into the leadership role at Ford Motor Company. Mulally came to Ford from Boeing, where he had devoted almost forty years to rising through the ranks to become CEO of Boeing Commercial Airplanes. He knew the people, he knew the industry, and he was instrumental in making Boeing an aerospace giant. When he joined Ford, he was hurled into a maelstrom of trouble.

The year was 2006, and American auto companies were on the ropes. Ford was losing market share to European and Asian automakers; the company had reported the largest annual loss in its history, $12.7 billion; and it was slashing thousands of jobs. People both inside and outside the company questioned its future.

"People were terrified; Ford was losing money," Mulally recalls.[1] "They saw their company going away. But they were not all on the team—it was a very small leadership team. Only a few were included on the team; not everybody knew what was going on."

Mulally's years at Boeing had given him intellectual tools, namely a curiosity that asks the right questions and an adaptive mindset to handle the situation. His mandate was clear: save the company. To do so, however, he needed to find a new direction. The company needed to reinvigorate its identity and rethink its product line. It needed to reinvent itself.

Ford's new shared direction was the One Ford plan, built on a compelling vision, comprehensive strategy, and relentless implementation. The Ford leadership team came together around Henry Ford's original compelling vision to open the highways to all mankind, making mobility accessible to everyone. To deliver on the vision, they developed a comprehensive strategy to serve all markets with a complete family of vehicles with best-in-class quality, fuel efficiency, safety, smart design, and value, built on global platforms. Mulally introduced the Business Plan Review process to relentlessly implement the plan, guiding the team in evaluating the external environment, monetizing opportunities, identifying areas that require special attention, and adjusting the plan as necessary.

The success of the One Ford plan would require that all the company's stakeholders work together, meaning everyone would be included—all would participate and understand the plan. The team's success in building a global automotive leader would be measured by a host of participants and observers. Customers, dealers, investors, suppliers, union officials, and communities, as well as employees themselves, would provide feedback on progress.

The One Ford plan called for a mobilizing of the team to take decisive actions. They would aggressively begin to restructure the company so that it could operate profitably even in a climate of declining demand and regularly changing car models—serving all markets with a full family of best-in-class Ford and Lincoln vehicles. Another effort was aimed at accelerating development of new models. A third action was directed at the company's financials to ensure that there was capital to implement the plan and a healthy balance sheet to support it. Finally, everyone committed to work together effectively as one team.

The company's goal was ambitious: build exciting cars, make the company economically viable for the long haul, and create growth that generates profits. It was a clear target, with many pieces.

Mulally sums up how they tackled it: "We look at the plan, we look at the forecast against the plan, the risks and opportunities, which we monetize. And then all the areas that need special attention, knowing that every quarter, every year, we're going to deliver a better plan," he says. Alan offers an example. "We took a point of view about fuel efficiency and quality and connected vehicles to where the world is going to go. This is what people are going to value, so we are actually designing our cars to be ahead, to satisfy the customer on every one of these."

Even with a clear direction, Mulally found that getting to the destination was going to be a challenge. He had to lead people by showing them precisely how to get there.

Mulally describes the approach: "We came together around a compelling vision, we came together on a comprehensive strategy, and we came together on an implementation plan in a most fundamental, respectful way, guided by our expected behaviors."

As the new CEO, one of the first things Mulally did was gather the top executives for a status report. He walked into the room that had on the board a simple rating system: managers were color-coding their reports—green for good, yellow for in trouble, and red for failing. He remembers sitting in an early meeting and being astonished. "The projected losses were $17 billion, and all the charts showed green!"

In order to make changes, Mulally had to get people to talk about what was really going on. It took repeated meetings before people understood that honesty would not cost them their job. The meeting in which one manager's chart was colored red opened the floodgates to a new reality. The manager wasn't fired, and his division's troubles were talked about openly and frankly. Mulally showed the executives that they were fighting this battle as a team.

"It has to be about the company, and, when you're together like this, everything has to be in the open. It is so important to hold two things in your head simultaneously: acknowledge the current reality and have a better plan for the future."

The executive team reviewed charts weekly. "By doing this every week, all 320 charts, you know what needs attention. So during the week, everybody was trying to figure out how to help each other so they could turn a red to yellow or a yellow to a green. It was almost like a celebration," he describes.

Through building mutually rewarding relationships and encouraging people to be generous with their time and ideas, Mulally gave them the tools to pursue a united strategy. Although his colleagues probably did not realize it, Mulally was applying a leadership philosophy he had developed decades earlier. He has a three-pronged approach to motivating and leading people. It begins with a well-articulated, compelling vision—something big, bold, and within everyone's grasp. Developing a comprehensive strategy is the next piece. This is hands-on engagement of people—meeting, talking, making plans, revising plans, making more plans.

His approach to devising a strategy reveals strong vocational health. His personal mastery of the forces the company had to contend with enabled him to identify industry and economic trends and to use them as ideas for new approaches. For instance, the company's focus on Ford and Lincoln prompted him to shed Jaguar, Land Rover, and Volvo.

Shaping strategy is a ceaseless process that Mulally refines as he leads people to the third phase, implementation. This stage is propelled by persistence and drive, and not only is he relentless in his determination to make things happen, but he does this by engaging people. Although the *Seattle Times* once called him "Mr. Nice Guy,"[2] he's also a guy with a titanium spine. He can be brutally honest and, in the same breath, enormously supportive.

At heart, his implementation depends on a collaborative effort. Here is where his social health comes into play. "It is all about the people," he declares. "I want to treat people like I want to be treated. Being myself enables others to be themselves." The success of this approach is evident in the high employee satisfaction ratings. At Boeing, they reached 65 percent; at Ford, they hit 87 percent.

His authenticity is apparent to all. We have known him for more than eighteen years and have seen him weather dark times and achieve enormous success. He has been constant throughout—the kind of person who eschews affectation or pretense and doesn't pontificate or dispense wisdom. He even has a personal version of the Healthy Leadership Model, what he calls One Life/Life's Work. In everyday terms, it means that he applies his approach to getting things done—direction coupled with strategy, plus implementation—to every facet of his life. For instance, Sunday mornings at home, he brings the family together to review what they'd done and to look at the week ahead.

"First of all, we would clean up the house, getting everything put away, get ready for another week," he describes. "Then we would go through everybody's calendar, and we'd build into the calendars what we needed to do to support each other."

Running Ford Motor Company the past seven years has been a hard job, with a steady stream of crises, both micro and macro. From the recession in America and Europe to the rapidly changing demands of motorists everywhere, he has been truly battling a hurricane. And his approach paid off—no required bailout money and record revenues and profits. Today, Ford is profitably growing around the world. It is the number-one selling brand in the United States, with the freshest product lineup in the country. The company repaid the $23.6 billion it borrowed to finance its plan, and the satisfaction scores are high among customers, dealers, suppliers, and employees. Alan was also named *Fortune* magazine's Businessperson of the Year.

His personal character is what has enabled him not just to get through the tough times but also to make significant improvements. His immutable leadership philosophy united with his healthy roots have made him the ultimate grounded individual.

WARNING SIGNS	WINNING SIGNS
• People often argue over priorities, decisions, and direction. • Individual efforts are at odds with each other. • Teams develop goals independent from broader goals. • Individuals are not held accountable for the organization's goals. • People exhibit a "me first" mentality.	• People have a clear road map for success. • Individual efforts align with the organization's goals. • Teams are aligned with organization's goals. • Individuals have a say in the direction of the organization. • People's aspirations are compatible with those of the organization.

WHERE ARE YOU GOING?

Forging a shared direction is both a concept and an action. It's offering a vision of the future and bringing people together so that everyone can contribute and succeed. Think about what you are doing and how your company is moving ahead. Use these suggestions for actions to take to get started or build momentum:

- **Evaluate the scope and boldness of your vision.** Consider whether your values and vision for the future are consistent with those of your team and company. Have you asked others for input so that the vision reflects shared dreams? Think about whether your vision is aligned with everyone's mission and goals.
- **Ensure that you have a strategy and plan for implementing your vision.** Try to break down the process into as many steps

as possible so that people have a clear picture of what actions are involved and what the areas of responsibility are.

- **Resist the drift.** Once you have a vision and implementation plan in place, do not turn your back on it; don't let yourself drift along. Create a system for regular monitoring. As the environment changes, which it always does, be prepared to make adjustments.

CHAPTER 25

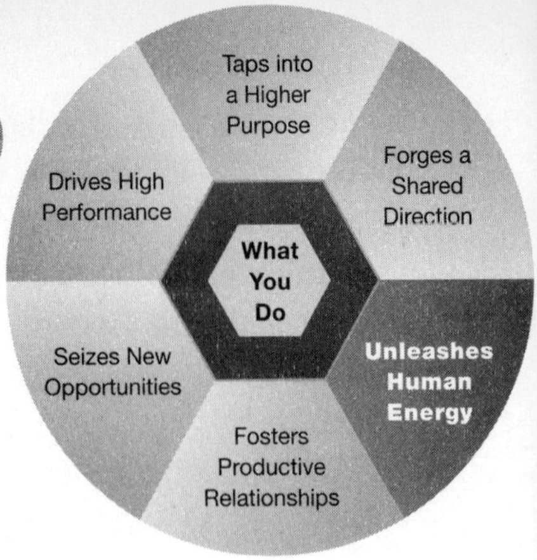

Unleashing Human Potential

How many times have you heard leaders say, "People come first"? And how many leaders actually align their actions with this principle? Not many, because it's easier said than done.

The big hurdle for many is that although they believe that a company's success depends on its people, they don't always know how to engage people. They are clumsy and awkward, sometimes clueless, when it comes to unleashing human potential because they try to apply a style of leading that may have worked decades earlier but not today. This outdated, ineffectual approach avoids anything personal or purely human and relies on the power of reason, numbers, and faceless communication.

Today's workers are younger, better educated, more mobile, and determined to have a full, rich life in which work is not a separate, boring enterprise but an activity that gives them meaning and value as individuals. They want to be engaged as people, and this means touching their hearts and minds. They need to be treated as individuals whose emotions are probably a bigger part of their internal lives than are their cognitive abilities.

Engaging employees as whole people instead of merely names and numbers allows them the freedom to show their talent, be innovative, and pursue success. It motivates them to pass their enthusiasm on to the customer. We have seen companies do this very successfully, as you will read further in David Novak's story. Three tools are particularly effective in engaging employees and unleashing potential.

Perhaps number one on the list is *appreciating and recognizing* people. It is a truism of human nature that we all desire to be acknowledged and praised for who we are. It makes us feel valued and special; it makes us feel good. Another approach is through *teaching and mentoring* people. Developing people, whether formally or informally, signals that they are capable of learning and worthy of attention and personal growth. "Nothing succeeds like success" goes the saying, and even small victories help a person feel more committed.

The third approach is about *protecting and stretching* people to unlock their full potential. This means giving them jobs that challenge them just enough and encouraging them to take risks, while reassuring them that missteps or failure won't jeopardize their position. To understand how profoundly these approaches uplift and propel a company, read about David Novak.

The Bounty of Unleashing People's Potential

- Greater employee commitment
- Increased confidence and willingness to improve performance
- Enhanced focus on learning and growth
- Decreased turnover and increased loyalty
- Improved ability to attract talent
- Lower recruiting costs

LEADING FROM THE HEART

Putting people first is more than a slogan for David Novak. The lifeblood of the company he leads—the world's largest quick-serve restaurant conglomerate in the world, with almost thirty-eight thousand establishments in 120 countries—is an agenda that makes employee recognition its top priority.

Novak's philosophy is unambiguous and apparent in every facet of company operations. "People have a deep-down, innate desire to be recognized for what they bring to the party at every level of the organization," he declares. "Our unique secret sauce is probably our focus on recognition."[1]

Novak recalls the encounter that forever changed his way of leading. Before Yum! was created, he was CEO of KFC and Pizza Hut, which were subsidiaries of PepsiCo. As part of that job, he regularly visited individual operations to talk to frontline employees. He was in St. Louis at six one morning, having donuts and coffee with a group of route salesmen and asking how the St. Louis market was faring. As soon as he asked the question, people at the table began to praise one of their own, a man sitting at the end, Bob.

Novak recounts, "Everybody started raving about this guy. They were going, 'This guy's phenomenal,' telling how they went out with Bob and he showed them more in one day than what they learned in the first four years. They went on and on about this guy, for ten minutes. It was Bob this and Bob that. And I looked down at the end of the table where he was, and he was crying.

"I said, 'Bob, why are you crying? All these people are saying these great things about you.' And he said, 'I've been with this company for forty-seven years, I'm retiring in two weeks, and I didn't know people felt this way.' "

Novak was stunned. "At that point, I said if I ever have a chance to lead a company, I am going to make recognition the number-one value. I didn't want to have more Bobs in the world."

Novak was good to his word. As the leader of three global restaurant chains, KFC, Pizza Hut, and Taco Bell, he has instituted far-reaching recognition award programs. At first, there was push-back. "When I started giving away these awards, people said it wouldn't work in China, it wouldn't work in India, for all these different cultural reasons. That's crazy—people love it everywhere. People love recognition. It's the one thing that everybody wants."

What makes Novak's recognition efforts especially powerful are the awards he gives. No formal plaques or gold watches for Yum! people. Both his awards and those made by company leaders running franchises and regional operations are highly personal. They reflect the personality of the giver and often include a dose of fun.

Leaders at KFC give outstanding employees rubber chickens. High performers at Pizza Hut are dubbed a "Big Cheese" and get cheese heads. The standouts at Taco Bell get the "Sauce Packet Award." People anywhere in the company noted for "walking the talk"—backing up good words with positive action—get a set of gigantic plastic dentures.

Novak's commitment to recognizing people is not just company policy; it's part of his daily life. He surrounds himself with reminders of all the good people who make up Yum! The walls of his office are plastered with hundreds of framed photos, mostly groups of employees being recognized. His favorite shows two thousand restaurant managers on the Great Wall of China doing a Yum! cheer.

Although recognition is the centerpiece of Novak's efforts to put people first and give employees the support they need to succeed, it is not the only approach Novak uses. He is also an enthusiastic and purposeful teacher and mentor.

Through a company program he developed called Taking People with You, he has personally taught more than four thousand people over the course of fifteen years. Every year, he devotes entire weeks to sharing his knowledge and skills with managers around the world. Applying his masterful vocational health, he develops people's change thinking, problem-solving, and management skills.

"My higher purpose," he states, "is to teach people how to lead the right way. I think my greatest joy is helping people discover how they can achieve their greatest in their own careers. To make teams perform at a higher level, to gain greater joy—that's really what my purpose has been."

Novak's teaching both adds another layer to his people-centered agenda and illustrates the vibrancy of his healthy leadership. The teaching allows him to express his spiritual health and devotion to a higher purpose, and it showcases his deep-rooted emotional and social health. Novak learned early in life how to relate to people, build mutually rewarding relationships, and be an authentic, regular guy. Because his father was a government surveyor, the family frequently moved. Novak had lived in twenty-three states by the time he was in seventh grade.

"Mom would say, 'You better make some friends, cause we're leaving in a hurry.' I learned how to size up situations fairly quickly and decide who I was going to be friends with. I worked on it, especially with people who had positive energy. I loved what they had," he says. David became comfortable with reading human emotions, understanding what makes people tick, and inspiring them to greatness.

Novak's efforts to put people first have not only made him a beloved leader but also paid off for Yum! Brands. For the past nine years, the company has logged 13 percent growth every year, and its earnings per share have been growing 10 percent per year. One of his more notable people-driven successes has been in China, where Yum! recently added eight hundred restaurants and continues to grow.

Clearly, David Novak's approach to leading makes people feel better and the company perform better. Deeply caring and intensely competitive, he loves well and competes well. By leading with his heart, he has merged his love of people with caring and compassion to accomplish much more than rigidly formal old-style leaders. This is also probably one reason *Chief Executive* magazine named him CEO of the Year in 2012. He has given the business world a real-time lesson in how the soft stuff trumps the hard stuff.

WARNING SIGNS	WINNING SIGNS
• People are underutilized in their jobs.	• People feel challenged and stimulated by their jobs.
• Individual development is haphazard.	• Individuals have clear career and developmental paths.
• People do only what is necessary and no more.	• Everyone contributes his or her best self every day.
• Individual contributions are overlooked.	• Individuals are appreciated for their unique contributions.
• People rarely seek out learning or growth opportunities.	• People like learning and acquiring new skills.

WHAT CAN YOU DO TO UNLOCK PEOPLE POTENTIAL?

Certainly David Novak's story provides a rich trove of ideas for engaging employees and helping them develop as people and leaders. The possibilities for actions you can take are unlimited. Before you begin, step back for a broader perspective on ways to create an atmosphere that realizes human potential.

- **Pay attention to perceptions.** People see the world through their own lens. Let people know that what they are doing is important to you and that they possess qualities that can make them outstanding performers. Believe in your people and help them believe in themselves.
- **Get the right people in the right jobs.** It's amazing how many people are in the wrong jobs. People will succeed when a leader considers their unique talents and takes the time and trouble to

put them in a position that can showcase their abilities. Character, timing, and opportunity are a powerful combination.

- **Ensure that your leadership is personal.** Don't be afraid to reveal your personal side and emotions. Be as open, honest, and real as situations allow. Make a point to learn people's names and something about their life outside of work. Let them know that you care about their feelings and personal lives.

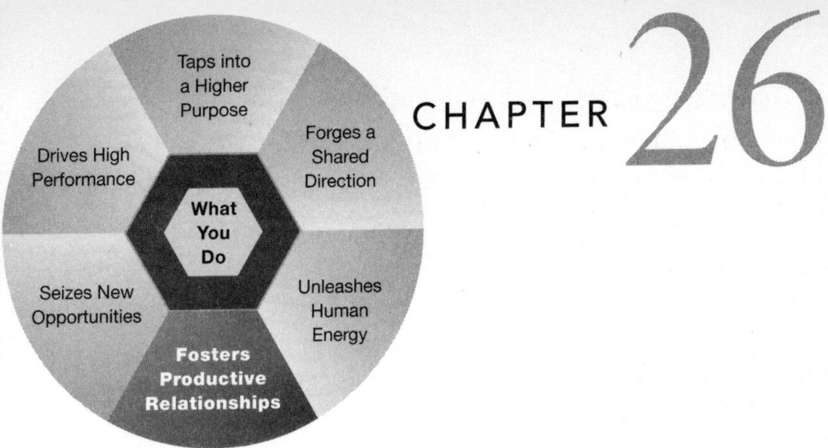

CHAPTER 26

Fostering Productive Relationships

Relationships, more than commerce, more than employment, even more than money, are at the heart of business. The grounded leader knows this instinctively. Relationships with bosses, coworkers, customers, competitors, suppliers, the community, and even the environment are what make people's lives enjoyable and gratifying. In a business context, healthy relationships are the essential fuel for productivity.

A productive relationship requires the stamina of robust physical health. Otherwise, you do not have the energy to engage and keep up with people. Emotional health functions as the glue in a productive relationship, empowering you with the awareness and positive feelings needed to sustain a connection. It's intellectual health that enables you to understand someone else's perspective and appreciate his unique qualities. The role of social health is obvious in your authenticity and the ability to empathize with and relate to others. With vibrant vocational health, you inspire and challenge people to excel to their highest capabilities. Spiritual health keeps that drive to succeed in perspective. It suffuses you with the recognition that the best relationships can be bigger than individuals and touch the world around you.

The healthy leader fosters productive relationships in a variety of ways. Reaching out with heartfelt generosity, whether through a small token of appreciation or by conceding an important negotiating point, immediately drops people's defenses and opens the door. Straight talk, a willingness to share power and control, and being considerate help people trust you. People like doing business with people they like. Making deep connections is the secret sauce that adds value to the lives of everyone involved. And it's an opportunity to leave people a little bigger and better than you found them. Sally Jewell, as you will read, has been doing just this for decades.

The Upside of Healthy Connections

- More profitable joint ventures
- Greater ability to leverage partnerships
- Deeper relationships with customers
- Increased loyalty
- Strong cross-functional ties
- Improved community connections

MAKING CONNECTIONS WITH STAKEHOLDERS AT EVERY TURN

When we first interviewed Sally Jewell, we knew she had a remarkable capacity to forge relationships that both enhanced the lives of people around her and improved the organizations she led.[1] Our opinion of her was recently confirmed by President Obama, who has chosen her to be secretary of the interior. Her ability to connect with people on all levels both inside and outside her organization propelled her achievements at the company she most recently led, REI (Recreational Equipment Inc.), and will be invaluable as she reaches out to the wide spectrum of constituents at the Department of the Interior.

Sally Jewell took over the CEO spot at REI in 2005 after a circuitous route through petroleum engineering, finance, and environmental activism. She immediately found good use for her background in balancing competing demands from disparate groups of stakeholders. A successful national retailer of outdoor equipment and clothing for hiking, climbing, camping, bicycling, paddling, and winter sports, REI is a privately held co-op. Founded in 1938, it has nearly eleven thousand employees and has been ranked as one of Fortune's 100 Best Companies to Work For since 1998. Its sales in 2012 grew by approximately 9 percent to $1.9 billion; that same year, it returned a dividend of $104 million to 5.1 million active co-op members.[2]

Although REI's primary stakeholders are its member-customers and employees, Jewell has teamed up with competitors, communities, and environmental organizations in order to build relationships that not only benefit the company but also enable it to pursue larger, common goals. As a self-described "servant leader," she has been adept at reaching "across the aisle" to find win-win solutions to problems. Her story is a classic case study in how to build productive relationships using well-developed physical, social, and spiritual dimensions.

From the beginning, Jewell looked to strengthen connections with those closest to her: company employees. She knew that getting the employee piece of the business right was the key to getting the customer piece right. Engaged employees freely give the extra effort that's key to productivity. Full and honest communication was the route she used.

"So I started sharing the fundamental building blocks of the financial side of our business at regular town meetings. It was like a bucket of ice water on employees. They didn't realize that our performance had been declining on a number of key measures for several years. We had to help employees understand that a co-op had to be successful financially in order to survive. We had to dispel the notion that a co-op is just a friendly organic gathering of people who don't have to follow the same growth pattern as the rest of the capitalist world," she explains.[3]

In addition to conducting town hall meetings, Jewell reinforced ties that bind the company by holding regular Let's Talk sessions. These also revealed how she builds mutually rewarding relationships. The sessions were regular dialogues during which people talked about what was happening and where the company was going. They were a chance to talk about customer relations, share successful ideas, and inspire and motivate people.

She says, "You take a good idea that starts from elsewhere around the company and roll it out to the company, then give credit or recognition to the store that came up with that, which makes them feel great. It also tells other employees, 'Hey, we would really like you to be thinking about this, because we don't have all the answers.' "

Another aspect to her relationship building was deftly balancing competing demands on REI. The company's mission as a retailer of outdoor gear and equipment is to promote use and enjoyment of the environment. However, Jewell also recognized that there is a limit to how much traffic a park or hiking trail can take before it begins to degrade.

Jewell describes the balancing act: "You want people to appreciate nature, but you don't want them to love it to death. You want to advocate for trails and easily accessible places for people in urban areas to get out so they can appreciate it, but you don't want it to become so overrun that it becomes inhospitable to wildlife and becomes trampled."

Her philosophy of balancing advocacy for nature and promotion of outdoor recreation has been translated into a number of REI programs that strengthen company relationships and contribute to the environment. Her commitment to making connections for a better world, and her giving generously of her time and effort to promote this, reveal the depth of her spiritual dimension.

One example of a successful partnership is REI's involvement with Volunteers for Outdoor Colorado, a recipient of an REI Stewardship Leader Grant. Another is the effort to maintain outdoor spaces in each of New York City's five boroughs, where REI employees work side by side with local high school and college students.

Then there's the PEAK (Promoting Environmental Awareness in Kids) program in which REI seeks to instill socially responsible values in the next generation by educating them in the principles and ethics of environmental stewardship.

REI employees are essential to these programs, and they also contribute by forging their own ties with communities through extensive volunteer work. "They are going out in their communities and doing trail work. They are taking their favorite nonprofit organization that does a great job on a local level and they are recommending them for a grant, and REI is funding that organization," says Jewell.

To give you a few statistics: in 2012, programs supported through REI grants engaged nearly 397,000 people in 2.8 million hours of volunteer work on public lands.[4] Volunteers maintained 54,000 miles of trails and 94,000 acres of local parks and public recreational spaces.[5]

"Those are things that I am so unbelievably proud of," Jewel declares. "And not because they add up to some big numbers and they feel like collectively we are making a difference, but because they are part of it by doing something in their own communities that is making a difference." And then there's the fact that REI has a record low turnover of 26.6 percent, compared to the average retail industry rate of 63 percent.

Jewell has tapped into people's inherent desire to improve the planet and has unleashed their energy so as to better serve REI's customers. She knows REI's customers well, because she is very much like them, placing a high value on physical health and body-mind awareness. She embraces an outdoor lifestyle and loves to snowboard, ski, and climb mountains. She calls kayaking one of her hobbies and does regular morning workouts to keep herself in shape.

The role of the physical dimension in her leadership is apparent in how REI promotes its business and its philosophy. "People are becoming busier; they have less opportunity to take care of themselves," she says. "We are in a vicious cycle with our consumption behaviors and the consequences on the environment and on our health not being sustainable. The opportunity is, how do you make that vicious cycle into a virtuous cycle? That is what I want to talk about with REI, and I do regularly. I think we are in a wonderful position to be significantly influential in being part of the solution as opposed to being part of the problem."

Jewell has clearly developed the skill of fostering productive relationships into a fine art. Her relationship-oriented leadership has propelled REI to become a global enterprise and an influential retailer as well as an advocate for a balanced approach to protecting the environment.

WARNING SIGNS	WINNING SIGNS
• People work on their own in an atmosphere of protectiveness. • Individuals hide some of themselves while at work. • People are uncomfortable with diversity and competing viewpoints. • Everyone provides his or her business partners with only just enough value to meet targets. • People work together only when necessary.	• People work collaboratively in an open, supportive environment. • Individuals are true to who they are while on the job. • People welcome diversity and competing points of view. • Everyone provides the highest possible value. • People enjoy working together.

ARE YOUR RELATIONSHIPS TRULY PRODUCTIVE?

You already have relationships—everyone does. And many of them take place at work. However, they may be lacking the necessary depth or aspects that could shape them into lasting and mutually beneficial experiences. Here are suggestions for taking your business relationships to the next level:

- **Get closer to your customers.** Cultivate acquaintances and turn familiarity into friendships. Strive to be honest, open, and authentic. Listen more. When encountering problems, never lose respect for others' point of view. Inspire your people to be company ambassadors.
- **Use diverse teams to yield better solutions.** Ask people about their strengths and weaknesses and how they can complement one another. Emphasize the importance of communication in team building and team maintenance. Promote diversity and different viewpoints. Give team relationships legitimacy by sharing freedom and responsibility.
- **Broaden your horizons.** Think about relationships in terms of your connections to the larger community and the physical world around you. Find ways to work with people outside your company, such as competitors, toward common goals. Be socially responsible and look for ways to implement relation-based solutions. Encourage people to volunteer. Protect our fragile environment.

CHAPTER 27

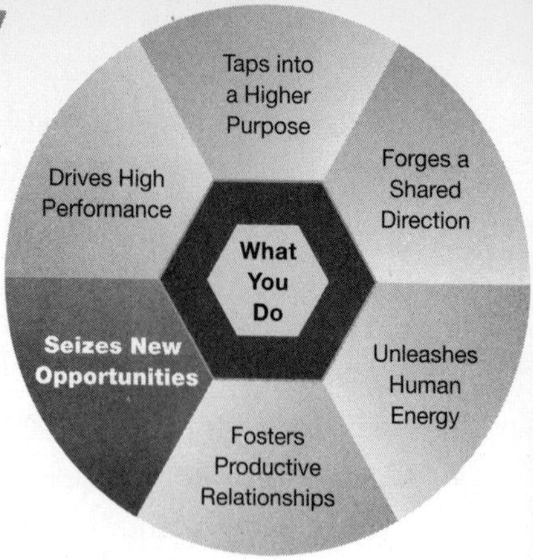

Taps into a Higher Purpose
Forges a Shared Direction
Unleashes Human Energy
Fosters Productive Relationships
Seizes New Opportunities
Drives High Performance
What You Do

Seizing New Opportunities

Change and upheaval are the new normal in this time of economic volatility, instant marketplace shifts, and technological innovations. A healthy leader navigating through the storm always need an eye on what's directly ahead, making sure there's a firm foundation of innovation and imagination. An essential aspect of leading is finding new avenues for both corporate and individual growth.

The imperative to find new opportunities for growth is a little like what Woody Allen said about a relationship: "It has to constantly move forward or it dies." Great organizations are always learning and innovating. Leaders who are committed to growing their companies have a distinct advantage. Whether it comes from acquisitions, organically from inside, or as the result of small improvements in performance, growth begets an expanding customer base, fends off competitors, and fosters innovation.

Because recognizing possibilities and opening new markets is so vital, a full complement of healthy roots is essential. Pursuing a promising concept, an innovative strategy, or an unfamiliar market can be unnerving. A leader has to operate in the short and long terms simultaneously and to be optimistic yet realistic, curious yet decisive.

Only the most grounded individual has the personal qualities needed to plunge ahead successfully.

The role of such a leader is to act as a catalyst, to be an essential spark in a process. This leader functions as both an initiator and a primary driver—without his push, a company stagnates. In research we mentioned earlier with fifty top managers at companies like Best Buy, Corning, General Electric, Hewlett-Packard, and Raytheon, we discovered that the growth leaders acted as catalysts by stimulating a chemical-like reaction that sparked growth and top-line results.

Leaders can seize new opportunities and grow their companies in various ways. A growth mindset is essential. Such leaders are always scanning the horizon for new possibilities. Thinking and acting like an entrepreneur is also part of the package. A leader cannot be afraid of taking chances even when she doesn't know everything. She has to be comfortable experimenting with what works and what doesn't, and learning how to launch new efforts.

Another source of growth arises from changes in the environment. The growth-minded leader is always looking for new trends and tapping into the best thinking and practices around the world. At the same time, he builds deep relationships with customers early to identify new opportunities, and uses existing resources inside the company to get started quickly. One leader whose business operates in the thick of constant economic and social change is Ben Noteboon. As you will read, he has leveraged broad trends into phenomenal growth for his company.

Benefits of Seizing New Opportunities

- Increased innovation
- Faster growth
- Enhanced ability to capitalize on opportunities
- More market share
- Greater resilience in down markets
- Improved community ties

LEVERAGING TALENT FOR GROWTH

To understand how growth has become an integral part of Noteboon's leadership at Randstad Holding, you need to know a little about the industry he operates in. This Amsterdam-based company is a global provider of temporary and permanent staffing, the second-largest such organization in the world. It is reshaping the world of work.

HR services is one of the fastest-growing industries in the world, and Randstad's people fill assignments in education, secretarial services, banking, information technology, engineering, and finance. Every day, the company provides an average of 581,700 staffing employees in thirty-nine companies. In short, the company specializes in talent and growth. It has learned firsthand that for a company to be successful in the service industry, it must identify what's working well and multiply that.

Randstad was not always this vibrant. When Noteboon became CEO of Randstad in 2003, the company was limping along. Failed forays into e-commerce had distracted its leaders. Noteboon set about to steer the company back to its core business and use its biggest and best asset, its people, to develop opportunities for growth. The steps he took began with assembling teams of people with complementary competencies.

"We spend a lot of money on training our people—from our on-board training to our own business school. We saw that we did not learn from each other, so we created something called Strong Concepts. We try to capture the best practices for whatever we do—all our activities, our operations, cash collection. It's not a choice—you will execute according to our concepts, or you will execute somewhere else," he declares.[1]

"It's a highly practical way for consultants to be able to become successful a lot faster than if they would have to reinvent everything themselves. Obviously, if you have consultants across the world and I can increase the average by 5 percent, I'm going to be the winner because nobody else will be able to do that," he explains.

Noteboon's practicality and people smarts reveal strong emotional, social, and vocational health. He has a positive approach to growing the company through its talented people. If you want to grow your company 10 percent a year, then each person must grow 10 percent. And he understands how to motivate people by challenging them enough to grow and succeed and not become discouraged.

"If there's no trust between people, you will never have a discussion about a topic. There will always be other ideas, thoughts, intentions behind that discussion. If you have a good team and people know each other, they will respect each other's strengths and they will know each other's weaknesses," he says.

Noteboon has been adept at leveraging talent in the company, sparking growth that has made it a powerhouse. Noteboon's Dutch cultural roots are distinctive. His leadership reveals a strong commitment to individual initiative and collaboration. He uses "we" much more than "I" and devotes considerable effort to helping others acquire skills and training so that they, too, can find opportunities for growth.

Noteboon learned early in life the value of persistence and taking chances. As a kid, he studied judo. Success came quickly, and soon he became a local champion. Then reality hit. "I went to districts and got thrown all across the mat because I didn't know what the hell I was doing. I was crying and disappointed. But you learn that if you really do your utmost, you fight like crazy, and even if you've lost, you'll get another opportunity."

His fearlessness and willingness to take risks are facets of his emotional health. "I would never risk something that would jeopardize the existence of the company, so I always monitor that the risk is not too big. When you put people under pressure, if they act out of fear, they always make mistakes. So we never act out of fear." This is the same tactic that successful entrepreneurs use. It's called "affordable loss." They only invest in what they are willing to lose at any point in time.

Noteboon has grown Randstad from within. He has cultivated and trained its talented pool of people and given them a higher purpose. Knowing that growth for growth's sake is a losing proposition, he has created something bigger than market share to work for.

"We strongly believe that companies have no reason to exist if they don't add value to society," Noteboon declares. This value begins with the quality of Randstad's people. "You will not build a culture by mercenaries who come in to make cuts and leave again. You need people that are fundamentally motivated to be able to build a better company and a better world."

Make no mistake: Noteboon is committed not just to growth but to *profitable* growth. "If you do it right, one reinforces the other. It's simultaneous promotion of all interests, including our own. You cannot have a successful company without having successful employees. You cannot have a successful company if there's no social acceptance of how your company functions. Because then your company will be put out of the system," he says.

Noteboon's philosophy also shows his spiritual health and commitment to social responsibility. The company "walked the talk" on this principle when it teamed up with Voluntary Service Overseas (VSO), an international development organization that fights poverty around the world. It provides local organizations with volunteers to work in education, health care, job training, and governance. This is where Randstad comes in.

"We take many unemployed people and provide them with work and a social life, an economically better life," Noteboon explains. "To just give money is easy. If I give one euro, all the value of what I gave is one euro—that doesn't help. So we have a synergy with VSO because it is sort of a staffing company in the third world. We can recruit people from anywhere in the world, which for them is a big cost."

You may be wondering how successful Noteboon has been in his efforts to develop new opportunities for growth at Randstad. At the beginning of his tenure as CEO in 2003, the company was active in twelve countries with revenues of $5 billion. Today, it is a $22.8 billion company with forty-five hundred branches in more than thirty-nine countries.

And Noteboon isn't done. He sees room for growth all around. "Companies need to be efficient and invest in capital—money in labor, an efficient workforce that automatically means a flexible workforce. We see lots of opportunities."

WARNING SIGNS	WINNING SIGNS
• People let mistakes escalate into setbacks. • Teams focus more on process than on creating value. • People fail to recognize or utilize what's available to succeed. • Individuals are reactive and often resistant to change. • Leaders miss or ignore growth opportunities.	• People recover quickly from mistakes. • People focus on creating value every day. • Teams are effective at leveraging everything. • Individuals partner with customers to discover new solutions. • Leaders run fast to launch growth opportunities.

DO YOU RECOGNIZE GROWTH OPPORTUNITIES?

What makes growth leaders like Ben Noteboon special are the ways they think, see, and act in the midst of a rapidly changing business environment. Growth requires both attitude and actions, along with the ability to take chances while knowing when to retreat and regroup. These moves can help you develop the mentality needed to accelerate your company into finding new markets and yielding better results.

- **Envision faster growth in your organization.** Imagine what's possible if you unleash growth in your company. Emphasize speed, urgency, innovation, customer contact, and experimentation. Leverage your company's existing capabilities. Learn quickly and establish a growth agenda.

- **Identify and deploy cadres of growth leaders.** Support high-potential growth leaders from across the company. Encourage numerous small bets and experiments. Help leaders learn from their failures and successes. Coach and celebrate these growth leaders.
- **Create a culture that unleashes growth.** Eliminate bureaucracies and procedures that get in the way of experimentation and innovation. Reinforce processes that make growth a priority. Create growth teams. Partner with customers as a vehicle for growth. Push people to develop a mental bias for finding growth opportunities.

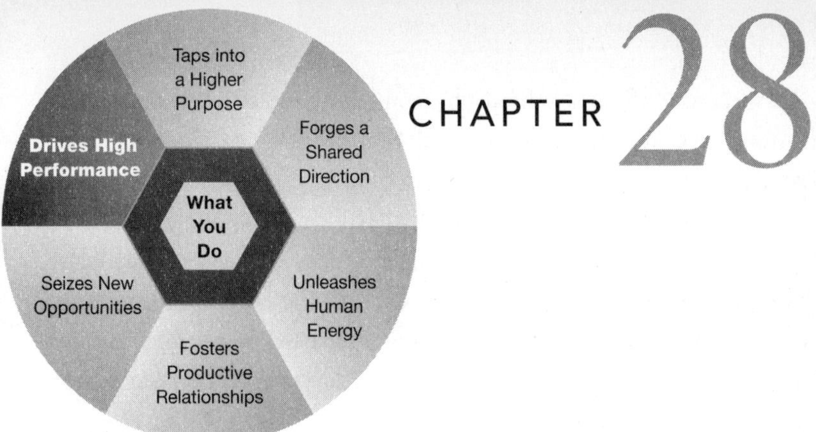

CHAPTER 28

Driving High Performance

The numbers are put up on the scoreboard by people's behavior. If you really want to get the best out of people and unleash their potential, you need to put a behavioral lens on what's going on. And many times, if you want to change someone's behavior, you need to change your own behavior.

These are the words of a technology entrepreneur who's been around the track a few times, having been involved in the telecommunications industry since its infancy. You'll learn more about him in a moment, but right now we want to focus on what it takes to drive people's performance. As he cogently summarized, what pushes performance is individual behavior. And when we dig deeper, we find that what shapes behavior is inside a person. It's those deep, thick roots below the well-grounded tree. When your healthy roots are strong and fully developed, that's going to determine what you do.

High performance is the result of a holistic synergy among all six types of health. Without all of them working together, performance suffers. Without physical health, you lack the speed to respond. An absence of emotional health cuts into resilience and creates fertile ground for too much negativity. Intellectual health is vital to your ability to adapt. A leader with weak social health is unable to mobilize people inside the business. A person who lacks enough drive and is unable to keep up with the competition reveals weak vocational health. And it's vibrant spiritual health that gives a leader the ability to show people a higher purpose, something bigger than personal needs, to inspire them.

A leader with a full complement of healthy roots pushes performance to ever-higher levels of achievement by taking ownership of his role in leading. He creates a culture of freedom and responsibility so that people feel that they can make a difference and know that they are accountable. He makes bold commitments, then acts with speed, urgency, and agility. And all the time, the leader is constantly raising the bar on learning and execution, and measures only what matters. John Kealey, the entrepreneur we just quoted, has done this not just once but repeatedly.

The Rewards of Driving High Performance

- Better and more consistent customer service
- Fewer product defects, errors, or mishaps
- Enhanced reputation in the marketplace
- Increased focus on continuous improvement
- Greater willingness to identify and fix problems
- Higher performance from each person

A SERIAL ENTREPRENEUR DRIVES PERFORMANCE

John Kealey's first day as CEO of iDirect Technologies brought an unpleasant surprise. He found a pile of checks made out to the start-up company's suppliers sitting on a bookshelf in the CFO's office. A few pointed questions to other executives solved the mystery: the company did not have enough cash in the bank to fund its satellite router and telecom services operations beyond a couple of pay periods. The cash-flow crisis galvanized Kealey to take action perhaps sooner than he originally planned.

An accountant by training, Kealey has spent most of his professional life building technology companies. He had been president of Metromedia Paging Services; president of MobilComm; a founder of TenFold Communications; CEO of Vivismo, a software company that IBM purchased; and, most recently, CEO of Decision Lens, a Web-based software company. However, it was during his years with iDirect that he was able to apply his well-honed healthy roots to dynamic leadership actions. The phenomenal results he produced made iDirect, according to *Inc.* magazine, one of the fastest-growing private companies.

A first step was applying both his intellectual and social health to the cash crisis. Within a week of his arrival, he brought together all the employees for a meeting. He did not mince his words. "I told them up front that we had enough money in the bank to pay the next two payrolls, but I didn't know where the money would come from to meet the third payroll," he recounts.[1]

"Obviously my statement made a lot of people nervous. But that was OK. That is the reality of our business. If there are people who can't handle the reality, that's fine. They need to know, so that they can make the appropriate decisions in their life. But more importantly, I thought that there were some answers out there to our problems, and I didn't have them. But the people in front of me probably had some."

Kealey's honesty, combined with experience with the financial ups and downs of new ventures, signaled that everyone had to work together and step up in terms of effort and ideas. Soon, people were offering suggestions on how to alleviate the cash-flow problem. For example, the controller put forth the idea of exchanging a security deposit with a tenant who was downsizing space, and using that money to tide them over. Speaking of the experience, Kealey concludes, "It made everyone realize that we could get through this difficult time and execute the right plan."

Kealey's approach to producing great results in a company is somewhat counterintuitive. Despite his background as a CFO numbers guy, he does not focus on the financial scoreboard. He knows that what drives performance are people and a culture that motivates them. His leadership strategy entails five basic directives:

- Get the facts.
- Change yourself first.
- Tell people the truth.
- Drive teamwork.
- Eliminate excuses.

One of our first customers asked me recently how big we want to be. I said I want to be really big. Later it bothered me that I answered that way. Now I just want to be a great company.

—Kevin Plank, CEO, Under Armour[2]

Getting the facts was a critical part of his approach to solving the cash-flow problem. As he studied the company, he realized that it was trying to operate two distinctly different businesses. It was both a satellite router company, which is a software business, and a telecom, or services, business.

"One of my first observations was that we had a lot of satellite router expertise and a lot of people who came from the world of building and selling products like routers, and we really didn't have a lot in the way of telecom services expertise."

With these facts in hand, he shifted his own thinking and behavior. He also set about creating a company culture where employees had the necessary freedom, and accountability, to retool their attitudes and actions.

"You have to spend your energy with people to influence their behavior, and not worry about the financial scorecard as much. It'll come along. Just make sure you've got the right team executing the right plan, and you'll get the results."

Teamwork became a touchstone for company employees. Before Kealey refined the company's identity to focus on routers and software development, employees functioned in two different cultures. There were engineers and there were salespeople, and the two rarely interacted.

Kealey recounts, "We started to bring them together to different meetings and getting them to realize that teamwork was important. And they got along fine. They realized that they wanted to work together. Pretty soon our salespeople were taking engineers on sales calls. The engineers would go meet with customers and return back to the office and say, 'Wow, this really isn't a bad experience! I like it. I get along with the sales guys.' So when we got wins, everyone felt the positive energy. It brought people together."

Kealey insists that excuses for poor performance will not be tolerated. He combines this attitude with giving employees enough control and support to get things done. He recalls with satisfaction how employees embraced this atmosphere of accountability. In one instance, a supplier in Idaho was hit by a snowstorm and had no way to make a critical delivery of equipment.

"Our head of operations, an ex-military person, took charge. I was away and didn't even know what was going on at the time. He hired a private plane, had all the seats taken out, got a pilot, and flew the plane to Salt Lake City, where they had diverted the trucks. All the inventory was flown to our warehouse in Virginia so we could ship it to our customers," he says.

Another challenging situation required employees from across the company rallying to work together, take charge, and solve a huge problem. A supplier had sent iDirect a shipment of defective parts, so the company had to shut down production and redesign a product with parts that were on hand and not defective. The production team was already stretched thin when they discovered that there were not enough people to manufacture and test the redesigned product.

Kealey recounts what happened next: "So the engineers taught everybody how to complete the testing. They taught our receptionist, and she worked the night shift doing some of the testing. Then she came into the office first thing in the morning to do her regular job. It was a magical time when no one was willing to fail and everyone came together as a team."

Kealey's people-based approach to driving performance produced results quickly. The company began to grow exponentially, making deals with satellite IP and broadband giants like Intelsat, Telesat, and SES. Within five years, company revenues soared 1,600 percent to over $120 million.

Kealey's accomplishments and iDirect's performance did not go unnoticed. He was selected by *Via Satellite* magazine as Satellite Executive of the Year and was an American Business Awards finalist for Executive of the Year in 2011. The company was sold to Singapore Technologies for $165 million in three-and-a-half years. Since then, Kealey has moved on from iDirect to become the CEO of Decision Lens. Still, the lessons of iDirect, where he used his internal life to propel growth, will always be integral to his leadership.

"I was very fortunate to have those experiences where I was able to understand my own personal psyche. It allowed me to see just how much impact my behavior has on other people. That forces me in many situations to ask: OK, what am I doing? Why is my behavior creating this? So whenever I'm a little frustrated, I say to myself: don't get more frustrated, just change your own behavior, and you'll probably be able to influence how others act and treat you. That's helped me turn negative energy into positive thinking."

WARNING SIGNS	WINNING SIGNS
• People are expected to follow strict guidelines.	• People have the freedom and flexibility to get the job done.
• Many people let small commitments go unmet.	• Everyone meets his or her commitments.
• Individuals rarely put forth extra effort to get things done.	• Individuals and teams do whatever it takes to get results.
• People are often confused about what is expected of them.	• People understand what is required of them.
• Individuals and teams are rarely singled out for recognition.	• Individuals and teams are rewarded for achieving business goals.

DO YOU DELIVER ON PERFORMANCE?

Performance can be measured in a variety of ways, yet improving and accelerating it all begins with the people in your company. Look around your organization for where you can apply your healthy leadership. With a firm grasp of who you are, discover how you can enlist others in the quest for higher performance.

- **Solidify what you know and admit what you don't know.** Learn how to gather facts and information from people. Be curious and open to learning from others. Instead of apologizing for weaknesses, hire people to help shore them up. Share power and responsibility. Promote trust and collaboration. Hold people accountable.
- **Keep your eye on both the present and the future.** Address day-to-day issues in the context of current tactics and future plans. Communicate openly and honestly about your vision and

provide a road map for getting there. Instill a clear mental image of success in everyone around you.

- **Balance urgency with compassion.** Set big goals and push people to get ahead while providing them with support. Create a culture where creativity and thoughtful risk-taking are rewarded. Build trust by demonstrating respect and appreciation for others. Encourage participation and learning. Create just enough anxiety.

WHY HEALTHY LEADERSHIP MATTERS

You have just met six executives who are leading healthy, high-performing organizations. Large consultants like IBM, Accenture, PwC, Booz & Company, and McKinsey, as well as leading academics and thought leaders, have confirmed that some combination of the practices described in these chapters is essential for building high-performance organizations. What has been missing is discussion of the ingredients of leadership that enable these actions to be put into practice.

We hope that by having read this book, you now have a better of understanding of why and how these leaders are succeeding and outperforming their competition. They understand deeply the connection between who they are, what they do, and how they perform. They see the world with clear eyes, think with an open mind, feel positively about themselves and others, and act in constructive ways. Most important, they nurture the roots of healthy leadership.

Whether you lead a team or an organization, performance matters. It is the ultimate measure of your success. Your challenge is to achieve this performance consistently and sustainably over time.

After interviewing hundreds of top executives around the world, we have noticed something interesting: the most successful leaders have a very distinct way of viewing their businesses and creating sustainable competitive advantage. It has to do with the way they believe value is created inside an enterprise. This mental model is the secret to their organizational success.

All organizations have four agendas:

1. **The finance agenda** includes cash flow, investments, capital structure, financial markets, equity, debt, dividends, and financial management.
2. **The marketplace agenda** focuses on customers, competition, distribution, reputation, suppliers, sales and marketing, alliances, and branding.
3. **The operations agenda** covers research, development, manufacturing, operations, planning, product development, processes, technology, and knowledge management.
4. **The human agenda** centers on higher purpose, values, leadership, talent management, engagement, motivation, communications, learning, and execution.

As a seasoned professional, you know that every good leader must master all four of these agendas. The agendas may change in priority over time, but all four are absolutely critical for success. Great leaders learn to balance them and excel at each of them separately and together.

So here's the secret: the healthy leaders always start with the human agenda—the values, the leadership, and the culture of their business—and the finance agenda is the scorecard for success. So what do they see and know that is different from other leaders? They understand that

- How employees feel about their company influences how they treat their customers.
- Corporate reputations (brand, customer satisfaction, community relations) come from the internal reputations of the leaders.
- The most desired customers demand that their suppliers be employers of choice.
- Human capital is their biggest expense and their most appreciable asset.

- Innovation and new product development require deep creativity, human ingenuity, and collaboration.
- Process management (six sigma, quality, lean manufacturing) depends on people working together.
- Intangible and intellectual assets (proprietary processes, knowledge, goodwill) are created by curious, engaged people.
- Great execution depends more and more on the human side of leadership.
- Increasing numbers of people want to work for healthy companies that unleash the human spirit.
- The success of alliances and acquisitions depends on the management of healthy relationships.
- Globally literate people are essential for cross-border and cross-cultural ventures

These are the *leading indicators* of business today. And healthy leaders understand this from the inside out.

If business is to regain the legitimacy that it has lost in the last twenty years . . . we must change our leadership and management paradigm.

—Michael Beer, professor emeritus, Harvard Business School[3]

Grounded
A Change in Consciousness

There is much to absorb in this book. We've tried to break new ground for you, introducing fresh perspectives and some unfamiliar concepts, maybe even radical ideas. For some among you, the book may have spoken directly to how you see yourself and confirmed everything you believe in and how you live your life every day.

Leading is a difficult job, and like most leaders, you are probably swamped with work. So you may be wondering where to start after the experience of reading the book. The answer is not unlike the theme of this book: begin with inside yourself.

Our society, encompassing thousands of organizations around the world as well as millions of personal lives, is at a historic tipping point. We are at the crux of an evolutionary shift as changes in the nature of our world along with our personal development accelerate at breakneck speed. And as is true for all organisms when confronted by seismic shifts in their environment, we can either adapt or become extinct. Of course everyone wants to adapt, and we believe that as a society and as leaders, we can do this by changing how we feel, think, and act in the world. Leadership is personal. So make a commitment to become a healthier, more conscious person.

The voyage of discovery consists not of seeing new landscapes but in having new eyes.

—Marcel Proust

The process begins with applying an evolutionary lens to your world. This entails seeing the bigger picture and understanding how every facet of your leadership affects not just you but people around you and even sends ripples into larger spheres. A facet of your evolutionary lens is the recognition that you have more choices than you realize. As a leader, you can do much more than act. You can change the way you see the world and your place in it by examining your thought processes, your emotions, and how you interact with others. In short, you can tap into a new level of consciousness.

Cognitive neuroscientists conclude that the self-conscious mind contributes only 5 percent of a person's cognitive activity. The implication of this is that people are largely unaware of 95 percent of their thoughts, feelings, decisions, and instincts. For you to expand this 5 percent requires you not only to examine your internal dialogues but also to elevate them from instinctive, survival-driven fear reactions and automatic thinking patterns into deliberate self-awareness, into full consciousness.

This means turning off your autopilot and choosing to direct your mind toward all the choices you have. It means choosing to attend to the healthy roots of your leadership and having the courage to be who you truly are. It means choosing to sow the seeds of healthy leadership throughout your organization and community by building healthy teams and forging healthy connections. Last but not least, reaching a new level of consciousness means choosing to step outside yourself, recognizing the implications of living in a global community, and making a positive contribution.

As a leader, you have enormous influence. You are in a position to make a lasting impact and become a more masterful leader, not only of your particular organization but also in a larger context. You teach by example; and by embracing a more healthy, conscious style of leadership, you show the world that we are entering a new phase of evolution. By discovering and demonstrating your true self, you can lead the way into a new age, a time of health and prosperity.

Healthy Companies has created several websites—www.healthycompanies.com, www.healthyleaders.com, and www.bobrosen.com—to receive your comments and reactions to this book. We hope you will visit us and share your thoughts about what you've read. We welcome your personal stories about your own voyage of discovery into the roots of healthy leadership.

Be well and good luck on your journey.

Notes

Chapter 1

1. Farber, Henry S. *Employment Insecurity: The Decline in Worker-Firm Attachment in the United States.* Working paper, Princeton University, 2008. http://www.princeton.edu/~ceps/workingpapers/172farber.pdf.
2. Dediu, Horace. "60 Percent of Apple's Sales Are from Products That Did Not Exist Three Years Ago." Asymco (blog), October 19, 2010. http://www.asymco.com/2010/10/19/60-percent-of-apples-sales-are-from-products-that-did-not-exist-three-years-ago/.
3. Kroodsma, David. "CEO of Manpower: We Have Entered 'The Human Age.'" The Blog (blog), January 25, 2011. http://www.huffingtonpost.com/david-kroodsma/ceo-of-manpower-we-have-e_b_813920.html.
4. Booz & Company. "The Heat Is (Back) On: CEO Turnover Rate Rises to Pre-Recession Levels, Finds Booz & Company Annual Global CEO Succession Study." May 24, 2012. http://www.booz.com/global/home/press/article/50560531.
5. Wainscott, Jim. Interview by Healthy Companies. April 11, 2012.
6. Gantz, John, and David Reinsel. "Extracting Value from Chaos." International Data Corporation, June 2011. http://www.emc.com/collateral/analyst-reports/idc-extracting-value-from-chaos-ar.pdf.
7. Orovic, Joseph. "JPMorgan CEO Jamie Dimon Issues Mea Culpa over $2B 'Egregious Mistake.'" *International Business Times*, May 13, 2013. http://www.ibtimes.com/jpmorgan-ceo-jamie-dimon-issues-mea-culpa-over-2b-egregious-mistake-698144.

8. International Telecommunications Union. "SMS Update 2011." June 12, 2011. http://www.ictdata.org/2012/06/sms-update-2011.html.
9. Hesselbein, Frances. Interview by Healthy Companies. April 10, 2012.
10. "The Dating Game." *Economist*, December 27, 2011. http://www.economist.com/blogs/dailychart/2010/12/save_date.
11. "Global MBA Ranking 2013." *Financial Times*, 2013. http://rankings.ft.com/businessschoolrankings/global-mba-ranking-2013.
12. Quoted in Huso, Deborah. "Leading the World's Largest Democracy." *Success*, July 12, 2012. http://www.success.com/articles/print/1876.
13. Ouye, Joe Aki. "Five Trends That Are Dramatically Changing Work and the Workplace." Knoll Workplace Research, 2011. http://www.knoll.com/media/18/144/WP_FiveTrends.pdf.
14. Ibid.
15. Mathas, Ted. Interview by Healthy Companies. April 30, 2012.

Chapter 2

1. Hardy, Jim. Interview by Healthy Companies. May 4, 2012.
2. Wagreich, Samuel. "Risk-Takers: This Is Your Year." *Inc.*, January 24, 2013. http://www.inc.com/samuel-wagreich/lessons-from-davos-how-to-take-on-risk-to-innovate.html
3. Schievelbein, Tom. Interview by Healthy Companies. June 29, 2012.
4. Bellevue College. "Cell Signaling and Communication." Accessed March 11, 2013. http://scidiv.bellevuecollege.edu/rkr/Biology211/lectures/pdfs/CellSignals211.pdf.
5. Lipton, Bruce. *The Biology of Belief: Unleashing the Power of Consciousness, Matter, & Miracles*. Carlsbad, CA: Hay House, 2005.
6. Begley, Sharon. *Train Your Mind, Change Your Brain: How a New Science Reveals Our Extraordinary Potential to Transform Ourselves*. New York: Ballantine Books, 2007.
7. Childre, Doc. *The HeartMath Solution: The Institute of HeartMath's Revolutionary Program for Engaging the Power of the Heart's Intelligence*. New York: HarperOne, 2000.

Chapter 3

1. Dispenza, Joe. *Evolve Your Brain: The Science of Changing Your Mind*. Deerfield Beach, FL: Healthy Companies International, 2008.
2. Agus, David B. *The End of Illness*. New York: Simon & Schuster, 2012.
3. "From Soup to Negligee: Success According to Victoria's Secret's Lori Greeley and Campbell Soup's Denise Morrison." *Knowledge@Wharton*, http://knowledge.wharton.upenn.edu/article.cfm?articleid=2724.

Chapter 4

1. Jamison, Judith. Interview by Healthy Companies. September 19, 2012.
2. U.S. Department of Energy Genome Program's Biological and Environmental Research Information System. "Insights from the Human DNA Sequence." Accessed March 11, 2013. http://www.ornl.gov/sci/techresources/Human_Genome/publicat/primer2001/4.shtml.
3. Rosen, Robert H. *Just Enough Anxiety*. New York: Portfolio, 2008.
4. Chopra, Deepak. *Reinventing the Body, Resurrecting the Soul*. New York: Three Rivers Press, 2009.
5. Smith, Michael, Susan Bartlett, Roy Ziegelstein, and Joseph Marine. "Research Pilot Studies." Johns Hopkins Center for Mind Body Research. Accessed March 13, 2013. http://www.jhsph.edu/research/centers-and-institutes/johns-hopkins-center-for-mind-body-research/research/.
6. Noakes, Tim, Alan St Clair Gibson, and Estelle V. Lambert. "From Catastrophe to Complexity: A Novel Model of Integrative Central Neural Regulation of Effort and Fatigue During Exercise in Humans: Summary and Conclusions." *British Journal of Sports Medicine*, February 2005. http://www.ncbi.nlm.nih.gov/pmc/articles/PMC1725112/pdf/v039p00120.pdf.
7. Childre, Doc. *The HeartMath Solution: The Institute of HeartMath's Revolutionary Program for Engaging the Power of the Heart's Intelligence*. New York: HarperOne, 2000.
8. Ibid.
9. Ibid.
10. Kerger, Paula. Interview by Healthy Companies. July 5, 2012.

Chapter 5

1. Nally, Dennis. Interview by Healthy Companies. May 1, 2012.
2. Kurth, Krista. *Running on Plenty at Work: Renewal Strategies for Individuals*. New York: Renewal Resources Press, 2003.
3. Epel, Elissa, Jennifer Daubenmier, Judith Moskowitz, Susan Folkman, and Elizabeth Blackburn. "Can Meditation Slow Rate of Cellular Aging? Cognitive Stress, Mindfulness, and Telomeres." *Annals of the New York Academy of Sciences*, 2009. http://www.ncbi.nlm.nih.gov/pmc/articles/PMC3057175/.
4. Brown, Eryn. "Sleep Deprivation Has Genetic Consequences, Study Finds." *Los Angeles Times*, March 1, 2013. http://articles.latimes.com/2013/mar/01/science/la-sci-sleep-genes-20130302.

5. Griffin, Morgan. "10 Health Problems Related to Stress That You Can Fix." WebMD. Accessed March 11, 2013. http://www.webmd.com/balance/stress-management/features/10-fixable-stress-related-health-problems.
6. Schlifske, John Dennis. Interview by Healthy Companies. May 29, 2012.

Chapter 6

1. Johnson, Bill. Interview by Healthy Companies. May 29, 2012.
2. Crowley, Chris, and Henry S. Lodge. *Younger Next Year: Live Strong, Fit, and Sexy—Until You're 80 and Beyond.* New York: Workman, 2004.
3. Rath, Tom. *Wellbeing: The Five Essential Elements.* New York: Gallup Press, 2010.
4. Campbell, Heather M., Nasreen Khan, Catherine Cone, and Dennis W. Raisch. "Relationship Between Diet, Exercise Habits, and Health Status Among Patients with Diabetes." *Research in Social and Administrative Pharmacy*, June 2011. http://www.ncbi.nlm.nih.gov/pubmed/21272540.
5. Story, Colleen. "Can Exercise Reverse or Prevent Heart Disease?" *Healthline*, April 8, 2012. http://www.healthline.com/health/heart-disease/exercise-prevent-reverse-heart-disease.
6. Rath, *Wellbeing.*
7. Tamkins, Theresa. "Study: Can More Sleep Help Fight off Colds?" Health.com, January 12, 2009. http://news.health.com/2009/01/12/study-sleep-help-fight-off-colds/.
8. Centers for Disease Control and Prevention. "Fact Sheets-Alcohol Use and Health." Last modified October 1, 2012. http://www.cdc.gov/alcohol/fact-sheets/alcohol-use.htm.
9. Polidori, Maria Cristina, Gereon Nelles, and Ludger Pientka. "Prevention of Dementia: Focus on Lifestyle." *International Journal of Alzheimer's Disease*, 2010. http://www.hindawi.com/journals/ijad/2010/393579/.
10. Gaman, Walter. "Executive Health a Top Priority for Stock Holders." *Corporate Wellness Magazine*, January 1, 2011. http://www.corporatewellnessmagazine.com/article/executive-health-a-top-priority.html.
11. Trust for America's Health. "Prevention for a Healthier America: Investments in Disease Prevention Yield Significant Savings, Stronger Communities." Accessed March 11, 2013. http://healthyamericans.org/reports/prevention08/.

12. Health Fairs Direct. "Corporate Health and Wellness Event: Return on Investment." 2012. http://www.slideshare.net/Healthfairsdirect/corporate-wellness-program-return-on-investment.
13. Jimenez, Joe. Interview by Healthy Companies. June 18, 2012.

Chapter 7

1. Ryan, Tim. Interview by Healthy Companies. August 2, 2012.
2. Orr, J. Evelyn, Victoria V. Swisher, King Yii Tang, and Kenneth P. De Meuse. "Illuminating Blind Spots and Hidden Strengths." Korn/Ferry Institute, October 2010. http://www.kornferryinstitute.com/reports-insights/illuminating-blind-spots-and-hidden-strengths.
3. Bergman, Nomi. Interview by Healthy Companies. June 7, 2012.
4. Musselwhite, Chris. "Self Awareness and the Effective Leader." *Inc.*, October 1, 2007. http://www.inc.com/resources/leadership/articles/20071001/musselwhite.html.
5. Rosen, Robert H. *Just Enough Anxiety*. New York: Portfolio, 2008.
6. Quoted in Sandberg, Sheryl. *Lean In: Women, Work, and the Will to Lead*. New York: Knopf, 2013.

Chapter 8

1. Parrado, Nando. Interview by Healthy Companies. June 12, 2012.
2. Vaillant, George. *Spiritual Evolution: How We Are Wired for Faith, Hope, and Love*. New York: Three Rivers Press, 2008.
3. Vaillant, George. "Positive Emotions, Spirituality and the Practice of Psychiatry." *Mens Sana Monographs*, December-January 2008. http://www.ncbi.nlm.nih.gov/pmc/articles/PMC3190563/.
4. Scheier, Michael F., and Charles S. Carver. "Optimism, Coping, and Health: Assessment and Implications of Generalized Outcome Expectancies." *Health Psychology*, 1985, *4*(3), 219.
5. Sharot, Tali. "Optimism Bias: Why the Young and the Old Tend to Look on the Bright Side." *Washington Post*, December 31, 2012. http://articles.washingtonpost.com/2012-12-31/national/36103321_1_divorce-lawyers-divorce-rates-rosy-future.
6. Blue, Lisa. "Is Our Happiness Preordained?" *Time*, March 12, 2008. http://www.time.com/time/health/article/0,8599,1721954,00.html.
7. Yount, Kathleen. "The Geography of Happiness." *UAB Magazine*. Winter 2007. https://www.uab.edu/uabmagazine/winter2007/cover/geography.
8. Harbaugh, William T., Mayr Ulrich, and Daniel R. Burghart. "Neural Responses to Taxation and Voluntary Giving Reveal Motives for

Charitable Donations." *Science*, 2007, *316*(5831), 1622–1625. http://www.sciencemag.org/content/316/5831/1622.abstract.

9. Rabbitt, Linda. Interview by Healthy Companies. June 29, 2012.
10. Davidson, Karina, Elizabeth Mostofsky, and William Wang. "Don't Worry, Be Happy: Positive Affect and Reduced 10-Year Incident Coronary Heart Disease: The Canadian Nova Scotia Health Survey." *European Heart Journal*, 2010, *31*(9), 1065–1070. http://www.ncbi.nlm.nih.gov/pubmed/20164244.
11. Jones, Dewitt. *Celebrate What's Right with the World.* [DVD]. St. Paul, MN: Star Thrower Distribution, 2007.

Chapter 9

1. Sumedho, Bhikku. *The Four Noble Truths.* Hertfordshire, England: Amaravati, 1992.
2. Rosen, Robert H. *Just Enough Anxiety.* New York: Portfolio, 2008.
3. Diffley, Atina. Interview by Healthy Companies. July 16, 2012.
4. Haidt, Jonathon. *The Happiness Hypothesis: Finding Modern Truth in Ancient Wisdom.* New York: Basic Books, 2006.
5. Puzziferri, Mike. Interview by Healthy Companies. March 29, 2012.
6. Begley, Sharon. *Train Your Mind, Change Your Brain: How a New Science Reveals Our Extraordinary Potential to Transform Ourselves.* New York: Ballantine Books, 2007.

Chapter 10

1. Petters, Mike. Interview by Healthy Companies. April 24, 2012.
2. "21 Quotes from Davos You Should Read." ChiefExecutive.net, January 31, 2013. http://chiefexecutive.net/21-quotes-from-davos-you-should-read.
3. Kashdan, Todd. *Curious? Discover the Missing Ingredient to a Fulfilling Life.* New York: Morrow, 2009.
4. Kang, Min Jeong, and others. *The Hunger for Knowledge: Neural Correlates of Curiosity.* Accessed March 11, 2013. http://lawweb.usc.edu/centers/scip/assets/docs/neuro/Camerer.pdf.
5. Gardner, Howard. *Frames of Mind: The Theory of Multiple Intelligences.* New York: Basic Books, 1983.
6. Liedtka, Jeanne, Robert Rosen, and Robert Wiltbank. *The Catalyst: How You Can Become an Extraordinary Growth Leader.* New York: Crown Business, 2009.
7. Hermann, Ned. *The Creative Brain.* New York: Brain Books, 1989.

8. Birla, Kumar. Interview by Healthy Companies. January 18, 2006.
9. Birla, Kumar. Email to author. October 10, 2012.

Chapter 11

1. Kashiwazaki. Interview by Healthy Companies. September 25, 2012.
2. Kahneman, Daniel. *Thinking, Fast and Slow*. New York: Farrar, Straus & Giroux, 2011.
3. Lipton, Bruce. *The Biology of Belief: Unleashing the Power of Consciousness, Matter, & Miracles*. Carlsbad, CA: Hay House, 2005.
4. IBM. *Capitalizing on Complexity: Insights from the Global Chief Executive Officer Study*. May 2012. http://c.ymcdn.com/sites/www.plexusinstitute.org/resource/resmgr/files/ibmcapitalizingoncomplexity.pdf.
5. Dweck, Carol. *Mindset: The New Psychology of Success*. New York: Ballantine Books, 2006.
6. Kegan, Robert, and Lisa Laskow Lahey. *Immunity to Change: How to Overcome It and Unlock the Potential in Yourself and Your Organization*. New York: Ballantine Books, 2009.
7. "21 Quotes from Davos You Should Read." ChiefExecutive.net, January 31, 2013. http://chiefexecutive.net/21-quotes-from-davos-you-should-read.
8. Rozanski, Horacio. Interview by Healthy Companies. April 3, 2012.

Chapter 12

1. Knudstorp, Jørgen Vig. Interview by Healthy Companies. May 2, 2012.
2. De Bono, Edward. "Lateral Thinking." 2013. http://edwdebono.com/lateral.htm.
3. Rosen, Robert, Patricia Digh, Marshall Singer, and Carl Phillips. *Global Literacies: Lessons on Business Leadership and National Cultures*. New York: Simon & Schuster, 2000.
4. Perman, Stacy. "How Failure Molded Spanx's Founder." *BloombergBusinessWeek*, November 21, 2007. http://www.businessweek.com/stories/2007-11-21/how-failure-molded-spanxs-founderbusinessweek-business-news-stock-market-and-financial-advice.
5. Communication from Stephen Parker, Healthy Companies International. February 2012.
6. Bernardin, Tom. Interview by Healthy Companies. September 6, 2012.

Part II, Section D

1. Edelman Consulting, "2013 Edelman Trust Barometer Finds a Crisis in Leadership." January 1, 2013. http://www.edelman.com/trust-downloads/press-release/.

Chapter 13

1. Samet, Ken. Interview by Healthy Companies. February 10, 2012.
2. George, Bill, Peter Sims, and David Gergen. *True North: Discover Your Authentic Leadership*. San Francisco: Jossey-Bass, 2007.
3. Rosen, Robert, and Lisa Berger. *The Healthy Company*. New York: Tarcher, 1992.
4. Kosh, Mitch. Interview by Healthy Companies. March 28, 2012.
5. Brown, Brené. "The Power of Vulnerability." TED Talks, December 2010, http://www.ted.com/talks/brene_brown_on_vulnerability.html.
6. Schlichting, Nancy. Interview by Healthy Companies. August 21, 2012.

Chapter 14

1. Brooks, David. *The Social Animal: The Hidden Sources of Love, Character, and Achievement*. New York: Random House, 2011.
2. Loof, Per-Olof. Interview by Healthy Companies. January 6, 2012.
3. IBM. *Leading Through Connections: Insights from the IBM Global CEO Study*. May 2012. http://www-935.ibm.com/services/us/en/c-suite/ceostudy2012.
4. Grant, Adam. *Give and Take: A Revolutionary Approach to Success*. New York: Viking Adult, 2013.
5. Rizzolatti, Giacomo, and Laila Craighero. "The Mirror-Neuron System." *Annual Review of Neuroscience*, 2004, *27*, 169–192.
6. Iacoboni, Marco. "Imitation, Empathy, and Mirror Neurons." *Annual Review of Psychology*, 2009, *60*, 653–670. http://www.ncbi.nlm.nih.gov/pubmed/18793090.
7. Goleman, Daniel, and Richard Boyatzis. "Social Intelligence and the Biology of Leadership." *Harvard Business Review*, September 2008. http://hbr.org/2008/09/social-intelligence-and-the-biology-of-leadership/ar/1.
8. Dasborough, Marie T., Neal M. Ashkanasy, Eugene Y. J. Tee, and Herman H. M. Tse. "What Goes Around Comes Around: How Meso-Level Negative Emotional Contagion Can Ultimately Determine Organizational Attitudes Toward Leaders." *Leadership Quarterly*, 2009, *20*(4), 571–585. http://www.academia.edu/2673494/What_goes_around_comes_around_How_meso-level_negative_emotional

_contagion_can_ultimately_determine_organizational_attitudes_toward_leaders.

9. Anonymous. Interview by Healthy Companies. November 28, 2011.
10. McTaggart, Lynne. *The Bond: Connecting Through the Space Between Us*. New York: Free Press, 2011.
11. Mosley, Eric. "Incentives vs. Recognition: How Do You Get Your Workers Engaged Again?" *Forbes*, November 19, 2009. http://www.forbes.com/2009/11/19/incentives-recognition-engagement-leadership-ceonetwork-employees.html.
12. Dunn, Elizabeth, and Michael Norton. "Paying Workers More Doesn't Always Pay Off." *Washington Post*, May 19, 2013.
13. Ramirez, Michael. Interview by Healthy Companies. May 18, 2012.

Chapter 15

1. Berkman, Lisa F., and S. Leonard Syme. "Social Networks, Host Resistance, and Mortality: A Nine-Year Follow-up Study of Alameda County Residents." *American Journal of Epidemiology*, 1979, *109*(2), 186–204. http://aje.oxfordjournals.org/content/109/2/186.abstract.
2. Brody, Jane. "Forging Social Connections for Longer Life." *New York Times*, March 26, 2012. http://well.blogs.nytimes.com/2012/03/26/forging-social-connections-for-longer-life.
3. Hawton, Annie, and others. "The Impact of Social Isolation on the Health Status and Health-Related Quality of Life of Older People." *Quality of Life Research*, 2011, *20*(1), 57. http://www.ncbi.nlm.nih.gov/pubmed/20658322.
4. Berkman and Syme, "Social Networks, Host Resistance, and Mortality."
5. Holt-Lunstad, Julianne, Timothy Smith, and Brad Layton. "Social Relationships and Mortality Risk: A Meta-Analytic Review." *PLOS Medicine*, 2010, *7*(7). http://www.ncbi.nlm.nih.gov/pubmed/20668659.
6. Lengauer, Christoph. Interview by Healthy Companies. March 27, 2012.
7. Cross, Rob. "Six Myths About Informal Networks—and How to Overcome Them." *MIT Sloan Management Review*, April 15, 2002. http://sloanreview.mit.edu/article/six-myths-about-informal-networks-and-how-to-overcome-them/.
8. Cross, Rob. *The Hidden Power of Social Networks: Understanding How Work Really Gets Done in Organizations*. Boston: Harvard Business Review Press, 2004.

9. McAfee, Andrew. “What Sells CEOs on Social Networking.” *MIT Sloan Management Review*, February 7, 2012. http://sloanreview.mit.edu/article/what-sells-ceos-on-social-networking.
10. Bughin, Jacques, Angela Hung Byers, and Michael Chui. “How Social Technologies Are Extending the Organization.” *McKinsey Quarterly*, November 2011. http://www.mckinseyquarterly.com/How_social_technologies_are_extending_the_organization_2888.
11. “21 Quotes from Davos You Should Read.” ChiefExecutive.net, January 31, 2013. http://chiefexecutive.net/21-quotes-from-davos-you-should-read.
12. Schoomaker, Eric. Interview by Healthy Companies. July 30, 2012.
13. Seligman, Martin. *Flourish: A Visionary New Understanding of Happiness and Well-Being*. New York: Free Press, 2011.

Part II, Section E

1. Jobs, Steve. “ ‘You've Got to Find What You Love,’ Jobs Says.” *Stanford News*, June 14, 2005. http://news.stanford.edu/news/2005/june15/jobs-061505.html.

Chapter 16

1. Rosen, Robert, and Paul B. Brown. *Leading People: Transforming Business from the Inside Out*. New York: Viking Adult, 1996.
2. Gallo, Carmine. “Google's Marissa Mayer: 3 Leadership Traits She'll Bring to Yahoo.” *Forbes*, July 17, 2012. http://www.forbes.com/sites/carminegallo/2012/07/17/googles-marissa-mayer-3-leadership-traits-shell-bring-to-yahoo/.
3. Fairlie, Paul. “All Generations Want Meaningful Work.” York University School of Human Resource Management, August 7, 2012. http://eon.businesswire.com/news/eon/20120807006251/en/meaningful/generations/older.
4. Kelly Outsourcing & Consulting Group. *Acquisition and Retention in the War for Talent: Kelly Global Workforce Index*, April 2012. http://www.kellyocg.com/uploadedFiles/Content/Knowledge/Kelly_Global_Workforce_Index_Content/Acquisition and Retention in the War for Talent Report.pdf.
5. Kuhlmann, Arkadi. Interview by Healthy Companies. July 9, 2008.
6. Covey, Stephen. *The 7 Habits of Highly Effective People*. New York: Free Press, 1989.
7. Pink, Dan. “The Puzzle of Motivation.” TED Talk, July 2009. http://www.ted.com/talks/dan_pink_on_motivation.html.

8. Rosen and Brown, *Leading People.*
9. Srinath, Ingrid. Interview by Healthy Companies. March 28, 2012.
10. Bell, Peter. Interview by Healthy Companies. March 26, 2012.

Chapter 17

1. Cornell, Brian. Interview by Healthy Companies. November 29, 2011.
2. "Erik Erikson: Eight Stages of Psychosocial Development." Collaborative Leadership Network. Accessed June 12, 2013. http://www.leadershipskillsandvalues.com/lessons-and-readings/erikson-s-life-cycle-theory.
3. Matthews, Jeff. *Pilgrimage to Warren Buffett's Omaha: A Hedge Fund Manager's Dispatches from Inside the Berkshire Hathaway Annual Meeting*. New York: McGraw-Hill, 2008.
4. Colvin, Geoffrey. "What it Takes to be Great." *Fortune Magazine*, October 30, 2006. http://money.cnn.com/magazines/fortune/fortune_archive/2006/10/30/8391794/index.htm
5. Mathas, Ted. Interview by Healthy Companies. April 30, 2012.
6. Clemmer, Jim. "Leadership and Learning Are Indispensable." *Expert Magazine*, September 22, 2007. http://www.expertmagazine.com/artman/publish/article_832.shtml.
7. Ibid.

Chapter 18

1. Koplovitz, Kay. Interview by Healthy Companies. September 28, 2012.
2. Gladwell, Malcolm. *Outliers: The Story of Success*. New York: Back Bay Books, 2008.
3. Gladwell, Malcolm. "What Is *Outliers* About?" Gladwell.com. Accessed March 13, 2013. http://www.gladwell.com/outliers/index.html.
4. Suri, Jeremi. "The Leaders We Need." October 7, 2012. http://jeremisuri.net/archives/1056.
5. Schwartz, Tony. "Our Unhealthy Obsession with Winning." HBR Blog Network (blog), August 1, 2012. http://blogs.hbr.org/schwartz/2012/08/our-unhealthy-obsession-with-winning.html.
6. "DBJ Special Report: Qwest's Joseph Nacchio and His Path to Prison." *Denver Business Journal*, May 3, 2012. http://www.bizjournals.com/denver/news/2012/05/04/dbj-special-report-nacchio.html?page=all.
7. Haidt, Jonathon. *The Happiness Hypothesis: Finding Modern Truth in Ancient Wisdom*. New York: Basic Books, 2006.

8. Helliwell, John, Richard Layard, and Jeffrey Sachs (eds.). *World Happiness Report*. Earth Institute, Columbia University, 2012. http://www.earth.columbia.edu/sitefiles/file/SachsWriting/2012/World Happiness Report.pdf.
9. Williams, Ray B. "Why Do We Have an Obsession with Winning?" *Psychology Today*, August 4, 2012. http://www.psychologytoday.com/blog/wired-success/201208/why-do-we-have-obsession-winning.
10. Flores, Raul. Interview by Healthy Companies. October 18, 2012.
11. Demetriou, Andrew. Interview by Healthy Companies. March 17, 2009.
12. Blacksmith, Nikki. "Majority of American Workers Not Engaged in Their Jobs." Gallup, October 28, 2011. http://www.gallup.com/poll/150383/majority-american-workers-not-engaged-jobs.aspx.
13. Hamel, Gary. "Exposing Management's Dirty Little Secret." CNN Money, June 25, 2012. http://management.fortune.cnn.com/2012/06/25/exposing-managements-dirty-little-secret/.
14. Towers Watson. "Employee Engagement in Practice: JTI Case Study." June 2010. http://www.towerswatson.com/assets/pdf/2423/tw-eu-2010-16710.pdf.

Chapter 19

1. Stephenson, Jack. Interview by Healthy Companies. April 2, 2012.
2. Palmieri, Tuchi. *Oprah, in Her Words: Our American Princess*. Charleston: BookSurge, 2008.
3. Millward Brown. "The Study: The Jim Stengel Study of Business Growth." Last modified 2012. http://www.millwardbrown.com/Sites/Brand_Ideal/The_Study.aspx.
4. Seck, Wai-Kwong. Interview by Healthy Companies. July 18, 2012.

Chapter 20

1. Kurowski, Cristoph. Interview by Healthy Companies. July 30, 2012.
2. Bussey, John. "Facebook's Test in China: What Price Free Speech?" *Wall Street Journal*, June 10, 2011. http://online.wsj.com/article/SB10001424052702304778304576375810359779964.html.
3. Ernst & Young. "Leading Across Borders: Inclusive Thinking in an Interconnected World." 2011. http://www.ey.com/Publication/vwLUAssets/Leading_across_borders:_inclusive_thinking_in_an_interconnected_world/$FILE/Leading_across_borders.pdf.
4. Bryan, Lowell L., Jane Fraser, Jeremy Oppenheim, and Wilhelm Rall. *Race for the World: Strategies to Build a Great Global Firm*. Boston: Harvard Business School Press, 1998.

5. Rosen, Robert, Patricia Digh, Marshall Singer, and Carl Phillips. *Global Literacies: Lessons on Business Leadership and National Cultures*. New York: Simon & Schuster, 2000.
6. Ibid.
7. Ibid.
8. Ibid.
9. Ernst & Young, "Leading Across Borders."
10. Diangienda, Armand. Interview by Healthy Companies. November 8, 2012.

Chapter 21

1. Bersin & Associates. "New Bersin & Associates Research Shows Organizations That Excel at Employee Recognition Are 12 Times More Likely to Generate Strong Business Results." 2011. http://www.bersin.com/News/Content.aspx?id=16023.
2. Rubenstein, David. Interview by Healthy Companies. August 3, 2012.
3. Zak, Paul J., Angela A. Stanton, and Sheila Ahmadi. "Oxytocin Increases Generosity in Humans." *PLOS Medicine*, 2007, 2(11), 1128. http://www.ncbi.nlm.nih.gov/pubmed/17987115.
4. Schwabel, Dan. "How to Build a Company People Trust." *Forbes*, January 9, 2012. http://www.forbes.com/sites/danschawbel/2012/01/09/how-to-build-an-company-people-trust/.
5. Pillay, Srinivasan S., and Rajendra S. Sisodia. "A Case for Conscious Capitalism: Conscious Leadership Through the Lens of Brain Science." *Ivey Business Journal*, October 2011. http://www.iveybusinessjournal.com/topics/leadership/a-case-for-conscious-capitalism-conscious-leadership-through-the-lens-of-brain-science.
6. Haidt, Jonathon. *The Happiness Hypothesis: Finding Modern Truth in Ancient Wisdom*. New York: Basic Books, 2006.
7. Aknin, Lara B., Michael I. Norton, and Elizabeth W Dunn. "From Wealth to Well-Being? Money Matters, but Less Than People Think." *Journal of Positive Psychology*, 2009, 4(6). http://www.tandfonline.com/doi/abs/10.1080/17439760903271421.
8. Shore, Debra. Interview by Healthy Companies. July 25, 2012.
9. Taylor, Bill. "Hire for Attitude, Train for Skill." *Harvard Business Review*, February 1, 2011. http://blogs.hbr.org/taylor/2011/02/hire_for_attitude_train_for_sk.html.
10. Campbell, Kenneth D. "Malden Mills Owner Applies Religious Ethics to Business." *MIT News*, April 16, 1997. http://web.mit.edu/newsoffice/1997/mills-0416.html.

11. McLaughlin, Corrine. "Spirituality and Ethics in Business." Center for Visionary Leadership, 2009. http://www.visionarylead.org/articles/spbus.htm.
12. PR Newswire. "Thousands of Marriott Employees Volunteer Worldwide During Company's Annual Spirit to Serve Our Communities Day." May 13, 2009. http://www.prnewswire.com/news-releases/thousands-of-marriott-employees-volunteer-worldwide-during-companys-annual-spirit-to-serve-our-communities-day-61844952.html.
13. Kaplan, David A. "SAS: A New No. 1 Best Employer." CNN Money, January 22, 2010. http://money.cnn.com/2010/01/21/technology/sas_best_companies.fortune/index.htm.
14. White, Allen L. "Business Brief: Intangibles and CSR." Businesses for Social Responsibility, February 2006. http://www.bsr.org/reports/BSR_AW_Intangibles-CSR.pdf.
15. Weiner, Jeff. "The Art of Conscious Leadership with Jeff Weiner, CEO LinkedIn Wisdom 2.0 2013." YouTube, April 3, 2013. http://www.youtube.com/watch?v=2xofOLqj2Zw.
16. "Stonyfield Farm Named to Ethisphere's 2011 'World's Most Ethical Companies.'" Stonyfield, April 2011. http://www.stonyfield.com/about-us/press-room/stonyfield-farm-named-ethisphere-s-2011-world-s-most-ethical-companies.
17. Epstein-Reeves, James. "The Six Reasons Why Companies Actually Wind Up Embracing CSR." *Forbes*, October 17, 2012. http://www.forbes.com/sites/csr/2012/10/17/the-six-reasons-why-companies-actually-wind-up-embracing-csr/
18. Ibid.
19. Ibid.
20. Ottman, Jacquelyn. "Tom's of Maine: Where CSR Is a Way of Life." *Greenbiz*, October 15, 2001. http://www.greenbiz.com/blog/2001/10/15/toms-maine-where-csr-way-life.
21. Klein, Paul. "Why Has Corporate Social Responsibility Stalled?" *Forbes*, October 22, 2012. http://www.forbes.com/sites/csr/2012/10/22/why-has-corporate-social-responsibility-stalled/2/
22. Toms Shoes. "One for One Movement." Accessed June 13, 2013. http://www.toms.com/our-movement/.
23. McLaughlin, Corrine. "Spirituality and Ethics in Business." Center for Visionary Leadership, 2009. http://www.visionarylead.org/articles/spbus.htm.
24. Polman, Paul. "Sustainable Growth—Building New, Long Term Business Models." Address to the Geneva Forum for Sustainable

Investment, June 8, 2012. http://unilever-rss.com/images/GFSI-Speech-08-June-2012_tcm13-288757.pdf.

25. Griffin, Jennifer J., and John F. Mahon. "The Corporate Social Performance and Corporate Financial Performance Debate." *Business and Society,* 1997 *36*(1), 5–31. http://business.gwu.edu/smpp/articles/griffin_mahon_1997_b_and_s.pdf.
26. McLaughlin, "Spirituality and Ethics in Business."
27. Pillay, Srinivasan S., and Rajendra S. Sisodia. "A Case for Conscious Capitalism: Conscious Leadership Through the Lens of Brain Science." *Ivey Business Journal*, October 2011. http://www.iveybusinessjournal.com/topics/leadership/a-case-for-conscious-capitalism-conscious-leadership-through-the-lens-of-brain-science.
28. Kleinfeld, Klaus. Interview by Healthy Companies. May 8, 2012.

Chapter 22

1. Kraemer, Harry. Interview by Healthy Companies. 2012.
2. Dispenza, Joe. *Evolve Your Brain: The Science of Changing Your Mind.* Deerfield Beach, FL: Healthy Companies International, 2008.
3. Begley, Sharon. *Train Your Mind, Change Your Brain: How a New Science Reveals Our Extraordinary Potential to Transform Ourselves.* New York: Ballantine Books, 2007.
4. Oh, In-Sue, Gang Wang, and Michael K. Mount. "Validity of Observer Ratings of the Five-Factor Model of Personality Traits: A Meta-Analysis." *Journal of Applied Psychology*, 2011, *96*(4), 762–773.
5. King, Martin Luther, Jr. *Strength to Love*. Minneapolis, MN: Fortress Press, 1963.
6. Frohman, Dov. *Leadership the Hard Way: Why Leadership Can't Be Taught—and How You Can Learn It Anyway*. San Francisco: Jossey-Bass, 2008; Ackoff, Russell L. *Handbook of Business Strategy*. Bingley, England: Emerald Group, 2005.

Chapter 23

1. Byron, Ellen, and Joann S. Lublin. "Embattled P&G Chief Replaced by Old Boss." *Wall Street Journal*, May 24, 2013. http://online.wsj.com/article/SB10001424127887324659404578501673304380076.html.
2. McDonald, Bob. Interview by Healthy Companies. April 18, 2012.

Chapter 24

1. Mulally, Alan. Interview by Healthy Companies. February 28, 2012.

2. Song, Kyung M. "Boeing's Mr. Nice Guy: Alan Mulally Steps into the Limelight." *Seattle Times*, April 8, 2001. http://community.seattletimes.nwsource.com/archive/?date=20010408&slug=mulally08

Chapter 25

1. Novak, David. Interview by Healthy Companies. August 20, 2012.

Chapter 26

1. Rosen, Robert. *Just Enough Anxiety*. New York: Portfolio, 2008.
2. "President's Message." Recreational Equipment Inc., http://www.rei.com/about-rei/presidents-message.html.
3. Jewell, Sally. Interview by Healthy Companies. February 1, 2007.
4. Recreational Equipment Inc., 2011. http://www.rei.com/stewardship/community.html
5. "President's Message," Recreational Equipment Inc.

Chapter 27

1. Noteboon, Ben. Interview by Healthy Companies. August 10, 2012.

Chapter 28

1. Kealey, John. Interview by Healthy Companies. 2010.
2. Plank, Kevin. "How I Did It: Kevin Plank." *Inc.*, December 1, 2003. http://www.inc.com/magazine/20031201/howididit.html.
3. Lagace, Martha. "High Ambition Leadership." *Working Knowledge*, September 15, 2011. http://hbswk.hbs.edu/item/6735.html.

Acknowledgments

Grounded is truly a work of love. Love for the higher purpose. For the people I have met over my career. For the ideas and lessons I have learned in my exploration. And for the possibility that this book might make a difference in someone's life.

No one is an island of self-interest. We truly are social animals. This book is a product of all those special connections I have made over the years. This is my sixth book on leadership and, in many ways, the culmination of thirty years' exploring the subject inside myself and sharing lessons with others. I am deeply grateful for these life experiences and to the many people who have touched me over the years.

To Jay and Cassie, who bring love into my life every day and teach me about the power of staying grounded at home and in far-off places around the world.

To our extraordinary writing team, Lisa Berger and Rae Thompson, dear friends with amazing minds and exquisite writing skills, who have helped bring the ideas in this book alive.

To my family, who on many days is actually a healthy family. Thanks for all the love and support you give me while I go into my introspective, introverted cave during writing season: Jay Fisette;

Barbara and Richard Keast; Dick Rosen; Randi, Ryan, Lauren, Chris, Sarah, Devon, and McKenna Tancini; Jerry and Margot Fisette; Lynne and Mark Salvaggio; Paul, Nancy, Kyle, and Melanie Fisette; Erin, Mac, Molly, and Harper McGinn; Amanda Salvaggio and Curtis George; and Michael, Katie, and Jack Salvaggio.

To my colleagues at Healthy Companies, who inspire and challenge me every day: Jim Mathews, Kathie Ross, Rick Auman, Dominick Volini, David Knauss, Nancy Williams, Kirk Blandford, Robin Altice, Dierck Casselman, Tony Rutigliano, David Rippey, Eric Sass, Leigh Shields, Ingrid Garay, Carol Olivera, Dyan Greggs, Gwen Sully, Bonnie Bell, Josh Suprenant, and the many coaches and consultants we work with around the world. My life would not be the same without you.

Thanks to Paul Squires, Rob Harris, Stephen Parker, Marc Kelly, Mark Smith, Paul Tate, Dawn Hyman, and Aimee Dawson for your early work on this project. Thanks also to Jim Moran, David Schner, Tom Waldron, Jim Cornehlson, Lyles Carr, Carlos Berio, Jonathan Peck, Tai Ito, Doug Hensch, Berard Tierney, Patrick Leonard, Jeff Akman, Bob Witeck, Pedro Nunez, Mark Treadaway, Bob Kenney, and Lance Wolf for supporting this project.

To my dear friend and agent Gail Ross, and Howard Yoon, for believing in me and my voice over many years. To Susan Williams and all my friends at Jossey-Bass/Wiley, who continue to lead the world in publishing great leadership books. And to Carolyn Monaco, Christine Fadden, Nancy Dailey, and Mark Fortier, who help us let the world know about our important work. Thanks also to Tom Neilssen and colleagues for supporting me over these many years.

To my good friends, who brighten my life and make the world a better place.

To the hundreds of leadership thinkers and writers who came before me. I am forever grateful for your being my teachers.

Finally, to the thousands of executives I have met and worked with over the years. Your passion for the work, your trust in sharing the real experience of leading, and your courage to be who you are has inspired me to write this book so that others can learn. Thank you.

About the Author

Bob Rosen—trusted CEO adviser, organizational psychologist, and bestselling author—has long been on a mission to transform the world of business, one leader at a time.

He founded Healthy Companies International over twenty years ago with the singular goal of helping top executives achieve their leadership potential. With support from a multiyear grant from the MacArthur Foundation, Bob and his colleagues began an in-depth study of leadership. Since then, he has personally interviewed hundreds of CEOs—in forty-five countries—in organizations as diverse as Ford, Motorola, Johnson & Johnson, Singapore Airlines, Brinks, Northrop Grumman, Toyota, Citigroup, PepsiCo, ING, and PricewaterhouseCoopers. He has become an adviser to many of these companies.

Bob has distilled his most critical findings into the Healthy Leadership Model, which shows leaders at every level how to develop six specific dimensions of themselves for greater impact. The Healthy Leader Model is the basis for his firm's ongoing work. Clients include Global 2000 corporations, government and nongovernmental organizations, and selected associations around the world.

Bob is a frequent media commentator who has been quoted in the *New York Times, Wall Street Journal, Fortune, Bloomberg Businessweek, Financial Times, Time, Chief Executive Magazine,* and more. Bob's books include *The Healthy Company, Leading People, Just Enough Anxiety, Global Literacies,* and *The Catalyst* (coauthor). He is also in demand as a global keynote speaker with a special focus on personal leadership.

Bob graduated from the University of Virginia. He subsequently earned a PhD in clinical psychology at the University of Pittsburgh. Bob teaches in executive education programs, and has been a long-time faculty member in the Department of Psychiatry and Behavioral Sciences at George Washington University's School of Medicine.

For more, including a self-assessment of your leadership profile, visit BobRosen.com.

Index

About Healthy Companies

Healthy Companies International was founded in 1988 by CEO adviser, organizational psychologist, and bestselling author Bob Rosen. Its mission is to transform the world's organizations, one leader at a time.

Thanks in part to a multiyear grant from the MacArthur Foundation, Bob and his colleagues began to research the characteristics of successful executives and their companies. Since then, the firm has conducted hundreds of in-depth interviews with CEOs in forty-five countries.

One of their most critical findings is that the executives with the most successful, sustainable organizations are fueled—and refueled—by daily attention to six particular aspects of their lives: their physical, emotional, intellectual, social, vocational, and even spiritual health. In other words, what sets them apart is their intensely *personal* leadership practice. "Who they are" drives "what they do" every day—and determines how they build their teams, organizations, and world-class outcomes.

Bob and his team have distilled this very personal approach into the Healthy Leader Model, which is the basis for the firm's work.

Every day, Healthy Companies advisers are coaching executives on optimizing their performance, helping organizations navigate through change, and guiding senior teams in building more productive relationships with their boards, with each other, and with their employees. The firm is also implementing leadership development programs at all levels within organizations.

Healthy Companies works with a wide range of Global 2000 corporations, government and nongovernmental organizations, and selected associations. Clients include New York Life, PricewaterhouseCoopers, Ralph Lauren, and MedStar Health.

Many of Healthy Companies' best practices can be found in Bob Rosen's bestselling books, including *The Healthy Company, Leading People, Just Enough Anxiety, Global Literacies,* and *The Catalyst.*

To sample the Healthy Leadership Model, including a self-assessment, visit HealthyCompanies.com.

Healthy Leaders build **Healthy Teams** create **Healthy Companies**

A SPECIAL OFFERING

Bring Bob and His Message to Your Organization

- *Sought-After Keynote Speaker*
- *Bestselling Author*
- *Founder Healthy Companies International*
- *Top CEO Advisor*

Confronted by constant change and economic turbulence, many leaders can find themselves ill-equipped to manage the challenges they face. A prevailing paradigm that focuses on short-term results without regard to sustainable performance sabotages who we are as healthy human beings. Few have seen alternatives, until now.

In this unique keynote, Bob proposes a new approach with the power to fuel–and refuel–some of the world's top leaders. It is a paradigm that speaks to our better selves by focusing on six personal dimensions: physical, emotional, intellectual, social, vocational, and spiritual health.

Bob Rosen is a trusted CEO advisor, organizational psychologist, and bestselling author. He has long been on a mission to transform the world of business, one leader at a time.

He founded Healthy Companies International over twenty years ago with the singular goal of helping top executives achieve their leadership potential. Bob has personally interviewed hundreds of CEOs—in 45 countries—in organizations across a variety industries.

Bob has an uncanny ability to tap into both the personal and professional sides of great leaders to uncover what lies beneath their success. He has a knack for synthesizing, organizing, and translating his discoveries into meaningful and practical insights and advice. And, as a consummate story teller, he skillfully integrates his own life experiences to reinforce his message.

For more information, please call (703) 351-9901 or go to BobRosen.com

BECOME A HEALTHY LEADER

VISIT **BOBROSEN.COM** FOR THESE FREE RESOURCES:

TAKE THE HEALTHY LEADER® ASSESSMENT

Begin with a look at who you are now with this snapshot of your leadership health across six dimensions: physical, emotional, intellectual, social, vocational, and spiritual.

INSIGHTS FROM THE HEALTHY LEADER® NEWSLETTER

Get access to hundreds of interviews with executives from around the world, as well as the latest research into leadership, management, neuroscience, psychology, and biology.

THE HEALTHY LEADER® TOOLKIT

Designed to build upon the opportunities identified in The Healthy Leader® Assessment, these tools offer a pathway to achieving the leadership legacy and results you envision.

BOB TALKS LEADERSHIP

Not all leaders are equipped to address the complexities of an ever-changing world. In this Webinar, Bob illustrates how who you are drives what you do, Bob makes it clear that we can develop the skills necessary to thrive in the face of uncertainty.

Transforming the World One Leader at a Time

DATE			

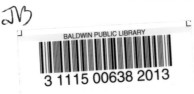